Wild & Free

Wild & Free

Frank Cooke
as told to
Jack Boudreau

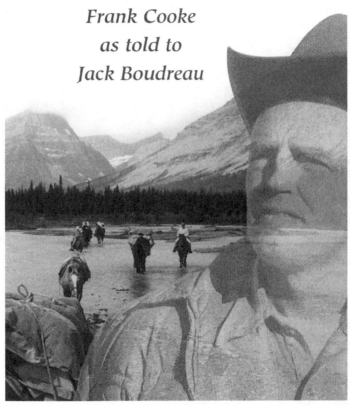

CAITLIN PRESS INC. 2002

Published by
Caitlin Press Inc.
Box 2387
Prince George BC V2N 2S6

Design by Warren Clark Graphic Design
Index by Kathy Plett
Maps by Rich Rawling
Photographs have been provided by a number of people including Frank
Cooke, his family, Earl Buck, Sharon Buck and many of the guides who
worked with Skook Davidson and Frank Cooke.

Caitlin Press acknowledges the financial support from Canada Council for
the Arts and from British Columbia Arts Council for its publishing
program. Also recognized is the Book Publishing Development Program of
the Canadian and the British Columbia Book Publishers' tax credit through
the Ministry of Revenue.

BRITISH
COLUMBIA
ARTS COUNCIL
Supported by the Province of British Columbia

THE CANADA COUNCIL | LE CONSEIL DES ARTS
FOR THE ARTS | DU CANADA
SINCE 1957 | DEPUIS 1957

Library and Archives Canada Cataloguing in Publication

Boudreau, Jack, 1933-
Wild and free / Jack Boudreau with Frank Cooke.

ISBN 1-894759-04-4

1. Davidson, Skook. 2. Cooke, Frank. 3. Hunting guides--British
Columbia, Northern--Biography. I. Cooke, Frank II. Title.
SK17.C65B68 2004   799.292   C2004-904861-9

Dedication.

It is the wish of Frank Cooke that this book be dedicated to his parents, his sisters and brothers, as well as his extended family. To all the guides and wranglers who served him so faithfully— Native as well as white—Frank states: "I couldn't have done it without you; you were among the best in the game and you proved it time and again."

Also, Frank stresses the need to honour his mentor and idol, Skook Davidson, "who taught me everything I know about packing with horses, traveling the mountains and taking care of things properly. Skook was without doubt the best pack train operator and woodsman I ever knew, bar none."

As this book goes to press, Frank added this final comment:

After a whirlwind divorce, I decided I needed a new women. I scouted around as I wasn't going to take off with just anyone. One day I ran into Joy McNeely, whom I had known for years. We started to travel together and here we are twenty years later and still together. She has been a great lady for me. I have no qualms about saying I love her very much.

Acknowledgements.

It has occurred to me that a book of this nature is never just the work of one person. Most certainly that is the case in this venture. Therefore I extend thanks to the many people who assisted me with pictures and/or information regarding the stories in this book. Without their assistance this book would not have been possible.

So it is with the deepest gratitude that I extend thanks to: Sharon and Doreen Buck, Irene Stangoe, Pritchard Common, Olive MacKenzie, Cecille Carroll, Maxine Koppe, J. Martin Benchoff, Stan Simpson, John Rasmussen, Bill McRae, Steve Marynovich, Cecil Reynolds, Willie Crosina, Brian Salmond, Ernie Harrison, Steve Buba, Eric Klaubauf, and Bill Hesse of Northern Thunderbird Air in Prince George. Singled out for special attention is the family of Frank Cooke who provided much of the information as well as most of the pictures contained herein.

Once again I must extend thanks to the *Prince George Citizen* for permission to reprint articles from the long ago.

Just as this book is going to print, a magnificent bronze plaque is to be placed in the Kechika Valley at Terminus Mountain to honour wilderness frontiersman Skook Davidson. Placed on this plaque is a brief story of his life as well as the poem he wrote with great feeling during the winter of 1949. To all those who assisted in the financial part of honouring this worthy pioneer, I must thank:

J. Martin Benchoff, Waynesboro, Pennsylvania.

Martin Benchoff Jr., Boston, Massachusetts.

Stan & Deb Simpson, Warburg, Alberta.

Margaret Humphries, Prince George, BC.

Clarence Boudreau, Penny, BC.

Doug Cameron, Prince George, BC.

When I was a young lad running around the mountains and learning to hunt, I used to read everything I could get my hands on concerning wildlife and hunting. Among the writers who commanded my attention were Jack O'Connor and Warren Page, both of whom traveled extensively and wrote about their experiences in outdoor magazines. Often involved in their adventures was a young wilderness guide named Frank Cooke, who guided in the beautiful mountains along the Kechika River just south of the Yukon Boundary.

This area is comprised of strikingly scenic mountains and for many years harboured some of the biggest Stone sheep to be found anywhere. Famous people traveled across the world for the privilege of seeking world-record Stone sheep, often considered the most sought after trophies on the planet.

Set in that remote wilderness at a place called Terminus Mountain was the legendary individual, Skook Davidson, who started the Diamond J Ranch in 1939. Skook was a renowned pack train operator who maintained about 200 head of horses on his wilderness ranch. He was, in my opinion, one of the most exceptional men to ever grace this province. And so it seems fitting that it was from Skook that young Frank Cooke learned the ways of packing with horses and traveling through endless miles of wilderness, and to this day he describes Skook as "the best packer and woodsman I ever knew, bar none."

Skook took young Frank under his wing and taught him the ways of the wild, and most important of all, how to treat and care for horses. Horses were Skook's love and to mistreat them in any way was guaranteed to force one to find a new source of employment. "He was strict but he was fair" is how Frank sums up their many years together.

Frank worked with Skook's pack trains for many years, surveying the Yukon Boundary, the Alaska Highway, and other projects. In the mid-1950s he went with Skook on their first guided hunt, which was the beginning of new careers for both of them. In 1964 Frank pur-chased the west half of Skook's huge guiding area, which was in effect—everything west of the Kechika River. This opened a new chapter in his life, for he soon found himself running a large guiding venture with up to 15 guides and hunts booked years in advance.

Frank sums it up this way, "Adventure, that's what it was, just one adventure after another; with the same satisfied hunters returning year after year. The advertising was free—just word of mouth—and it doesn't get much better than that."

There are also stories of Frank Cooke Sr., an early-day provincial policeman who, as his Inspector described, "Carried a punch like a sledgehammer in either fist." Several different bullies found them-selves lying flat on their backs wondering if anyone got the licence plate numbers of the trucks that just hit them. Frank Sr. became a leg-end in his own right by following law-breakers through the northern forests for weeks on end. His courage in the face of grave danger was proven on many occasions, and his ability to control violent people was beyond question. During his tenure as a policeman Frank Sr. staked several mineral claims, which netted him the equivalent of over $1 million in today's currency. After ten years with the provincial police force Frank Sr. retired and became a wealthy mining expert.

Since there are three generations of Cookes named Frank fre-quently mentioned in this book, I have referred to the policeman as Frank Sr., the guide outfitter as Frank, and the guide as Frankie or Frank Jr. Regrettably, Frankie was killed in an accident several years ago.

Although the Kechika area is the main focus of this material, many different areas of the North and Interior of the province are covered as well, such as the Cariboo, Omineca, Yukon and Northwest Territories. Also worth mentioning is the obvious affection I feel for the rugged open mountains of the North. This will be apparent to the reader when they notice my choice of pictures. As well, the admira-tion and respect I hold for horses and all they have accomplished in the North cannot be hidden from view; for me, and many others, they represent the largest part of the northern experience.

Because I am dealing with history, I repeatedly refer to First Nations People as Natives or Indians, often because I am quoting others. It should be apparent to the reader that no disrespect is intended. Many of the Native guides mentioned herein are repeatedly referred to as the best in the business by the outfitters.

One problem I ran into while researching this book concerned the many people who thought I would open a Pandora's box because of the many squabbles throughout the years between different guides and the authorities. I have repeatedly tried to reassure these people that I do not write to make people miserable; I believe that is what marriage is for.

So pull up a chair—if you like wilderness adventure—then sit back and read stories of courage, comedy, tenacity and a lot of plain damned foolishness.

Jack Boudreau.
September 2004

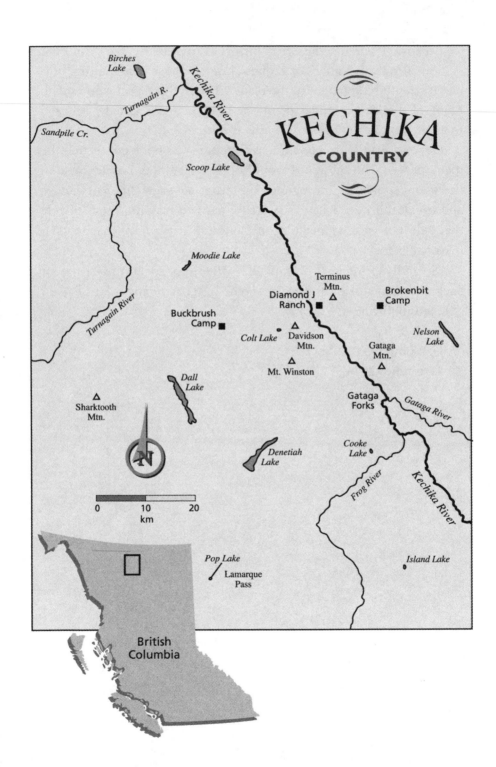

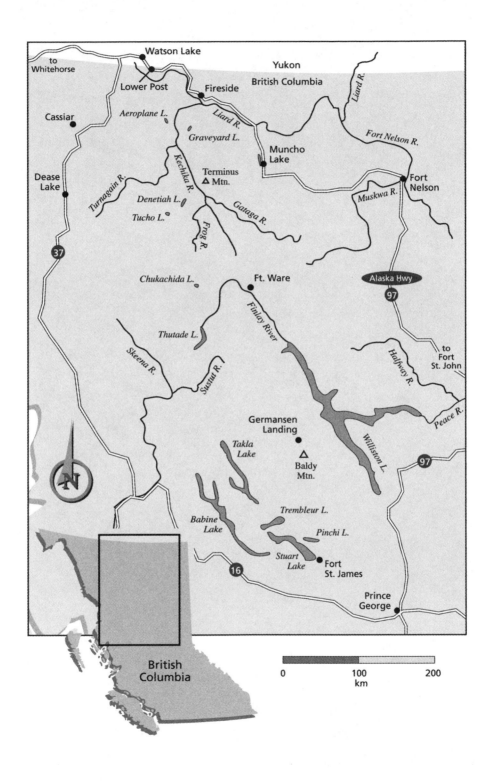

Chapter 1

Perhaps the best place to start this story is with Frank Cooke Sr., who worked in the woods as a logger and also as a longshoreman all along the coast of BC during the 1920s. These duties he continued with after he met Gertrude Churchill—a relative of Sir Winston Churchill—whom he married in 1925 in the city of Victoria. Frank Sr. was a powerful man and a great swimmer, which he proved when their salvage boat was cut in half by a ship. Frank swam in the dark and fog for six hours until rescue arrived. Just a short time later he experienced a major change in his life when he became a member of the BC Provincial Police.

On May 26, 1927 a son (also named Frank) was born to the newlyweds in Victoria. Seventy-seven years later in 2004, I was lucky enough to interview this outstanding woodsman. Frank started the interview with his earliest recollection of Victoria. "I was running along a ditch with my Uncle Pat, who was trying to shoot some birds with a slingshot. Suddenly my Uncle Art, a provincial policeman, came by and really gave us heck."

I asked Frank if he recalled when his father first joined the police force and he replied, "My first recollection of my father as a policeman was in Victoria, when Pat and I were playing in our backyard on Davida Street. Pat had been chasing me around the house and when we got to the front of the house a big policeman was opening the gate.

For some reason or other I was always afraid of policemen, so I turned and ran back around the house and hollered to my mother that there was a policeman at the front steps. By that time he was already in the front room and I realized it was my father. I went over and sat on his knee and then heard him say that he had been posted to Prince George and that he had to leave right away. My mother was pregnant at the time with my sister Lorraine and it must have upset her because I can remember her suggesting that it must be the end of the world to have to go way up into the Far North, but my dad just looked at her and smiled.

"My dad left for Prince George and went on duty January 5, 1932. It seemed like forever until we caught a midnight boat and traveled to Vancouver. From there we traveled by train to Prince George. I was five years old at the time and I can recall that mother had a terrible time with sister Lorraine because she had the whooping cough. When we finally arrived in Prince George, my father met us at the station and took us to our home on 10th Avenue."

"How did you adjust to Prince George?" I asked.

"Pretty well, I'd say. I remember an old Chinese man who owned a pinto horse and a cart. He owned a pig farm up toward the airport and every day he would collect slop from the restaurants to feed his animals. I was just crazy about animals so every chance I got I would ride around town with him and help him. Sometimes my dad would see me riding with him and he would just laugh. Mom didn't like it but dad used to tell her that at least they knew where I was all the time."

"Prince George was a small town then, compared to now." I offered.

"Yes, I think it had a population of about 3000 people at that time, and my dad was always busy as attested to by his daily diaries, which have been handed down to me. Times were tough in the Thirties, as there was a shortage of work. According to dad's diaries at least 90 % of the crimes were committed by transients. They would come to town riding the boxcars without any food. Many times dad brought

Gertrude Cooke and son Frank at Prince George, BC

them home where mom prepared food for them. I guess he felt sorry for them. My dad always had lots of wood in the back yard and they were happy to split wood in return for some food. At times when dad released prisoners from jail, he would hand them a dollar and say, 'I'm sorry, boys, I can't help you anymore; hit the road!' Some of the people dad helped came back into his life years later; some helped him attain financial security through mining ventures.

"Dad was very strict, yet considerate; he often gave a troublemaker several chances before arresting him. He had a way with people and they learned to trust him. Even the Natives in the community trusted and respected him completely. My mother used to worry at times because they always seemed to put dad on the tough and dangerous cases. Dad would tell me to take care of my mother and sister and I promised I would do my best. My dad was a big, strong man who would take off his uniform and mix it if reason didn't work. More than one man found himself on the ground after insulting my father or the law."

"His duties often took him quite far from home according to the reports I've read, Frank."

"Dad often had to go north or wherever else they sent him. He understood boats and rivers and what he didn't know, he picked up from others through the years. He could keep up to anyone in the woods. He just seemed to take command of the situation when there was serious trouble. It was just something he had in him and apparently his father was the same: a hardy, adaptable man. In going over dad's diaries it is apparent that he knew almost everything that was going on. He kept a list of many people, their names and where they were from. There were people from all over the world just rambling around, trying to find a way to earn a nickel.

"I started school in Prince George in 1934, and I had to learn to take care of myself. Perhaps I inherited some of this ability from my dad who certainly knew how to handle himself."

As I had found an interesting article concerning his father, Frank asked me to use it. It concerned a fight between strikers and police that took place near Prince George in May 1935. Take note that in those times police and game wardens assisted and substituted for each other as the situations demanded. I quote from the *Prince George Citizen* dated May 16, 1935:

"The striking unemployed men, who on May 2 refused the provincial government's offer of work at 40 cents an hour, came into a violent clash with the police shortly after 8 o'clock on Monday morning on the long hill to the east of the Fraser River bridge. Since the strikers refused to work for less than 50 cents an hour and other concessions, after receiving their relief

Const. Frank Cooke with moose.

cheques in advance, they have been picketing the public works garage in South Fort George from which other men on relief have been conveyed to work, but met with little success in persuading or intimidating others from going to work.

"Monday morning four trucks left the public works' garage for work on the highway to the south of this city under the direction of J. W. Miers, resident district engineer. At the head of the trucks was a car containing Inspector Van Dyk, and Game Officers Forrester and Copeland. Following the trucks was a police car in which were C. K. MacKenzie and Constables Cooke, Smith and Pomeroy. Near the top of the hill the workers on the trucks and the officers in the convoying cars were subjected to a barrage of stones from strikers along the roadway, and the game officers' car came up to a barricade thrown across the roadway. Officers Forrester and Copeland at once proceeded to remove the barricade when they were pounced upon by a group of strikers armed with clubs and throwing stones. Officer Forrester saw Officer Copeland greatly outnumbered and started to his assistance when he was felled with a blow on the head, which rendered him unconscious for the moment. When he came to, he found himself in a ditch by the roadside with a number of strikers still attacking him. It occupied probably three minutes from the time of the first outbreak until the police trailing the four trucks could come into action. A few shots were fired in the air and the disturbance was soon quelled. Officer Copeland had stuck gamely to one of the men who had attacked him throughout the beating the strikers administered, and Frederick Barker was the first of the strikers to be placed under arrest. He [Copeland] and Officer Forrester were the only police officers to suffer serious injury. Officer Forrester was badly bruised about the body and had his right arm broken with a blow from a club, but was able to be about in the afternoon with the broken arm in a cast. Officer Copeland was a more serious hospital case having been badly beaten over the head.

"When the barricade was finally removed from the roadway the trucks carrying the men who were willing to work proceeded to their destination, having defended themselves lustily when brought into close contact with the strikers. Later in the day the police made three other arrests. Heitman Johnson and Jack Rutledge were apprehended in the CLDL headquarters and Gus Edvall was arrested in his home.

"Sergeant McKenzie showed excellent judgement in his handling of a difficult situation with but six peace officers at his disposal, a situation which for a time appeared to be distinctly menacing. The firing of a few shots in the air, with the promise to bring the range closer if developments warranted, proved sufficient to quell the trouble. Inspector Van Dyk did not see much of the encounter between officers Forrester and Copeland. When the trouble started he tried to swarm up the bank at the side of the roadway to engage the men who were throwing stones, but the climbing was difficult and as often as he neared the top he was shoved down the slope again. He was busy all the time but escaped serious injury.

"The four prisoners, Frederick Barker, Heitman Johnson, Jack Rutledge and Gus Edvall, appeared before Stipendiary Magistrate Milburn on Tuesday charged with assaulting peace officers in the dis-

Constable Frank Cooke and Game Warden Copeland.

charge of their duties, and were given formal remand for eight days. Application for bail was made later when the magistrate fixed bail at $5000 with two sureties in each case of $2500. Some difficulty was experienced in the finding of satisfactory sureties and the accused were returned to gaol until the matter could be arranged."

The end result of this fiasco was an all-expenses-paid trip to jail, which gave the men plenty of time to contemplate their actions and their futures.

During the years when Const. Frank Cooke served in Prince George his boss had been Sergeant Colin Mackenzie. After his retirement as Inspector from the provincial police in 1970, Colin MacKenzie gave an interview to the *Prince George Citizen* during which he touched on Frank Cooke's career:

" . . . Though I say, unmatched in a canoe, on a horse or on snowshoes, Frank's quiet and non-committal air frequently disguised the fact that he packed a sledgehammer wallop in either fist. Maybe there are still some around who remember Prince George about 35 years ago [1935], and Art Bellos—a character, to put it mildly, of ill repute, who for a time held sway as the town bully. Which meant that, as a vicious, no-holds-barred brawler, he was frequently a trial to the police. Sometimes, even in a cell, he would keep up his fighting.

"It was on one occasion that Bellos, slapping one of his cringing prostitute friends, knocked her down. Then just to show that the age of chivalry wasn't entirely dead, he kicked her in the head. Though there were witnesses, their indignation didn't flash up to the point of interfering. However word of the affair did get around to the police and Cooke, then a rookie, was elected to bring him in. Frank found Mr. Bellos on a restaurant stool [Shasta Café] toying with his morning coffee. 'I would like a word with you outside' was the constable's quiet invitation. At which Bellos looked up at the uniformed figure, and as a slow smile spread over his face, remarked, 'Then you'll just have to wait until I finish my coffee, and I may be quite a time.'

"Cooke, in almost pensive mood, examined his fingernails, while some of the nearby customers apprehensively slid out of their seats and departed. In a quick and wordless move, Frank suddenly seized Bellos from behind, a hand on each elbow, and quickly propelled him to the street. There he freed him, and Bellos swung with more energy, I may say, than science, for the next thing he knew he was flat on his back . . . with a broken jaw. Two weeks later when he could articulate, he got eight months for kicking his lady friend, and five more for obstructing the police. Whether or not he ever returned to Prince George I cannot say, but one thing you can bank on—he never forgot Frank Cooke."

When Art Bellos managed to articulate again, he accused Frank Sr. of police brutality. At the hearing Frank was asked why he did not get assistance before confronting Bellos, as he knew Art was a troublesome type. Frank's reply was short and to the point, "When I joined the force no one told me that it would take six police officers to arrest one troublemaker." Art's charge went to the garbage bin where it belonged.

Further commenting on Const. Frank Cooke's ability, the Inspector added:

". . . A roistering gang, by all accounts, these Cooke Bros. (I believe there were seven of them) who, as kids, hunted, fished and rode hors-

Sergeant Colin MacKenzie and Const. Frank Cooke with police car.

es on the height of land above the Gorge, between Tillicum and the Admirals. So far as Frank was concerned it was in northern police circles that he became a sort of legendary figure. Six foot two, lithe and broad shouldered, he was not only handsome but he could also chew more snoose, drink more rum (without visible effect) and in addition outpace any three men on the trail.

"Once, from Prince George, assigned to check on a stricken trapper he covered a hundred miles of snowbound wilderness in three and a half days. Though today Frank is 61 and a prosperous mining expert, I notice he hasn't put on an extra pound."

Inspector Mackenzie's interview also touched on another story that concerned a ghoul of Prince George. The reporter wrote:

"However it wasn't only in demonstrations of physical fitness that Mr. Cooke displayed his worth. I can remember when, on one occasion, he delved into the realm of the mysterious—a real weirdo situation that might have intrigued Edgar Allen Poe. It was a story that started when then sergeant Colin MacKenzie was summoned to give evidence in some divorce proceedings. Seems that a man, whom we'll dub for convenience Joe Doak, was divorcing his wife who had been running around in rather abandoned fashion, which the police had occasion to note. Hence Mackenzie—for a brief moment on the witness stand—was quizzed by the plaintiff's lawyer.

"Joe got his divorce, but as he had children to look after, he advertised in a Vancouver paper for a housekeeper. A quiet, decent sort of woman answered the ad, but after a month or so with Mr. Doak she felt compelled to call on Sgt. Mackenzie to voice a complaint. Seems that Joe was getting amorous and making passes. In fact he chased her from room to room on occasion, which caused her to ponder (behind her locked bedroom door) whether her chastity would survive till payday. Mackenzie, of course, counselled her that she could leave her employment or, if she had been molested, lay a charge. However as they spoke, he sensed something more was burdening her mind and after further probing came a story as strange as any he had ever heard; and Mac had then been 20 years on the force. Seems that Joe Doak, in addition to being general handyman, was also the community gravedigger; the graveyard at that time being quite a piece out of town in a rather unfrequented spot.

"The astonishing story that fell from the lips of the woman was to the effect that Joe was robbing the dead after burial! She vowed he was bringing home clothing from the cemetery, and usually after a funeral. One man's coat, she said, was bloodstained and torn, and he had her wash and repair it. Some of the garments he made her alter and cut down for the children. Const. Frank Cooke was assigned the task of unravelling the tale and in a day or so reported he had discovered that one Mike Zuaven, beating his way on a CN freight, had been instantly killed when a string of cars went off the track near Urling, 46 miles west of McBride. Mike, still in his bloodstained clothing, had been buried four days later in the Prince George cemetery. Now his clothing, washed and repaired, had been found in Joe Doak's house and identified. How come? Well, there had only been three people at the interment and after Joe had thrown a few shovelsful of earth on the coffin, two of the witnesses departed leaving Joe to complete the job. But Joe didn't. He opened the coffin, took off the clothing, nailed down the lid and filled in the grave.

"Same thing with Mike Cosgrove, an indigent who died in hospital. His coat and pants landed in Joe's house, identified by Joe Saywright, the undertaker. A hospital nurse, who had checked the coat, identified it by some wheat in one pocket.

"The case of Henry Hedrick was strange, for not only was he a pauper but he had no clothes at all. In the economical standard of that day the government furnished coffins for indigents, but they didn't extend the largesse so far as clothing or a shroud. Which left government agent Milburn the right to exercise his initiative. He remembered a man being committed to Essondale [the asylum] years before, whose trunk was still in the courthouse vault. He remembered too, that it contained a blue suit. Though by now somewhat moth eaten, it was handed over for Henry's last rite. Queer to relate, a couple of days after the simple funeral, the man who owned the trunk turned

Frank Cooke and sister Lorraine, circa 1935.

up to claim it. Now in a normal state of mind, luckily he accepted Milburn's explanation. He was glad some use had been found for the suit, because it would no longer fit him. The arrest of the ghoulish Mr Doak followed, but curious to relate he wouldn't say how many coffins had been tampered with, or how long his grave robbing had been going on. Naturally there were a fair number of people in Prince George who wondered about their own kith and kin in the cemetery. Anyway not one further word came from the lips of Mr. Doak. A week later at a speedy trial before County Court Judge Robertson, Joe got three years on each of three charges of offering indignity to human remains. True to the simple style of that day Const. William Smith did the prosecuting, and Frank Cooke gave his evidence."

After we finished with the Inspector's account, I asked Frank, "This story about your father certainly proves that there were plenty of weird folks around back then, doesn't it?"

"It sure does. My father's diaries provide abundant evidence of that fact. But that just went with the job, though, as did another memorable case that dad was involved in. This concerned a Native who shot a white man named Hugo Stolberg up the Finlay River."

Since I had the newspaper articles, Frank asked me to quote them. They were taken from the *Prince George Citizen* of July 15th, 1937:

"In the make-believe of the picture making world it is always the Mountie who gets his man. But in the cold, hard world of the unexplored, poorly mapped area in Northern Omineca, Provincial Constable Frank Cooke is fast building up a reputation that needs no moving picture set-up to prove that he gets his man. The two-month's mystery of who shot trapper Hugo Stolberg through the arm at the head of the Finlay River 360 miles [576 km] north of Prince George May 20th last, was unfolded with dramatic suddenness on Monday at the Prince George Courthouse.

"Arthur Sampson, a Hazelton Indian, who had married into the family of Bob Patrick, alias Bob Bailey, of the Bear River Tribe, pleaded guilty to the charge of unlawfully shooting Hugo Stolberg, and was sentenced to two years in the Provincial Penitentiary . . . "

There was much more to this case that what the newspaper article suggests. This was clearly demonstrated by Const. Cooke's diary. The first mention of the Stolberg shooting appears in the diary dated June 1st, 1936. On that date Frank was already far into the forest on his search for the person(s) responsible for the shooting. Any person who thinks it was fun to be a police officer in those days should grab a packsack and follow Const. Cooke through the forest on his hunt for Stolberg's attacker.

First off, the weather was atrocious with rain drenching everything day after day. Through the Trembleur and Takla Lakes area he searched until he met some Natives that gave him valuable information. Armed with this new information, Frank continued through the forest. Some days 20 miles or more were covered hiking ever deeper into the wilderness. It strikes me that here was an exceptionally courageous individual who had to know that his life was in danger every minute of every day. But on he went through the Thutade Lake country where the only sign of man was a faint trail the Natives used to access their traplines. Many trails were traveled during his stay in the forests. The Sustut country as well as the Fort Grahame area was traveled during weather so terrible that the trails were covered with water and therefore unlikely to be used.

Whenever he met Indians along the trails, Frank questioned them in detail. He learned everything possible about the man he was trailing. He found out that Sampson carried a 351 self-loading Winchester rifle. He also knew that he had a three-inch scar on his face and where it was located. With all this information, Frank was in a good position if he happened to meet his quarry along those endless wilderness trails. And it was while camping along one of these faint trails that Const. Cooke had a break come his way. Arthur Sampson happened along and thanks to the adequate description the constable had received, he was recognized and taken into custody. But the journey was far from over, because they had to spend another week on the trail to get to Takla Lake where a boat returned them to Fort St. James. The date was July 7th and Const. Cooke had been in the woods for over five weeks.

But getting back to the court case, the trial dragged on for several hours during which time both men claimed ownership of the trapline. Stolberg, in turn, was accused of stealing traps from Sampson. Whether or not justice was done that day it seems impossible to know, but Sampson got two years and the case was finally closed.

When I discussed this story of his father's hunt for Sampson with Frank, he said, "According to the Indians, Stolberg had been trapping what they believed was their trapline, stealing their traps as well as their beaver pelts. Of course there were laws back then; you were not allowed to shoot at people or kill them. It's hard to remember, now, but I think he got out of jail early. I heard them say that dad testified for him in court and that helped him a great deal. But there was a part to the story that dad kept to himself. When he interviewed Sampson, he asked if he intended to kill the white man when he shot at him and Sampson answered, 'Frank, I aim at his back when he run over the bank, but God damn it, I got no front sight; I miss my aim and I shoot off his arm.' That's the story my dad told me."

"I have collected a substantial amount of information on the police career of your father, Frank. In fact, many of his manhunts are among the collection. But the one that intrigued me the most was the Fort

Nelson case, which was more in your father's normal line of work

"This memorable event in your father's career began on July 12, 1936 and went on for most of two years. It began the day that the Hudson's Bay Company at Fort Nelson was robbed. The thieves broke in and found two trappers bedded down for the night so they tied them up and forced them down into the cellar. The Hudson's Bay Company manager was away at the reserve at the time and had left his assistant, Tommy Clarke, in charge. So Tommy was also bound and gagged and forced to join the two trappers in the cellar, but only after he had surrendered the key to the storehouse where the furs were stored. Then the thieves piled bags of flour on the cellar door to give them time for a getaway.

"It took the captives almost three hours to escape the cellar, after which they notified the area policeman, Const. Clark. A search quickly showed that the furs had been carried to the river's edge and taken away by boat or canoes. Worse yet, Const. Clark was unable to pursue the thieves because his shipment of gasoline for the boat motor was 110 miles upriver, stranded because of low water. There was no means of communication in those days, so getting word to the outside world was a major undertaking."

"I remember the story quite well, Jack, because dad told it to us many times. He told me they sent an Indian by canoe to Fort Simpson 400 miles downriver, and a week later he arrived at his destination. Word was sent to the outside world through the radio station and soon police officers and game wardens descended on the area. When it was learned that all 29 heavy bales of furs were missing, the extent of the robbery became clear. The furs were valued at $34,000, which would be the equivalent of a half-million dollar robbery today, so the importance of solving this crime was made clear to all the officers involved. My dad, along with Constable William Forrester, flew out of Prince George with Pilot Ginger Coote on the start of what was to be a long, drawn-out investigation. Because the aircraft was fixed with floats and the spots where it could land were few and far between, a great deal of walking was involved. In one instance, dad walked over

100 miles in three days. In another part of the investigation he and a helper named Angus Harold rafted 80 miles of the Muskwa River while searching for evidence. Other police officers such as Monty Armstrong and Ernest Gammon were involved in the case, as well as game wardens Van Dyke, Copeland and Butler. The air searches were conducted by bush pilots Sheldon Luck and Ginger Coote.

"During the hold-up, the two trappers had noticed that the thieves were carrying a Savage rifle and an automatic pistol; this pointed the finger at area trappers Henry Courvoisier and Bert Sheffield. Further evidence was obtained while searching the cabins of the two suspects, and more was found at a camp two miles up the Nelson River. It appeared that the two men had used the camp for two days. As well, blue paint from a canoe was found on a tree near the shore. The police checked with a trapper who owned a blue canoe, and found out that it had been stolen about two weeks earlier. Dad said that this really puzzled the police because they realized that a canoe could not possibly carry all the furs. They knew a plane wasn't used because someone along the river would have heard it. For a while, the police thought that five or six people were involved in the theft, because of the work it took to move such a large amount of furs out of the area. Finally Game Warden Forrester found one of the camps used by the thieves and noticed that the campfire stakes were shaped in an odd fashion. He had seen this same style of stakes used before at campsites of the suspects.

"Dad told me that the police needed evidence to hold the men before they decided to leave the country. A bit of luck finally came their way when they found some un-prime furs in one suspect's cabin. This was enough evidence to hold the two men until better evidence was found.

"Just a few days later Const. Duke was at his radio in Fort Nelson when the two suspects came to town. He arrested them and they were flown to Prince George for trial. As it turned out, the suspects were only charged with possession of the un-prime fur. They got a small fine and were released. More time passed until the police found $4000 worth of furs in one of the cabins of the accused and they were arrested once more. But when the case went to court, the experts couldn't agree on the age of the furs; so they got off again.

Police found canoes sunk full of rock in the Nelson River and brought them to Fort Nelson for evidence.

"Finally, an Indian hunter stumbled onto the cached furs, most of which were spoiled. Then a pilot spotted two sunken canoes in the Nelson River. The canoes had been filled with rocks and sunk in an effort to hide them. They were returned to Fort Nelson to be used as evidence. The badly damaged furs had just been left in the woods nearby, and only about three miles from Fort Nelson. Once again arrest warrants were issued and Dad was sent north on another search."

As Frank remembered his father relating the events of the case, we had a great gab session going. I produced an abundance of newspaper articles for Frank's perusal. As a result, he agreed that I should quote the ending of the case directly from the *Prince George Citizen* dated October 21st, 1937:

"Henry Courvoisier and Bert Sheffield, northern B.C. trappers, pleaded guilty at Pouce Coupe last Tuesday to the robbery of $34,000 worth of fur from the H. B. Co. Post at Fort Nelson on July 12th, 1936, and were sentenced to five years in the penitentiary by Judge H. Robertson, of this city. The staff of the B.C. Provincial Police at Prince George brought to a successful conclusion a search for evidence that ranks with the detective thrillers of such writers as the late Sir Conan Doyle, and Edgar Wallace.

"Never in doubt in their own minds as to whom the guilty parties were from the time in 1936 that they first arrested Courvoisier and Sheffield, Sergeant E. Gammon and Const. Frank Cooke were faced with heavy odds to turn their circumstantial evidence into absolute proof of guilt.

"When their first investigation in 1936 led to the arrest of Courvoisier and Sheffield the accused were given a preliminary hearing and sent up to the higher court for trial. They were brought to Prince George in the fall of 1936 but at the October assizes were successful in having their case traversed to the spring assizes of 1937, and were allowed out on bail of $1000 each. Courvoisier and Sheffield went back to their trapline in the Fort Nelson area and shortly after sold a bunch of furs to the Hudson's Bay Post there. When these furs arrived in Edmonton it was suspected on examination that they were part of a lot of furs that were stolen from the Fort St. John Hudson's Bay Post in 1934 [a separate robbery]. The draft for $4000 in payment was stopped and Courvoisier and Sheffield were again arrested, and charged with being in possession of stolen furs. In May 1937, they were brought up at the spring assizes of the Supreme Court in Prince George, but were granted a stay of proceedings in the Fort Nelson fur robbery and stood trial on the charge of being in possession of stolen furs. Their council, A. McBride Young, won an acquittal from the jury and they were again turned loose.

"Going back to the Fort Nelson district, they [the accused] took in 1800 pounds of supplies by airplane. These supplies they unloaded from the plane on the shores of Henry Lake, informing the pilot that it was located about in the center of their trapping ground, and they would have to find their horses and distribute the supplies by pack-horse to their chain of cabins and caches on the trap line. Some weeks later the pilot, making a trip into the same territory, noticed that the pile of supplies had not been moved, and casually reported the occurrence to the police. The police immediately concluded that there was something amiss, as if Courvoisier and Sheffield intended to trap this winter they should have the supplies well spread by that time to their caches along the trap line. About this time the $34,000 worth of stolen furs was found on the banks of the Nelson River three miles below the Hudson's Bay post from which they were stolen.

"Sergeant E. Gammon and Const. Frank Cooke were immediately taken in by plane and the hunt started again. Weeks of intensive search in the trackless wilds of northern British Columbia failed to catch up with the wanted pair, but evidence was accumulated daily that told the officers they were on the right track. Such slight clues as blue paint on rocks along the shores of the rivers and creeks were noted and patiently followed, all suggesting that the pair were in the vicinity, as they were known to own a blue painted canoe. Finally the canoe was discovered filled with stones to keep it submerged in several feet of water. A horse track trail was next picked up and followed but led to a creek and all trace of it was lost. Finally getting to the top of a ridge and climbing a tree to get a look over the surrounding country to discover possible horse feeding grounds, as Courvoisier and Sheffield were known to have five horses somewhere in the country, Const. Cooke spotted a likely looking valley. On going there he found only three horses. Finally he picked up the trail of two horses heading out of the valley and evidently making for the south.

"Reporting to Sergeant E. Gammon the result of his reconnaissance, it was decided to get word out to headquarters that there was a possibility the two wanted men were heading for the south, and a hoped-for safe domicile in the U.S.A. It was this decision that brought about their capture by immigration authorities at Sweetgrass, Montana, and finally landed them in the penitentiary for five years. To those conversant with conditions in the wilds of northern B.C., the successful rounding up of the bandits is considered one of the cleverest bits of detective work by B.C. police."

"I met Henry many years later," Frank confided, "at that time he was running a stopping place at Steamboat Mountain on the Alaska Highway. He thought I looked familiar so he came to my table and asked my name. When I told him, he shook his finger and said, 'I knew you had to be; you look so much like your father.' He sat down and talked to me for a while and told me that dad and the other policemen had treated them very well after their arrests."

"Something that may interest you, Frank, is that there is a Courvoisier Creek about 50 km northeast of Fort Nelson. It appears that those two men covered a huge territory; I'm amazed at the size of their traplines. But I must bring your mother into the picture, because it must have been hard on her with your father gone for long periods of time." I suggested.

"My mother used to worry while he was gone. There was no communication and we didn't hear from him once for months. Mom used to cry sometimes and I always tried to comfort her, but it wasn't easy. I recall the time my dad had to take four criminals to Okalla. The road was terrible, so it took all day to get to Quesnel. The second day they got stuck and the convicts were working with poles helping dad get the car out of a mud hole. Suddenly dad started laughing and the men asked him what was so funny. Dad told them that he had never seen people work so hard to get to a penitentiary.

"Another time, dad caught a guy breaking the law and challenged him about it. The guy was arrogant as can be and he talked down to dad by saying, 'You can't be making much money; I'll give you a few dollars and you can forget about it.' Well there was just a big bang and that guy was flat on the ground. He learned the hard way that dad wasn't for sale."

"I have a story to tell about your father, Frank, and it comes from his police daily diaries, as well as from my home town. It concerned an elderly trapper named Charlie Hartsell who lived just a short distance from our home in the community of Penny, BC. In his later years, Charlie started acting strange and got into the habit of hollering at people that came near his cabin. As my older brothers and sisters had to pass right by his cabin door on their trips to and from school, this caused my mother no end of worry. My dad had been a trapper a few years earlier and consequently felt sorry for Charlie. Perhaps that is why dad frequently had soup or other foodstuffs taken to his cabin to help him out. On one trip, my sister Josie and brother Joe took soup to Charlie's cabin and suddenly he started chasing them around his wood stove, attempting to catch hold of them. By some good luck they managed to escape and that was the last of taking food to his cabin. But the worst was yet to come, for when he started pointing a pistol at people the police were notified and your father was sent to investigate. My mom told your father that on a few occasions Charlie walked to our home and talked absolute nonsense. Mom further told your dad that Charlie had taken to howling like a coyote and barking like a dog. Finally your father went to his shack, and his police diary describes how he went to the door and Charlie refused him entry. He coaxed for a bit and at last got him to come out on the step, at which point your dad rushed him and got the automatic handgun under his pillow. A further search of the cabin found some food and two $100 bills. On further questioning, Charlie admitted to yelling at people and said he was living on snowballs. When his investigation was completed, your father arrested him and took him away and may well have prevented a disaster by doing so."

"My dad told me that story many times and said that the trapper was a big, powerful man. He had another officer with him and I think his name was Pete Smith. For some reason the old trapper didn't like Pete—maybe he knew him—so dad asked Pete to leave. After he left, dad finally got the old man to come out on the step. As he talked to the old trapper, dad edged closer until he knew he could stop him before he could get back in the cabin for his gun. Then dad made a run at him, caught him before he reached his bed, and put him on the floor. Charlie roared like a wild man and dad had a terrible time trying to control him. When Pete saw that dad was in the cabin, he came on the run. It took the two of them to get a straight jacket on him and even then they had a tough time getting him out of the cabin."

"I don't envy your father for some of the dirty jobs he had to do, but I guess that just goes with the job. Did he ever have to shoot anyone?" I asked.

"No! But he said that he felt like it once. A little boy went missing and he was involved in the search. One of the areas he searched was near the river and he found a make-do shack with a piece of tarp for a door. He opened the tarp and there was a man with the little boy and he had his clothes off. Dad told me that was the closest he ever came to blowing someone's head off. I think that man got 10 years if I remember right."

After Frank and I finished discussing his father—Const. Frank Cooke, our conversation shifted to a man named "Skook" Davidson, who profoundly influenced young Frank Cooke's life in the years that followed.

Chapter 2

ONE OF THE MOST MEMORABLE INDIVIDUALS TO EVER grace the province of British Columbia was Jean-Jacques Caux, better known as Cataline. From the 1860s until about 1912 his mule pack trains delivered supplies to remote areas of the BC wilderness with dependability.

Cataline was truly one of a kind—a man of courage with an indelible memory. Unable to read or write, he could remember every article of trade in his 50- to 60-mule pack train. Freelance writer Cecille Carroll of Queen Charlotte City has many interesting stories to tell about this man, because her father, Paddy Carroll, worked for Cataline as a stevedore.

The Paddy Carroll story is memorable in itself, because of what he went through. Paddy left Bella Coola at the age of 22 and walked all the way through the Chilcotin country with only a .22 calibre gun. At the point of starvation, Paddy started eating whatever he could find in the way of food. One day he prepared a meal of mushrooms and succeeded in poisoning himself. But for the intervention of some Natives, he most certainly would have perished. They took him to their camp and nourished him back to health. Cecille assures me that her father felt indebted to the Natives for the rest of his life.

After his recovery, Paddy continued on his journey until he reached Hazelton where he began his employment as a stevedore for

Cataline. Paddy claimed that conversation was almost impossible with Cataline because he spoke a mixture of about nine different languages. Cecille noted:

"Carrying on a conversation with Cataline was next to impossible, for his original Bearnaise accent was peppered with a smattering of French and Spanish. Added to that were his gleanings from exchanges with various Indian tribes with whom he did business, and he also had adopted words from Mexicans, French Canadians, Irish, Germans, Scots, British and Chinese. My father said that Cataline swore with great dexterity in all languages."

One story goes that a group of toughs from 'outside' had consumed a few too many and started heckling Cataline. When they went too far, he walked quietly to the far side of the room and made a pointed exhibit of examining a small spot on the wall, drawing everyone's attention. Then he backed off about 15 feet, reached into his boot, pulled out his knife, and quick as a cat threw it directly into the spot. Swiftly recovering the knife, he spun around in a flash and addressed the astonished troublemakers in a rasping voice that rose from the depths of his barrel chest. 'Sacreedam—dat all I tell you dis time.' That ended the heckling.

In 1912 when Cataline headed north on his last foray out of Ashcroft, he undertook the unprecedented challenge of driving an outfit of pack animals strung out along the trail for well over one mile. It was the longest pack train ever known to leave the Cariboo.

The old boy never lost his gift for the theatrical, and so his final encore was established in a grand blaze of glory. Sperry Cline, the provincial police officer in charge at Hazelton, knew Cataline well, and claimed he was the toughest man—Indian or white—that he had ever known. Cline made that report after encountering the old packer along the Babine Trail. "It had been a frosty night, and Cataline was asleep at the side of the trail, his bed a manteau [canvas pack cover] spread on the ground. He was fully clothed, even to his spurs, and had no cover. A small fire he had started beside him had gone out. I stood for a few minutes watching his deep breathing . . . his hair, beard and clothing covered with heavy frost. Despite everything he was having a good night's sleep." According to legend, his circulation was so remarkable that he was impervious to the cold.

Apparently he wore leather riding boots, a fetching wide-rimmed sombrero, heavy wool trousers, a boiled shirt whose duration was the entire trip to a far-off place, a red kerchief tied around his neck, and an elaborately buckled bucking belt. An impressive figure, Cataline remained consistent throughout his career; he wore gauntleted buck-skin gloves, but he was never known to have worn socks, not even in winter . . .

There was one noted exception to Cataline never wearing socks. One winter day he came to the store in Hazleton wearing socks. It was during his last years and apparently there was a layer of slippery ice on the roadway. In order to prevent a fall, Cataline wore a pair of socks over his boots to gain a bit of traction.

Before I leave the story of Paddy James Carroll, it must be mentioned that he spent many years in the wilds and produced a book of his poems called, *Ditties of a Dog Musher*. With Cecille's permission I include one of his poems:

The Pack Train
In the lead of the jingling primitive train
The cargadero rides,
On the switch-back trail by the glacier's edge,
On the rugged mountainside.
In the canyon deep they wend their way
To the rushing river's rim,
 By the slumbering lake where the weird loon calls
And frisky rainbows swim.
Past staggering caches of Siwash camps
Where the leaning totems bow
To the gurgling river's tawny breast
And the mountain's rugged brow.

They list to the plaintive husky's wail
'Neath Aurora's dancing ray,
As they camp 'neath the stars on the lonely trail
In the mountains far away,
And the squeaking aparajoes sing
A song that is ever dear
To the hearts of lonely men who wait
Beyond the far frontier.

Cecille clarified some of the words in the poem:

"The words 'cargadero' and 'aparajoes' come from the Chinook language that was used extensively in the Cataline camp. They are, of course, of Mexican origin. Apparently Cataline hired as many of these packers as he could find, for they were the very finest of packers . . . "

During his tenure as a packer, Cataline took on a young man named John Ogilvie Davidson, who started out as a bellboy, but quickly learned the art of packing and became a legend in his own right. An exceptionally powerful individual, he was given the name Skookum, which in the Chinook dialect means strong or powerful. Skookum was later shortened to Skook, a name that stuck with him throughout his life. This unique individual left a legacy capable of filling several books.

Perhaps the best way to introduce this man who became known as "Skook" is by starting way back in 1904 when he left his home in Longside, Scotland at the age of 13 and came to Vancouver, BC. Over a period of several months, Skook made his way north to the goldfields of the Cariboo, where his life took a profound turn when he met wilderness packer Cataline in Ashcroft. He hired on with the famous packer as a bellboy and quickly learned about pack trains from the king of pack trains himself. But the friendship was put to the test when Skook began eyeing a young Native lady that Cataline had taken a shine to. One day as they were loading up the train, Skook was walking by Cataline when a boot came out and tripped him. He landed face down and when he rolled over, he found Cataline's knife against his throat. In his buggered up language he got the point across to Skook with words equivalent to "Stay away from her, Scotty, she's my woman."

Then for emphasis Cataline moved the knife in an up and down motion that could not be misunderstood. When asked how he dealt with the situation, Skook replied, "I made wide circles around her after that."

Another thing that must be mentioned is that Cataline had the strange habit of finding dual use for a bottle of booze. He would take a stiff drink and then pour an equal amount on his head. "Some for the inside man and some for the outside man" was his motto.

During the time that Skook worked with Cataline, two other Prince George pioneers were also in his employ—famed surveyor L. C. Gunn, and George Williams, who was one of the best white-water men to travel the rivers of BC.

While some sources state that Cataline gave up packing and retired in 1907, I must respond to that assumption by pointing out that Quesnel's *Cariboo Observer* carried a brief note in its November 7th, 1908 edition:

"Jean Caux [Cataline] passed through on his way to Ashcroft."

Anyway, after he parted company with Cataline, Skook toyed with prospecting and also worked as a ranch hand in the Cariboo area where he met and became friends with a veterinarian. For a period of time that is lost in history, Skook drove the vet to and from ranches in the area with a team of horses and buggy. During this time he learned a great deal about horses from the vet; knowledge he put to good use in later years.

When his tenure as an assistant to the vet came to a close, Skook bought an eight-horse team and took up freighting for a year, then sold the horses in Ashcroft. After a long, serious bout of partying, he joined the 11th Canadian Mounted Rifles as a scout during the First World War. Often referred to as the most promoted soldier in the war, Skook made Sergeant 17 times, but always managed to get demoted again. He finally left the army with the rank of Corporal and a painful wound in his hips where he had stopped a bullet.

After the war, in fact while he was employed as ranch boss for the 158-Mile ranch, Skook met a young lady named Lil Crosina. Statuesque and pretty, she captured Skook's heart. The relationship must have become serious, because Skook asked for her hand and the young lady accepted, but with a condition: Skook had to quit drinking. The price must have been too high for Skook to accept, because he kept drinking and moved on. He didn't forget her, though, and according to a story that has survived the years, he sent her a rocking chair on her birthday. After several of these chairs had been received, the lady quizzed Skook as to the meaning of all the chairs. His reply was "I like to picture you sitting in those chairs thinking about me."

Olive (Lock) MacKenzie of Miocene, BC. remembers Skookum Jack Davidson as he was known then. During that time he served as

boss of the 158-Mile Ranch, which was also known as Mountain House. According to her he earned the reputation of not being entirely reliable. On one occasion Skook gave her a cutter with a broken runner. She had the runner fixed and used the sleigh to go to school as well as to give neighbourhood sleigh rides during the winter months. Her memories of Skook are limited as she was only about eight years of age when Skook left the area

Lil Crosina and her brother Bill, 1916.

after serving as ranch boss for a few years. This fits in well with his arrival in Fort St. James during the summer of 1920.

Throughout the years countless stories have emerged as to the origin of the name Skookum as applied to Davidson, but many are incorrect. Olive assures me that he was known as Skookum before he ever left the Cariboo in 1920. (I believe that the name Skook came about during his time with Cataline.) Olive also confirmed what many other people have stated—that Skook was a bugger with booze and the ladies.

Skook first arrived in Fort St. James in 1920 and quickly made friends, as he did everywhere he travelled. In a short time he became partners with pioneer rancher Earl Buck in a freighting venture, servicing the gold fields to the north and west. Earl claimed that on one occasion Skook got into a row while drinking and asked Earl's assistance to help clean up the bar. At some point a woman phoned the police, but by the time they arrived on scene, everything had been settled and the place was quiet. Skook met the police at the door and said, "We don't need you guys; we do our own policing around here."

Striegler and Skook Freighting.

Whatever his faults for partying too much, Skook earned the reputation of a great freighter. Along with his counterpart, Fred Streigler, they got the freight to its destination no matter how cold the weather or how deep the snow.

One of the stories that followed Skook throughout his life concerned a fight he had with six Americans back in 1920. Skook was employed by the BC Government at the time and was on a trip to the BC Coast. He was drinking in a bar in Esquimalt when the six American sailors came in and began bragging about how they won the war. Skook listened for a time and then waded into the group with fists flying and his voice roaring out, "This is one war you're going to lose." Although it is claimed that Skook won the fight, it is also claimed that he spent a few days in jail.

Skook carried on the packing tradition established by Cataline, to the point where he became a legend in northern BC. In one instance it was reported that he took a mile-long pack train of horses on a 500-mile trip all by himself and arrived right on schedule.

Often forest travelers would hear his voice echo through the forest long before his pack train arrived. His drinking habit, which sometimes went on for days, became his trademark and revellers would often delight to the news that Skook had arrived in town, because they knew it was going to be party time.

After several years spent freighting, Skook's love of adventure led him to try other lines of work, such as his short

Left to right Ethel Hamilton, Dolly Crosina, Ivy Lock, Skookum Jack Davidson, Olive Lock (Mackenzie), Bob Burgess, Louis Crosina (Lil's Dad), Bill Lock, Jimmy Hargreaves at 158-mile House, circa 1919.

tenure as a trapper. This episode began when he arrived in Dome Creek, BC, in 1932 and purchased a trapline in the Herrick Creek area. That summer he and a friend named John Gaspery took some of Skook's ever-present horses and travelled through what was then Blunder Pass (McCullagh Pass) to prepare the area for a winter of trapping. When they attempted to return home, they found themselves confused because the area was socked in solid with fog. Skook wasn't stymied very long, though, because he sent one of the horses ahead and they followed it. A short time later they were on the trail toward home.

Skook then spent that winter trapping with little success, as it was a winter of heavy snowfall during which the fur hardly moved. There was a bright side to the adventure that has added yet another humorous event to his legacy. During the spring of 1933 Skook made his way off his trapline and arrived in Dome Creek, his heart set on doing some heavy duty partying. Sometime earlier he had ordered two bottles of rum from the liquor store in Prince George, and he knew they would be waiting in the post office on his arrival. When he went to claim his booze from postmaster Scotty Stewart, he was in for some

Scotty Stewart, 1925.

bad news. It was a Sunday, and Scotty informed him that the post office never opened on a Sunday. Skook attempted reason for a while and when that didn't work he grabbed a fry pan and clobbered Scotty over the head with it. The result? That was the only time in the history of Dome Creek that the post office opened for business on a Sunday.

It was also in Dome Creek that Skook's reputed strength was out to the test. This happened when a group of trappers fresh from the forests decided to do some wrestling, more or less in fun. One of the men Skook took on was Frank Gleason, an ex-trapper and at the time, storekeeper in Dome Creek. Frank was renowned for his physical strength, and frequently displayed it by carrying 45-gallon drums of fuel around on his shoulders. In relating the outcome of the duel, Frank's brother, Chris, told me that as far as he knew Skook was the only man to ever take Frank in a wrestling match.

After Skook left his trapline in the upper Herrick Creek, he gave it to his friend Cecil Reynolds of Terrace, BC, in lieu of wages for work Cecil had performed earlier. That winter Cecil and his brother John trapped the area, with the same results Skook had experienced. Worth mentioning is a near-tragedy that the two brothers experienced when they went along the trapline without their snowshoes. They had just made camp for the night when it started snowing and by morning when they hit the trail again it had snowed almost two feet. The men struggled through the raging snowstorm and made it back to their cabin at the point of collapse; a valuable lesson learned to never travel in winter without their snowshoes.

Totally disappointed with the trapline, Cecil sold it, this time to a young man named Ernie Mix. During the summer of 1935 Ernie went to explore his new area, traveling from Dome Creek through Blunder Pass to his trapline. When the area got socked in, Ernie learned why the pass had been so named because he got lost. Several weeks later he reached civilization by arriving in the community of Aleza Lake perhaps 80 miles (128 km) from his trapline. So it seems apparent that Skook did the right thing when he said goodbye to that area.

Before we leave Cecil Reynolds, there is another story that must be told. This concerned the time he and Skook boarded a passenger train after going on a binge for several days. Both men intended to carry on with the party but they had a problem in that they were unable to find a seat. Suddenly Skook spoke to two men in a nearby seat, "You fellows get out of here and let us sit down." The two men looked at Skook and immediately left the seat, whereupon he turned to the man in the adjoining seat and said, "You get the hell out of here, too." The other man followed suit, leaving Cecil and Skook with plenty of room to continue partying.

During all the years that Skook spent freighting and packing with horses he had many adventures, some of which were not quickly forgotten. One such incident was carried in the *Prince George Citizen* on January 6th, 1938:

"One of the pioneer packers and freighters in Northern Omineca, J. O. 'Skook' Davidson arrived in Prince George last Thursday by airplane for medical treatment for a broken arm and horse kicks to the body. Skook has been freighting with four- and six-horse teams and packhorses in the North Country since before the war and while others have brought in tractors and other mechanical freighting gear, he sticks to horse transport for the most part. He brought in a couple of trucks last summer, but still thinks he can get farther with his horses with present road conditions in the north.

"Last week while going over an icy piece of road near Manson Creek his sleigh skidded, throwing him under the feet of one of the wheel horses. The horse kicked strenuously, breaking one of Skook's arms at the elbow, and landing several heavy blows to his body. He was dazed for some minutes after the mix-up, and lay on the side of the road before reviving. He then made his way to the Consolidated Mining and Smelting Co.'s camp at Slate Creek, and arrangements were made to fly him out to Prince George for medical treatment.

"After spending a few hours with the doctor here Skook left the following morning for Manson Creek to supervise his job of keeping supplies moving to the different mining camps for which he freights. Skook is one of the most popular characters of the North Country, and his many friends hope he will not be long without the use of his arm. Many of his buddies in the 48th Battalion with which he went overseas, there winning the D.C.M. and Military Medal with Bar, are extending sympathy to him in the unfortunate accident and wishing him well."

Whether the accident had any bearing on what followed is perhaps a matter of opinion, but on January 20th, 1938, just 14 days after he was admitted to hospital, the following article appeared in the *Citizen*:

"J. O. Skook Davidson, pioneer packer and freighter in Northern Omineca, passed through Prince George from Manson Creek on last Thursday's train for Vancouver to take delivery of a 60 H.P. International diesel tractor to be used in handling freight during the winter over Baldy Mountain. Skook has a contract from the deGanahl interests for the movement of 150 tons of supplies into Germansen Landing along with his other regular contracts."

Some people assure me that the tractor was required to keep the road open over old Baldy Mountain during the winter, because the previous winter men had been forced to shovel the nine feet of snow off the road by hand. While it may seem impossible for men to shovel nine feet off a road, several different people have assured me that it definitely happened.

Skook freighted in the Fort St. James and Omineca area until 1939, when he headed north with pack trains to assist with the BC/Yukon Boundary surveys. One of the packers who went along on that trip was a man named John Rasmussen, who still resides in Fort St. James, BC. John worked with Skook from 1939 until 1944 and confirmed that Skook really was a character, and just as rough and tough as they come.

During our conversation John mentioned Clayton "Slim" Pawnee, another woodsman who had worked with Skook's pack trains. He also confirmed a story I had heard from others that Slim had been terribly

Ludwig Smaaslet, Johnny Rasmussen and Fred Forsberg with Skook at Terminus Mountain, 1939.

wounded during the war. John described Slim as a good man and a great guy. John also informed me that when the summer surveys were completed that they intentionally brought the horses back to the Kechika Valley because Skook knew horses could over-winter there. Two trapper friends named Fred Forsberg and Ludwig Smaaslet had taken horses into the area several years earlier, so they informed Skook of the valley's potential. When I asked John if he spent a winter with Skook in the valley he told me that on one occasion he got caught in the valley by the winter snow and walked out on snowshoes to Lower Post, a distance of about 120 miles (192 km). Skook walked out with him and then returned to the valley alone.

When I questioned John about his years in the North, he told me about a pack train trip he was on when he fractured his ankle. After his injury, he crawled for about four miles until he reached the pack train, where he was taken by packhorse to Watson Lake. From there he was flown by airplane to the hospital in Whitehorse, Yukon.

Another neat story John told concerned the tropical valley that had been reported by prospector/pilot Colin "Lucky" Caldwell in

1929; a valley with hot springs that had been reported years earlier by another prospector who had been considered "gone in the head" when he reported the same phenomenon. Anyway, when their summer surveys were completed in 1939, John and a fellow packer named Ronnie Campbell decided to visit this famed area. They asked the Hudson's Bay man at Lower Post if he knew how to find the area. The man appeared surprised, but suggested they contact a Swede named John Olson who traveled the rivers while trapping that country. When contacted and asked to guide the men to the "tropical valley" the Swede replied, "I wouldn't call it a tropical valley, but I have seen bullfrogs in there that are bigger than porcupines."

Well, the men were guided to the spot, which required a 20-mile hike through the woods, and when they got there all they found was a couple hot springs. John thinks that they were kind of led down the garden path, so to speak, but he figures it was worth it anyway.

Remembering stories I had heard about Skook, I asked John, "I've heard so much about the fights Skook got into when partying. Did you ever get involved in any of those fights?"

"Oh, sure. When you traveled with Skook there was no way

John Rasmussen, Slim Pawnee and Skook, 1940.

around it. I remember back about 1942 when we finished packing for the summer and ended up at Germansen Landing. We got a big party going and later that night the fists started flying. The next day there were black eyes and bruises everywhere. It was a sad looking camp. Then we heard Skook shout, "Look at this fellow; there's not a mark on him." Then we heard a big splat and down went Big Jerry Affie, one of the packers. Somehow he had got through the night without fighting—maybe he hid in the woods. The next day he had two big shiners so Skook patted him on the back and said, 'now you're one of the boys'."

"Anymore stories about Skook?" I quizzed.

"Yes. I've got a story that was told to me by Major Charles who was an engineer on the surveys. He was in the war with Skook and they were in England on a furlough when Skook decided to visit his mother in Scotland. Major Charles went with him and while they were visiting, Skook's mother asked Skook if he still had the Bible she had given him when he left home at age 13. Skook assured her that he had it in his pack. Then she asked if he had ever read the verse of comfort that she had noted inside the front cover and insisted he read when in trouble. Again, Skook assured her that he read it every time he needed comfort and it always helped him find peace. At that point his mother opened the Bible to the designated page and there was the 10£ note she had put there when he first left home. Caught with his pants down, so to speak, Skook was speechless. According to Major Charles, Skook's mother rather enjoyed the moment.

"Major Charles had another cute story as well. Skook's mother told him that when John [Skook] was young his parents pressured him to become a priest. When asked why he didn't, Skook replied, 'I would have but I never liked wine; I've always preferred hard liquor'."

"Talk to me about the pack trains, John. Did you fellows eat quite well out there?" I asked.

"No. Sometime it was the same thing over and over. We had a boss named Norman Stewart who was a cheapo. It got to be a poor joke around camp when someone would ask the cook what was for chow, because he would either say macaroni and cheese or else cheese and macaroni. But it's surprising how a person can eat anything when they are working hard and it all tastes okay.

"I remember the time we got a moose and the cook prepared a big roast. Not only did the men gorge themselves on it at the table, but we also took a pile of it back to our tents. One of the packers was a big man named "Slim" Pawnee, and the cook used to tell people that on one occasion "Slim" ate a whole moose in six days. But as far as food goes, there wasn't a great variation, although they always made sure we ate prunes every day for obvious reasons."

"I suppose you knew Charlie and Paul Bloomfield, John, I have a picture of Charlie out with a pack train when he was still a young man." I said.

"Of course, they lived here for many years. They were with us on the surveys. In fact, their parents were some of the original pioneers in Fort St. James as they arrived here way back in 1919."

"I presume you didn't have much in the way of medical attention on those surveys." I asked.

"No. I remember an engineer named Bill Moffat. On one of the surveys he and two helpers were at a survey station on a mountain-top when they got hit by lightning. Bill got hit the hardest but managed to survive. The next year he got sick up on a big hump off the Liard River. We carried him down near the river on a stretcher but we had to put him down to cut through some willows. I remember he told us, 'Don't be too long, boys.' We were only gone about 20 minutes, but when we got back he was dead. The body was flown to Whitehorse and then to Vancouver. But when his body arrived in Vancouver his wife let it be known that Bill's desire was to be buried on his last station. So back he came—all the way up the Liard River and we carried that ten-day-old body back up that same ridge. Skook Davidson helped us carry him back and when we were ready to lower him into the ground, the edge of the grave gave away and Skook dropped right under the coffin. We had to haul it back up a ways in order to get him out. Then Skook gave his famous eulogy, 'Better you than me, Bill; lower away boys.'

"After we finished burying him, Skook pulled out his pistol and fired several shots over the grave. Another thing, there was a plaque put up on that hump to honour Bill and as far as I know, it's still there."

"Did you lose many horses back in the wilderness?" I asked.

"I remember Skook lost a horse once. He had gotten that horse from the Peace River Country and one day it went missing. Skook always felt that the horse might have gone back home."

"I assume that you worked with Frank Cooke on the surveys as well; is that correct?" I asked.

"Yes. But sometimes we were in different areas. I mean people were spread out all over that country. Yes, I knew Frank and his father the policeman, too, but I have a story about Frank when he was still a young lad that is rather funny. On occasion Frank used to come out to the Cassiar Ranch about 15 miles from The Fort (Fort St. James), to assist the men in whatever they were doing. For some reason Frank was always after the crows and would beg the men for a gun so he could take a shot at them. One day the men consented and sent Frank

Charlie Bloomfield near Manson Creek, 1935

out with a double-barrelled 10-gauge shotgun. When 12-year-old Frank pulled on the crows and fired, he used both barrels at once. We watched through the window of the bunkhouse and suddenly there was a tremendous explosion and Frank was blown over backwards and stretched right out on the ground. For some strange reason Frank never bothered the crows after that."

"What is your final assessment of Skook after working with him for many years?" I asked.

"He was a good, strong character who commanded respect. He didn't drink when he was working, but a summer's survey was always capped with a knock-em-down, drag-em-out party, and you never forgot them, that's for sure."

Chapter 3

AS THE LIVES OF YOUNG FRANK COOKE AND SKOOK Davidson were to become so closely entwined in later years, I questioned Frank at length, starting with the memories of his father.

"I recall the day when my dad came home from work in Prince George and told mom that he had the opportunity to move to Fort St. James and run the office there. Mom said, 'Well Frank, whatever seems right with you.'

"Dad moved to The Fort on April 24, 1937 and we left about two months later; we packed everything and took the train to Vanderhoof where dad met us. We traveled by truck to The Fort over a very tough road and it took us eight hours to cover the 42 miles. Dad had a little house for us right on the bank of Stuart Lake, and there was a small police station nearby. It had a cell in one corner with two bunks in it, and there was a well and pump where we got our water.

"There were a lot of Indian people on the reserve at that time. They were not allowed to buy liquor and this led to many problems. They always managed to get liquor or simply made their own, which caused many fights on the reserve. My dad stayed away unless someone came and said there was a serious problem over there. Then dad was forced to go and straighten things out. I recall just after we arrived in The Fort when dad and I went for a walk through the

Reserve with my dog, Dick. It was about a mile and a half walk through the area. When we got about half way through, three Native men walked up to us on the wagon road. One of them—a tall guy who looked pretty tough to me—walked up to dad and asked, 'What are you doing here?'

"Dad replied, 'I'm the policeman here.'

"My dad wasn't in uniform, instead he was wearing coveralls and an Indian sweater, but he did have his police hat on. The Indian poked him in the chest with his finger and told him, 'We don't need any white policemen around here.' Then he made it clear that we should get lost.

"When dad didn't move, this man took a swing at him and I heard a big 'splat'. When I looked, the man was lying flat on his back on the road. Then dad turned to the other two and said, 'I'm the policeman here.'

"They left us and we carried on through the reserve walking slowly. Dad never had any trouble with them after that. In fact, they would come and ask him for help when things went wrong. Dad treated

Four prospectors—Dan Rottaker, Frank Cooke, Manuel Rottaker and George Neilson at Pinchi Lake, 1939.

them fair and won their respect in return. I sure learned a lesson from my dad that day—if you are in the right, you never back down.

"My dog, Dick, was a Mackenzie River husky and I don't know what I would have done without him. Dad built a toboggan for him and he used to pull my sister Lorraine and I to school, a distance of about three and a half miles. I would turn him loose and he would wait all day for us and then pull us back home. He was one of the greatest work dogs I have ever seen, and I have seen a lot of them and worked some of them when I trapped the Liard River many years later. Dick was a good one."

"What are some of your other memories from those days?"

"I recall back in 1937 when my father and Russ Baker—the man who ended up president of Pacific Western Airlines—went to Prince George to get mom and my new sister, Gloria. I was on the wharf to meet them when they arrived back home. It was exciting to have a new addition to the family."

"Tell me about some of your early woods' experiences." I suggested.

"Well, I think it was the next year during summer holidays from school that I went with about 40 men to Aiken Lake from Germansen Landing. It was a government relief program. They were cutting road by hand and Skook was there with about 30 head of horses that belonged to Bert McCorkell's Ranch, about 16 miles from The Fort. That was the first time I worked around Skook and because I had heard so many stories about him, I was a bit overwhelmed. Skook's horses were used to pull slips [small earth movers] and things like that. A school chum of mine named Craig Smith came along and we all spent the summer up there. It was an adventurous summer for me.

"One of my most important memories takes me back to 1938, because that was when two brothers named Dan and Manuel Rottaker, along with two friends named Andy Ostram and George Neilson, arrived in Fort St. James. They camped on the creek near town and some women complained about their presence there so dad went to investigate. When the introductions were complete, dad asked what they were doing in the area. The men confided that they were prospectors looking for cinnabar, urged on by a government report of deposits near Pinchi Lake. I was with my dad and he was so interested in what the men had to say that we stayed and they talked for several hours. Dad drove them to Lawrence Dickenson's store, where Lawrence kicked in a lot of grub in exchange for an equal share. As well, dad supplied them with some money. The agreement said that they would be equal partners in whatever was found. Pilot Russ Baker also had the government report and was intent on staking the area—he was flying for Canadian Airways at the time—but the lake was rough and Russ could not take off with the airplane."

"We got up at 4 a.m. and headed out across the lake, which was very rough, as Stuart Lake can be. I was standing in the bow and my dad was running the motor. It got so rough that we were forced to give up and return to shore. Two hours later it was still rough when we tried again. We went 14 miles up the lake and unloaded all our gear. Then we walked over to the Pinchi deposits and staked the claims. Just as we finished up the weather lifted and Russ Baker flew in to stake the claims. He was too late, though, as we had them all sown up.

"If you ever check an encyclopedia, you will find that the Pinchi Mercury Mine was the largest on this continent and one of the largest in the world. Dad and the boys did quite well when it was sold to Canadian Mining and Smelting a couple years later. Dad noted that the $21,000 each felt good in his briefcase. This was a great sum of money back then, probably the equivalent of $400,000 today."

"I've looked at all the paper work of your dad's business dealings, Frank, and I have to admit that he did exceedingly well. Just the payments from his shares of the Pinchi Mine amounted to $114, 379.00 over the next eight years, which would equal a couple million dollars today. As well, he had a great many other shares and partnerships that made him financially independent. It is no wonder he left the police force; he could afford to. But tell me a bit more about The Fort back then."

Frank Cooke Sr. and Lawrence
Dickenson with $42,000.00 on
Granville Street, 1946.

Frank Cooke Sr. and Lawrence
Dickenson with $42,000.00 on
Granville Street, 1946.

"I remember that my dad used to go on patrols up Stuart Lake to the Tachie and Pinchi Indian Reserves, and then through Trembleur Lake and up to Takla Landing. I loved to go on these patrols with him and that is where I learned to run a boat and motor.

"Sometimes dad would go with Skook Davidson or Earl Buck when they would freight loads of supplies into Manson Creek or Germansen Landing. There were a lot of men of different nationalities working in the mines at that time and dad had to keep track of them. There were also many trappers and others spread throughout the area. Dad had all their names recorded—how they were doing, what they needed and when they were expecting to come out to town. That way if they didn't show up, dad would check on their whereabouts or go looking for them. I learned a lot from watching my father—how he handled people and commanded their respect.

"I went to school in The Fort for several years and during that time I always had a saddle horse. I loved to ride down to Earl Buck's farm on the Necoslie River every chance I got. I spent quite a lot of time there with Claire and Earl Buck. I remember that he was the best shot I ever seen or heard of. He could throw pennies in the air and hit them every time with a Remington semi-automatic .22. He was also deadly with a pistol. He never aimed a gun; he just pointed it and shot. He was not very tall but he was certainly well built. Earl Buck was a great cowboy who came in first in five events at a rodeo held in Vanderhoof in 1927. He even went one better that day by riding a bareback bronco backwards without falling off. I will never forget him because he taught me a great deal.

"Earl first came to the area in 1923 by riding the rods, and then spent that winter trapping. After that, he freighted supplies from Vanderhoof to Fort St. James for several years. Claire joined him in 1930. Earl also worked with Skook on the Manson Trail and the construction of the road over Old Baldy Mountain [Baldy Mountain]. He freighted a lot in the early 30s and sometimes Claire would go along with him. Earl hauled supplies to the Sultry and Pioneer Mines and also up to the lookout for the forestry.

"Earl had an Indian chap named Justa Sam that used to travel with him; he rode a big horse called Snake. Earl's horse was called Torpe and mine was called Bessie. We used to ride along the Necoslie River where Earl had herds of black cattle. I also used to go out to the McCorkell Ranch toward Pinchi Lake every chance I got to see Skook Davidson when he was there. He packed and hauled with his horses for years along the Manson Trail. At that time I had no idea that I would spend many years working with him and that he would teach me so much about horses, packing and the woods. On his trips into The Fort I would often help him hook up his horses at the Hudson's Bay barn.

"I can still remember branding a horse at the old McCorkell ranch about 1936 or 37. I can see old Skook standing there with his hat

Earl Buck on Paso at Fort St. James, 1960.

on. It was the first horse I ever branded. I can still close my eyes and smell the smoke rising off the horse and hear Skook giving me hell and telling me how to do it. My dad was there of course—not in uniform, but just watching to see how I was doing.

"One of my best friends throughout those years was a lad named Craig Forfar. We used to enjoy helping the freighters look after their horses when they were in town. They were our heroes, you know. Anyway, Craig's parents owned a hotel with a small bar and all the freighters used to gather in there. Craig and I were too young to enter so we went in the back way to the kitchen and watched them through the door. They would set to drinking and after a while they would start fighting. It usually didn't take too long before my dad would appear and return order. He would tell them to straighten up and they would. Sometimes he would let them fight a bit as long as they fought fair, but if things got dirty or out of hand he would stop them. Looking back at it all, I'm convinced his bosses knew he had the ability to handle things and that's why he was sent to The Fort in the first place. If things were run then the way they are now, it would have taken a large jail to handle everyone. Dad had the brawn and the brains to handle any situation. He would often make it clear to people that he was not running a free boarding house so he would do whatever was necessary to get them home or to their camps or whatever."

"I've had more than a few of the old timers tell me that there were some tough guys around Fort St. James back then, Frank. As a matter of fact they mention Earl Buck and Roy Spencer as two of the boys who really 'got it on' as the saying goes. Apparently they got in a fight over a garden and while one guy told me it ended in a draw, another person swears that Earl Buck won the fight hands down. Yet another person told me that Roy wouldn't quit. Regardless, it is an established fact that Roy and Earl became great friends after their fight; the new friendship probably spawned by something called mutual respect. Herold Perison was another name that repeatedly came up. One fellow told me that those three guys and your father could have taken on the entire town."

Roy Spencer and Earl Buck, 1935.

"They were all tough guys, that's for sure. Perison used to be a wrestler before he came to The Fort, you know, and I've heard it said that Roy did some boxing years earlier."

In an effort to get more information on the early days around The Fort (Fort St. James), I visited Earl Buck's daughters, Sharon and Doreen, who still reside on the original land owned by Earl and Claire. They told me that the fight between their dad and Roy Spencer was a real barnburner that went on for a quite a while. It started because Roy was supposed to drive cattle to a distant pasture, but because he was in a hurry to visit his girlfriend, he just drove them a short distance. When Earl got back home he found that the cows had completely destroyed their garden—a serious loss in those days. So when Earl challenged Roy that it was his fault, the fight was on.

An incident that caused deep worry to the Buck family surely must be mentioned here. It was a thing that happened to many families years ago and was a constant worry to the pioneers—children getting lost in the forests. Doreen recalls the time when she was 14 years old and went by horseback to bring in the horses. Her nine-year-old brother Ronald rode along with her into an adventure they would long remember. After a thorough search, they finally found the horses about 20 miles (32 km) up the Necoslie River. The horses refused to head toward home, though, so the chase was on. After several futile attempts to turn them toward home, the horses crossed the river. Doreen had been warned by her father to never cross the river under

Doreen Buck at about 16, 1947.

any circumstances, but because they had expended so much effort up to that point, they did not want to return home empty-handed. They followed the horses across the river and then began a game of catch-me-if-you-can. Several times they caught up with the horses but each time they tried to get around them, the horses circled. With darkness approaching, Doreen led the way back toward where she thought the river should be, but she couldn't find it.

At one point she recognized a tree and three meadows that were repeatedly in their path and this forced her to accept the fact that they were lost and travelling in circles. With darkness approaching and a rainstorm in progress, she made the necessary decision to camp for the night. Fortunately she had two matches with her, so after gathering witch's hair lichen from the trees, she struck a match and got a fire started. In the last moments before full darkness, she and her brother gathered enough firewood to keep a small fire going throughout the night. Then they unsaddled the horses and watched as they sank to the ground totally exhausted.

As they sat in the dark by the small campfire the sound of raindrops falling in the woods around them spooked Doreen, but she put on a brave front so as not to frighten Ronald, who somehow managed to fall asleep in his exhausted condition.

When Earl arrived home that same evening, Claire advised him that the children were not home and at once he said, "They're lost; make me a lunch because I'm going after them."

It was a 20-mile (32 km) ride for Earl to get to where the horses had crossed the river, but he found their tracks and lit a large tree on fire in an effort to direct the children. As it turned out, the fire was out of their line of sight so it was of no value, but even if they had seen it, they couldn't have moved in the darkness. Sometime around 3 a.m. Doreen heard what she thought was an animal howling in the distance so she roused Ronald from his sleep. They listened for a minute and realized it was their father shouting far away in the distance. He was too far away to hear their shouts, though, and because it was so dark, they could not head in his direction. With no other option, they sat by the fire until daylight. At first light they saddled the horses and just got going when they heard their father shouting again. Somehow he had managed to follow the horses' tracks in the darkness to their general location, and so they were reunited.

But they were not out of trouble yet, because after traveling through the woods for half the night, their father was now lost, too. It took another hour or so of wandering around the woods until the

Guides Sharon Buck and her son Wade Christian with Yukon moose.

river came into view. Several hours later they reached home where they and their exhausted horses needed a well-earned rest.

Sharon also has a story about this same area and another hunt for the horses. On that occasion their mom's brother—Bud Shaver—went along with Earl and several other men. Toward evening Earl and Bud stopped to spend the night in a cabin 20 miles from nowhere; a cabin that once belonged to a man named John Wallin who had passed away years earlier. With full darkness upon them, they ate their lunch by the dim light of a Grease Glim (a lighted wick in a tin filled with bacon grease). As they sat in the cabin, Earl went into great detail concerning John's death; he also added that there were reports of people seeing John's ghost around the cabin area. Suddenly an eerie noise emanated from another room and Earl shouted, "It's John Wallin; come on in, John!"

By that time, Bud, who had freaked right out, had his gun in his hands and was ready for business. He finally calmed down when he learned that one of the other men had crawled in through an open window and was portraying the ghost of John Wallin.

Both women tell a story about a man called Duncan Bill and a feud that involved their father. Apparently Duncan had a dog that frequently roamed with a pack of dogs that ran wild in the Fort St. James area. After several dog attacks on his cattle, Earl caught them in the act and shot Duncan Bill's dog. In return, someone shot Earl's three-year-old stud horse. A short time later Duncan Bill was found dead with his head burnt off in a campfire. Immediately speculation raged in the area that he had been murdered. When Const. Frank Cooke investigated, he is reported to have stated, "It's obvious what happened here—Earl Buck shot Duncan in the head and then burnt his head off to destroy the evidence."

Both Buck girls state that they used to ask their father if he did it, but he neither acknowledged nor denied it. Instead he made it a point to just smile at them and let them wonder. But other sources in the area figure that Earl got a lot of mileage out of that story and so he just let it ride. Some people say that it was possible that Duncan may have fallen into the campfire because he was an epileptic. Whatever the truth may have been, the cause of death was never established because the fire destroyed all the evidence.

Doreen has a special memory from the pioneer days. It concerns a night the family spent outdoors when the temperature hovered at –60 degrees. Their family was in the process of moving from their winter cabin to their home farm when the cold spell moved in. Forced to camp beneath the trees, Earl put up a lean-to by using a tarp, and then spent the entire night cutting firewood to try to provide some heat to the family, as well as 100 head of sheep, some milk cows and horses. During the night the smoke and ashes coalesced on the trees above them and large balls of soot tumbled down on the campers.

Somehow they made it through the night—the sheep and cows with some frozen tails and ears—plus two sheep with badly singed wool from crowding the fire too closely. In retrospect, it is just another memory from the so-called good old days.

When I mentioned Skook Davidson's name, immediate laughter ensued and the two women had some stories to add to the never-ending collection already on record. According to what Skook told their family, he was assisted in leaving the Cariboo area about 1920 because of his habit of borrowing things and not returning them. In that particular case it was a borrowed horse that was given to another party rather than returned to the owner.

Several people around The Fort recall the time Skook borrowed a heavy fur coat from a man named Ernie Burden in

Constable Cooke and Skook, 1937.

Prince George. The coat was needed to fend off the cold on his return trip to Vanderhoof. A year later the lender was visiting in Vanderhoof when he spotted a man named Pat Patterson wearing what appeared to be his coat. He approached Pat and asked how he had obtained the coat and his obvious answer was, "Skook Davidson gave it to me." Skook was always known for being generous, but sometimes it was with the property of others.

Sharon and Doreen recall the time their father, although a close friend to Skook, got taken. It happened because a woman from England requested Skook pose for a painting. But Skook just had a ratty old hat, so he borrowed Earl's new Stetson. Some time later Earl asked Skook when he intended to return the Stetson, at which point he was informed that the Stetson had gone on to England with the woman. Skook was the kind of fellow who could get away with such actions because he was such a likable fellow.

But the keeper occurred one night at a community dance when Skook had a woman all wrapped up in his arms on the dance floor. He was chewing gum at the time and because of his close proximity to the woman, her hair got into his mouth. Unable to separate the gum and hair, Skook did the only thing possible and spit it out. Suddenly this poor woman was standing on the dance floor with a big wad of gum knotted up with her hair. I guess it's safe to say that Skook didn't win any favours that night.

During our conversation Doreen and Sharon asked me if Frank had told me the story about the day they hanged the schoolteacher in Fort St. James. When I admitted he hadn't, they filled me in. It seems that the teacher was a weird chap who delighted in refusing to let the children leave the room, which often resulted in them peeing their pants or worse. Eager to get the rest of the story, I phoned Frank and asked for his version of the event.

"I forgot all about that," was his response. "We used to call him Biff Jones because he used to strike us on the head with a dictionary. But one day at school he went too far and started teasing my sister and pointed out to the class the big birthmark on her face. She was terribly self-conscious about it and he really hurt her feelings. I jumped up from my desk and went at him but he was much bigger than me so I was losing until another boy jumped up and helped me; then we gave it to him. I got sent home from school over that, and then my parents got a note from him. Dad called him into the police station and we went over things and straightened it all out about me, and then dad made it plain to him that if he ever mentioned the birthmark in class again that he would talk to him by hand.

"Things didn't get any better around the school, though, so one day Craig Forfar and I, along with three other kids, decided it was time to do something. There was a big tree out behind the school-house and the trail went under it; this was where we set the trap.

"I had been doing a bit of roping so I was elected to throw the rope, while the other four guys were supposed to do the pulling. Sure enough, after we waited for a while he came along and walked right under the tree. I threw the rope and got him and the other guys pulled and up he came, almost up to where I was. I looked at his face and I couldn't recognize him because his eyes were bulging out and his tongue was hanging out and he was turning blue. The sight of him scared me so much that I shouted to the boys to let go and they dropped him."

"Are you telling me that you actually had him off the ground?" I asked."

"Oh, he was free and clear all right."

"How did he respond after that?"

"You would never know it was the same guy. But he only stayed until the end of the term and then he left the area. I don't think I ever seen him again after that."

"I understand that Earl Buck kind of saved your bacon when you were working at Pinchi Mine, Frank, it that true?"

"Yes. Some money was stolen and I was accused of it. When I got back to the mine, Earl and I were currying the horses when he asked me straight out if I took the money and I convinced him that I didn't.

When we went into the cookhouse, the crew were grumbling about me and one real big man suggested that he was going to slap me around and get the truth. The way I recall it, Earl faced them and said, 'Frank said he didn't take the money and I believe him; anyone who tries to slap him will have to slap me first.'

"There was dead silence in the room after Earl said that; it was obvious that no one wanted to try slapping him around. A few weeks later they found out who took the money—it was one of the cook's children. Anyway, that man didn't have the decency to apologize to me so that tells you what kind of fellow he was."

"I have another question for you, Frank, did you ever visit the Hugh Gillis burial site on Old Baldy Mountain?"

"I sure did. I went by there with Skook. There was a cross on the trail there where a man named Hugh Gillis took his own life. Apparently he received a letter from his girlfriend stating that she had married his best friend, so he built a cairn out of rocks and then killed himself."

I know the story, Frank, but just recently I was given a poem by Sharon and Doreen Buck. Their father wrote it many years ago and when I read it, it seemed to me that Earl actually felt Hugh's sorrow. At the very least, Earl has immortalized one of the most memorable tragedies of the North with his poem, which is appropriately titled:

Gillis' Grave:
Back in the 1870s when Manson trails were new,
From the eastern part of Canada came a miner staunch and true.
He landed in on Manson's Creek when pay was at its best,
He worked from morn till evening and didn't stop to rest.
For two long years he panned the dust to fill his poke with gold,
And dreamed each night of his sweetheart, with whom he would
    grow old.
Now the lure of gold was in his veins; it was hard to leave his
    claim,

But waiting at home was a maiden fair that would someday bear
    his name.
To Manson Creek and the properties round, many prospectors went,
But the women at night in the halls so bright left many without a
    cent.
But it was different with this lad; he stayed in his cabin at night,
For with a sweetheart waiting to marry him, he didn't think it
    right.
His partner grew weary of this life, and decided not to stay,
Hugh bid his friend a last goodbye and these parting words did say,
"This poke of gold is for my girl, so she can buy a ring,
I'll stay and wash another poke, then come home in the spring."
All winter he tunnelled in the bank; he piled his diggings high,
And with the break-up in the spring him dream was looming high.
He filled his poke and bound it tight, and headed on the trails,
Three hundred miles he had to tramp before he reached the rails.
With Baldy Mountain in his path; he climbed it to the top,
And coming down the southern slope, to eat and rest he stopped.
A pack train coming from the south, with food, supplies and mail,
Met this miner where he'd camped beside the lonely trail.
He asked them if they had his mail, "Hugh Gillis is my name."
And as they scanned the letters, there was one addressed to same.
He took the letter and read it through; they saw his face go pale,
His eyes turned green with envy; it's a sad and bitter tale.
His partner when he'd reached their home, this maiden fair did
    wed,
With gold enough to build a home, they lived his life instead.
Hugh's step was slow as he gathered stones and built them in a
    pile,
They all stood round dumbfounded and watched him for a while.
They heard a shot and then they found poor Gillis lying dead,
He couldn't bear to go on home; he took his life instead.
They buried him in that lonely spot, many years have come and
    gone,

But the memory of that fatal place will always linger on.
Hugh's poke of gold is up there, where he buried it in the ground,
And since that day though many have searched, it never has been
     found.

After I had finished reading the poem to Frank, he responded
with, "Now you see what I mean about tragedy in the North. There's
just something about living up there that seems to get to people. I
don't think you would believe how many people have committed suicide up there over the years."

"I want to get back to your father, Frank, I notice from his daily
diary that he purchased his own boat and motor while he was in Fort
St. James. Why didn't the police buy it?"

"I was in the office the day Inspector Tom Parsons came to visit
dad—I happened to be in the office sweeping the floor at the time. He
had a funny English accent that I had trouble understanding. He told
dad that he wanted to use the police boat to go up the lakes, but
dad told him he would have to rent one from the Indians. When he
asked where the police boat was, dad told him he had loaned it to a
family of Indians so they could go up to Takla Lake. Then the
Inspector got huffy and wanted to know why the boat was being
loaned to the Natives or anyone else for that matter. Dad set him
straight by telling him that the police were too cheap to buy a boat so
he had purchased his own. The Inspector was not pleased about that
and left with the remark that he intended to do something about it. A
few weeks later dad got a check in the mail for the full price of the
boat and motor."

"As the only policeman in the Fort St. James area, your father was
often called to investigate criminal activity. I notice in his diaries that
there were many cases of people bootlegging to the Natives."

"If dad found out that a white man was bootlegging to the Natives
he would go to his place and tell him straight out that if got caught
he would end up in Okalla. I distinctly remember one man who sold
a bottle of rum to a Native that had just walked out about 90 miles

from way up the Middle River to sell his furs to the Hudson's Bay Company. I knew the Native very well and I believe he is dead now. Anyway, as my father came along he found this man staggering, so drunk he could not walk. My dad took him into the office and questioned him as to where he got the liquor. When he got his answer, he asked how much he had paid for the bottle. When the man said he had paid $50, dad asked how much he got for his furs and learned he had received $100. Dad was disgusted; he just asked, 'How are you going to feed your family?'

"Dad locked him up for the night to protect him from himself, and then turned him loose the next day. He took him to the Hudson's Bay Store and helped him load up with grub to take back to his family. That Native became a good friend to my dad after that.

"After the Native left, my dad went over to the bootlegger's place

Constable Frank Cooke, left with HRH King George and HRH Queen Mary at Jasper, 1939.

and arrested him. I heard him say, 'Any man that will sell booze to someone for that price is not going to live around here as long as I am around.' Dad took him to Vanderhoof and he was sentenced to Okalla, I never did see him again."

"I have noticed the picture you have of your father with H. R. H. King George and H. R. H. Queen Mary in Jasper back in 1939. It appears obvious that he must have been held in high esteem to be placed in such a position of trust as to be their protector during their Canadian tour. I also found among your father's effects a letter from Prime Minister Mackenzie King congratulating the members of the Force for their duties surrounding the Royal Visit. This was done at the bidding of His Majesty the King. I assume you must feel a measure of pride at your father's accomplishments."

"Yes, dad was admired by the police force; I guess that's why they almost pleaded with him to stay on. But he was financially independent by then, so there was no point staying on."

"Do you have any other memories from your youth that you want to share, Frank?"

"Something I should mention is that I had a problem growing up in The Fort. People would often refer to me as 'the policeman's son.' When I would go to ballgames, play hockey, or anything else for that matter, a certain element would challenge me and I would have to defend myself. I had to fight to survive. It just seemed natural to me. I never had any training but I managed to hold my own. As you grow up into your twenties, the instinct is still there, so if you are hot-headed, you can get into a lot of trouble. I'm not sure it was good to be raised a policeman's son in a small town. The fighting ability did help me in later years, though, when I got up on the Liard River.

"After I started working with Skook Davidson, he gave me some advice by telling me that if I had to fight, then I should hit first and hit hard. I followed that advice and didn't take too many lickings. When my dad had to fight anyone he would knock him down and then stand back until he got on his feet; there was none of this hitting or kicking a man when he was down like there is nowadays. In fact, if you had hit a man when he was down back then, others would have straightened you out in short order. Once I had a fellow tell me that I must have a mean streak in me because I didn't take any guff from anyone. I let him know that if I had not stood up for myself that people would have walked all over me."

I have always been so intrigued by the adventures of Skook Davidson, I was anxious to query Frank Cooke about the years they had spent together. It didn't take much prompting to get him going.

"The way I remember hearing it, Skook bought that tractor in partnership with Herb Blackburn. Although it is hard for me to picture Skook running a tractor, he really did. Machinery wasn't his specialty, though, so he sold out to Herb and stuck with his horses. There were many tough pioneers around The Fort at that time. There was Dave Hoy who freighted along the lakes and rivers for many years and had some huge barges that could carry tractors or anything else you wanted to move. Dave and his family deserve a lot of credit for all they did for that country.

"Of course I put Skook in a class by himself. He was the proper man to travel the woods with if you wanted to learn something. Once when we were traveling he pointed out that a particular spot was a good place to winter horses. I asked him how he knew that the horses could survive the winter in that area and he told me, 'Kid, when the bottom branches of the trees point upward you know it is an area with little snowfall.' That's the way Skook was—very observant. Well, he spent the first winter at his new ranch in a tent—that was in 1939—and that was the start of the Diamond J Ranch right below Terminus Mountain. Skook didn't see anyone until spring when he heard two shots across the river. He answered with two shots and a while later Louie Boya, Amos Alec and their families appeared on the riverbank. Moose were very scarce at that time in the valley and those people were short of food. They stayed with Skook for a few days until they managed to get a moose. They got to be good friends with Skook after that.

"His first winter at the ranch he survived on some flour, 10 pounds of sugar and a pound each of tea and coffee. Obviously he ate wild game as well. It was cold but not too snowbound because the snow shadow made the place somewhat arid compared to surrounding valleys. When the temperature dropped to -50° he'd yell, 'It's hell on horses and the woodpile.'

"Skook added a new twist to his horse breeding program by mixing in some blood from BC Government horses into his herd. On one occasion he claimed that he tricked a provincial policeman into applying the branding iron. 'They can't arrest me for that' he used to say.

"Another trick Skook had up his sleeve was to give his guides the Diamond J haircut, which left you practically bald after a session in the bush. He called it 'a test to see if your girlfriend still loves you.'

"In 1941 Skook drove his horses down to Scoop Lake on the west side of the valley. He met the government surveyors and worked all summer with them. In 1942 he worked with his horses on the railway survey to Alaska for the United States Government. During that year Johnnie Rasmussen, Ludwig Smaaslet and Fred Forsburg worked with him."

"In 1943 Skook, John Rasmussen, Slim Pawnee and a man called Pat Cook walked from Fort Ware on down to Jim Beattie's Ranch on the upper Halfway river and stayed there about two months," Frank continued. "Then Skook bought about 40 head of horses from Jim and the next spring when the grass got green they drove the horses up the Peace to Finlay Forks and on to Fort Ware. They met a survey party there and I believe the man in charge was Dr. Campbell. They worked all summer up the Finlay, over to Caribou Hide and all through the Sustut. That fall they ended up at Bear Lake. They followed on down to Takla Lake where Dave Hoy had a scow business and he hauled their horses (I believe there were about 40 horses) on down to Fort St. James.

"After they arrived in Fort St. James, they took the horses on down to the old Bachon Ranch on the Necoslie to winter them there. By that time the Pinchi Lake Mercury Mine was operating and they used wood for power at the mine. This gave Skook and Earl Buck an opportunity: they got a chance to break and train a lot of the horses and then they moved them over to Pinchi Lake and got a contract to haul all the wood to the mine. The Indians were cutting the wood and they were hauling it. They built some bunkhouses and barns right there and I spent the winter driving a 4-horse team hauling cordwood for Earl and Skook. I was not very big at that time and the cordwood had to be piled 12 feet high. I used to have an awful time trying to stack it high enough. We used large hay hooks to stack it and I had my own outfit to look after. If I didn't get it loaded in time someone would always come and help me. When spring came we had 1,000 cords piled in one pile about two miles below the mill."

"I notice a picture of you with a deer you got on Vancouver Island, Frank. That looks like an exceptionally large deer for that area."

"That was the second largest deer taken on the island that year. So for a young lad, I was sure pleased." "About this time [1941] my dad

decided to quit the police force. The Inspector came to The Fort and said to dad, 'Frank, you have a great future on the police force, don't throw it away.' Dad told him that he was making big money from his shares in the Pinchi mine, and that he was fed up with all the red tape. He finally said, 'I'm done and that's that.' He purchased his discharge from the force for $100 and left the

Frank with his first deer, Upper Campbell Lake, Vancouver Island, 1941.

service September 30, 1941. My folks moved to Vancouver after he retired from the force."

"Did you stay at Fort St. James?" I asked.

"After a while I went to Vancouver and took a welding course, then worked in the shipyards for awhile. At that time I was the youngest welder on the coast. But I hated Vancouver; I just couldn't stand it. I wanted to go back north."

"Wasn't there a good story about you getting in an argument with your dad?"

"We got into it pretty hot one day and I got so angry I shouted, "Dad, one of these days I'm going to kick your ass for you!"

"Do you think you scared him?" I asked.

"No! He just smiled at me and said, 'Son, when that day comes I will be proud of you', so obviously I didn't scare him."

"So you returned to Fort St. James?" I questioned.

"That's right."

Chapter 4

FRANK TOLD ME A BIT ABOUT GETTING IN TROUBLE SO I
asked him to elaborate, which he did. "Sometimes a person gets in
trouble when they don't mean to; I know that happened to me. For
instance, I got myself into a lot of trouble before I threw the booze
away for good. There was the time I was driving my vehicle and was
pretty well loaded up when I got in a fight with a policeman. I woke
up in jail the next day and couldn't remember what had happened. It
took about five months before the case went to court and I ended up
with three months in Okalla. Actually I didn't spend much time there
because I was shipped to a logging camp in the Chilliwack Valley.

"Man, there were some weird people at that camp—every type you
can imagine. One fellow used to wear glasses without any glass in
them, so I asked him why he did that and he told me to bugger off. I
think there was about 1700 men altogether and some tough ones, too,
so when they told you to bugger off then that was the proper thing to
do. Anyway, one day the guy with no glass in his glasses sidled up to
me in a rather sneaky way and handed me a note. It explained why he
didn't have glass in his glasses. It was a long drawn out tale about how
the government—especially Premier Bennett—was responsible for
everything. I think he should have been in a nuthouse instead of in
that place. Another thing about that place—I never ate better food in
my life—yet the men were complaining all the time. They should

have tried a diet of goat and sheep such as I had in the Kechika and they would have thought they were in heaven."

"Any other tales of trouble?" I asked.

"Well, there was the time in the spring of 1944 when several of us got partying out at the McCorkell Ranch near Fort St. James. Bert McCorkell had rented the ranch to a couple fellows and they made a big batch of champagne. Craig Forfar was there, as well as John Rasmussen and Stewart Hoy. Skook was also there, because he was getting ready to head out with his horses for the Kechika Valley."

"Well, everybody got hammered that night including me; although I didn't let the others see me taking the drinks because they would have stopped me. When I got hammered that night I started thinking of my girlfriend, Frances Wilson, in The Fort and I decided to go see her. One of the men renting the ranch was named Phillip Robertson and he had a Fargo truck sitting in the yard with a load of seed grain on it. I had never driven a truck before but I got in and managed to get it started. That was a bad mistake, because I took off for The Fort about 20 miles away and never got there. I did manage to get to the Ocock River, though, and it had steep hills on both sides. I didn't know how to shift gears, so I got it going as fast as I could so that I would be able to climb the hill on the other side. There was a sharp curve just before the bridge and that's where I left the road and hit the guardrail dead centre. The truck stood on its nose and then did a flip to land upside down in the river with the seed oats flying in all directions.

"I must have got knocked out, because when I came to, I saw water running right through the cab. It was a hell of a mess with glass everywhere and part of the truck hanging from the bridge. Someone from Manson Creek happened along and gave me a ride into The Fort to the Wilson House. I was still drunk and I must have fallen asleep because when I woke up, the policeman, Bell Munkley, was there. He was not happy, I can tell you that. He examined me to be sure I wasn't hurt and then he really laid the law down to me.

"When the boys at the ranch woke up the next morning they realized that I had taken the truck so Phillip and Skook came by horseback looking for me. When they reached the Ocock River, they found the truck but didn't know if I was dead or alive. When they got to town, Skook and the policeman got into a row because he accused Skook of giving me booze, which he didn't. Skook really blew up at him and told him straight out that it was a damned lie, so he calmed down and let it go.

"Well, the end result of that adventure was that Skook and Lawrence Dickenson paid for the truck to be repaired in Prince George. My end of the bargain was that I would work for Skook at $50 a month until the bill was paid off. It was a big bill and that was a hell of a lesson for me. That is why I wintered in the Kechika with Skook, because I had no money to go anywhere. Maybe it was worse than going to jail because I sure had to toe the mark. Skook's methods were crude, but they were effective.

"When I look back on it, it was probably the best thing that could have happened to me, but I sure didn't think so at the time. I went from living in Vancouver with rich parents in a big, fancy house in Kerrisdale, to sleeping in a tent at −50 degrees looking after horses in the Rocky Mountain Trench 100 miles from nowhere. Believe me, that's a character builder."

I put the question to Frank, "So you headed north with Skook?"

"Yes, we moved the horses out in the spring of 1944 to the McCorkell Ranch and got things ready to go. Craig Forfar and John Rasmussen were with us, along with 40-head of horses. When we were ready to travel, Stewart Hoy, John, Skook and I pulled out for Manson Creek. We left our first bunch of horses with John at Germansen Landing, and dropped off the second bunch with Craig at Aiken Lake.

"One thing Skook taught me was to always make smudges for the horses when the flies were bad, and we always had to put rails around the fires so the horses couldn't burn their feet.

"Another trick we used was to put the camp on the back-trail side of where the horses were put out to feed. That way we would hear the bells if they tried to move back past our camp during the night. That saved a lot of time finding horses early the following morning.

"Well, we carried on to Moose Valley where we found a mowing machine and a hay rake that had been left by the Bedaux Expedition many years earlier. Skook told me that we were going to take the mower into the Kechika and I stayed awake all night trying to figure out how we could get the mower through the trees and across the rivers. I was 17 at that time and it didn't make sense to me. The next day we went to work and started tearing the mowing machine all apart and loading it on the horses. It was terribly rusted and it took us three days to get it apart and loaded. The wheels were put on one horse, but the main base was another story. We had a big, black half-Percheron mare called Topsy for the big load. Skook told me to gather an abundance of bunch grass that is so prevalent in the valley, and I did. We dried it by the fire and jammed it into gunnysacks and wrapped the sickle bar and pitman with these bags. Then we wrapped the base and laid hay sacks against Topsy's back so it wouldn't rub her. We would have taken the rake as well but we didn't have enough horses.

"We left seven head of horses at Thutade Lake with Stewart Hoy and carried on with that mowing machine. Then Skook and I, just the two of us with about 15 horses, carried on down to Fort Ware. We had to raft everything across the Finlay River at Bower Creek. Seven trips by raft, and each time we had to frog the raft back upstream to the starting point. We got by that river and then we came to the Fox River. It was at high water stage so we had some real fun crossing there.

"I was in for a big shock when we got to Fort Ware, because I had heard so much about it that I thought it was a big town. So you can imagine my surprise when we got there and all we found was an Indian Reserve, a Hudson's Bay house and store, and a bunkhouse."

When Frank stopped for a minute I interrupted by asking, "What was your biggest surprise on the trip up to that point?"

"I guess it would be the Indian children. They used to run and play along the rivers—the Natives always camped along the lakes and rivers you know—and the children never seemed to fall in. I couldn't believe it. They loved their children but didn't seem worried about them drowning. Yet in all my years in the North I only heard of one Indian child drowning and that was near Lower Post on the Liard River many years later. I often felt pity for the Indians, and Skook was so kind, if he saw the Natives were short of food he would always give them some of ours, and that often left us short. The children never had any candy to speak of so we used to share what we had. The stories that the Indian Agents took care of those people are not true. They often starved or were desperately short of food. Another thing I must mention: there were few moose and caribou in that country back then. The wolves played hell with them. There is much more game in those mountains now."

"Did you stay around Fort Ware?"

"We stayed for about a week. While we were there, Dick Corless, Jimmy Ware, Hamburger Joe and a carpenter freighted in some supplies from Prince George. They were going to build a new Hudson's Bay Store. Anyway, when we were ready to leave, we packed up our horses and traveled through Sifton Pass. Skook would only travel six hours a day because of the heavy load Topsy was carrying. In one place we came to a big fire that was lit by an Indian named McCook and Skook asked him what was going on. His response was a lesson in simplicity, 'Us makin moose country, you see. Pretty soon you see lots of fat-ass moose this place for sure.' That was my first taste of man-set fires and I had no idea at the time just what a gift they are to wildlife.

"We carried on to the Gataga River, which was booming high and wild, so we had to change our plans. We built a cache and put all the saddles, blankets and equipment in it. Then we put the mower beneath it and left it to be picked up later. We had quite a time crossing the Gataga River, which was high and wild because of all the rain.

We built a raft and drove the horses into the river. When they were about half way across, we pushed off with the raft, which should have been a little bigger because we were taking water. Skook bellowed at me to paddle hard and I sure did. Eventually we got across and then carried on right into the Kechika Valley.

"When I look back on it, it was an awful job rafting that mower and the other equipment across the Finlay and the other rivers we had to cross, and we had to build a raft for each crossing. It was a very rainy season and being that I was small for my age I found it hard to lift the mower and other equipment onto the horses every day. Also, we had to cut trail every day so I really found it to be a rough trip."

"What did you find for game on that trip?" I wanted to know.

"There was very little game at that time, although we did find quite a few sheep in places. We packed everything on to Medula Creek at the foot of Terminus Mountain, which is the last mountain in the Rockies, and we got into Skook's Diamond J Ranch about the 25th of August. Willard Freer—a Native that stayed with Skook—had spent the previous winter there and we expected a lot of grub to be there when we arrived, but there wasn't. This meant that I had to go up the mountain and shoot goats, sheep and blue grouse. That is where I learned to shoot the heads off grouse, because if you shot them in the body with a 30-30, there would be nothing left.

"During the fall, we built a cache and didn't see a soul until Willard showed up from Lower Post with some grub on October 15th. After the water went down in late fall, we returned to Gataga Forks and moved the mower and other supplies on to the ranch. Then Skook, Willard, and I took 30 horses to Fort Ware and it took us six days. The purpose for the trip was to get a winter's supply of grub, so we loaded up the horses with everything Skook thought we needed to survive the winter. The trip back to Terminus Mountain took 12 days because Skook would not push a loaded horse. I have to say this, though, you never saw a blemish or a sore on his horses; that's the way he treated them. Well, when we got back to the ranch we settled into the cabin for the winter. That was the winter of 1944/45."

"Did you have any contact with your parents during that time?" I wondered.

"Not a bit. I found out later that my mother hounded my dad continually to find me, but dad told her not to worry because Skook was a first class woodsman and would take care of me. Besides, there was no means of communication where we were at that time, and we didn't want to walk over a hundred miles for the mail.

"What did you do during the winter? I asked.

"We kept busy all winter, that's for sure. There wasn't much snow so we built snake fence and cleared land. Besides that we always had to cut and split a large amount of firewood. When you worked for Skook you got $50 a month so it didn't take long to figure how you stood financially. One of the jobs we had to do with regularity was move the horses. When the horses had pawed a meadow it froze and there was nothing for the horses to eat, so we would move them to a fresh meadow where they were able to paw up grass. If you don't force them to move, some of them will just stand under a tree and starve to death. The winter of '46 was a tough winter in the North and many horses were lost that winter, but we never lost a single horse to starvation, and Skook made darned sure of that."

"Did you work hard during the winter, Frank?"

"We worked six days a week and then took a bath on Saturday night. Skook and I did most of the outside work and Willard did the cooking. On Sundays I washed all our clothes. Willard was a nice fellow, but as I told Skook, he was the only man I ever knew that squatted down to take a piss."

"Did you ever have any disagreements with Skook?" I queried.

"I remember one of them. We were making smudges to keep the flies away from the horses and Skook hollered to me, 'Kid (he always called me kid), how would you like to make more smudges for me?'

"I must have been in a bad mood that day because I shouted back, 'How would you like to go to hell?'

"Skook walked over to where I was standing and said, 'Kid! I promised your father that I would make a man out of you or kill you in the process and I'm prepared to do either one!'

"He looked me right in the eye and I knew he meant it; I never gave him any lip after that. Another time I wasn't doing things quite as fast as Skook wanted so he shouted at me, 'Give it up, Kid, go back to Vancouver and become a pimp.'

"I remember the day he fired one of the crew and I told him to fire me too, because I wanted to get out of there. He shouted back to me, 'You're the one that has to stay because you will be taking over this outfit someday when you are ready; but you are not ready yet so do as you're told and no lip.'"

"Was he tough to work for, Frank?"

"Well I guess he was tough but at the same time I have to say he was fair. He was strict about a lot of things, such as when the Indians came to visit—he would trade grub for fur—he was worried about getting tuberculosis, so as soon as they left he made me wash the floor with Creolin [a disinfectant containing cresol]."

"Did it bother you spending the winter out there in the wilderness?"

"Well I can remember climbing Terminus Mountain several times right to the top. Skook had told me that the Alaska Highway was over in that direction so I thought if I could see it, that maybe I could walk out to it and get the hell out of there. But all I ever seen was endless mountain peaks. I have flown over those peaks countless times since those days, so I know that if I had been crazy enough to try, I never would have made it out alive at that age. That was a pretty tough upbringing for me—just a young boy—but I learned to be self-sufficient. I would take a tent and go down the valley about seven miles and camp out. I would check all the horses to see that they were fine and that the wolves were not bothering them. I had to be certain that I checked every horse because if I told Skook I had seen a certain horse in a certain place and I hadn't, then if Skook went the next day and that horse was miles from that place, I was in trouble. It was not easy to deceive him."

"Did you manage to find enough game to eat in the area?"

"There were very few moose at that time. The wolves kept them cleaned out, and as well, they played hell with Skook's horses. He lost 18 head one winter. We tried everything we could think of and we couldn't keep them away. We had all the bells in camp on the horses and we even tied clothes and different things on the horses but the wolves still attacked. But they made a mistake when they went after Skook's horses because he declared war on them for that. The next year he got poison from the Game Department and the wolves got some of their own medicine. But to feed the 14 sleigh dogs and us, it was mostly mountain sheep that we ate, because they used to come right down the mountain during the winter. We used many of them for dog food. They were lying around the yard and the dogs were chewing on the ends of their horns. I never dreamed that they would be worth so much money in years to come.

"We had a strange thing happen that winter. Skook and Willard were in the cabin making supper and I was out gathering firewood when I happened to glance down the river and saw a dog team coming on the run. When it got close I recognized Dan McCook, his wife Angel and their four children. After Dan tied his dogs and gave them each a frozen whitefish, he set up his tent and tucked his wife and children in bed. Then he came to the cabin with a sack of furs. Skook used to do a bit of trading with the Natives so he and Dan made a deal. I remember asking how far they had traveled that day and I think he said about 20 miles. Anyway, he laid out his furs, which, if I remember right, consisted of three mink, four weasels, a wolverine and two coyotes. The reason I remember is because I was so interested in that sort of thing. Well, Skook examined them and offered a sack of sugar, and a sack of flour, two tins of jam and a roll of snoose. And then, just for a bonus Skook threw in a pail of lard.

"The next morning we heard a knock on the cabin door and it was

Dan. He asked if we had any milk and Skook gave him a large can of powdered milk. Just as he turned to leave, Dan smiled and said, 'My wife had a baby boy last night.' Man, we were sure surprised. It must have been close to 50 below that night, so that gives you an idea just how tough those people were."

"Did you keep busy enough to avoid boredom throughout that winter?" I asked.

"You never had to worry about getting bored; Skook made sure of that. We built many miles of snake fence that winter and when spring came Skook and I drove the horses back out to Lower Post and on up the highway to start work on the BC-Yukon Boundary survey. It was really something to see the young colts swimming the rivers with their mothers, and some of them were only about one month old. During the summer I went on an advance party with two surveyors and twelve head of horses; we had a swamper who did the cooking while we went ahead and did the topographical for the main party

Skodini on tent pole.

who were coming behind. The first thing we did was cut a trail for 16 miles to the head of Teslin Lake. Because of all the muskegs, we fought flies like I've never seen before or since. We had to smudge the horses all night long, and what with getting up at daylight to gather and pack the horses, it was a test for any man. It was a damned tough summer for me, but I learned a lot from working around some good men."

Remembering a story I had heard earlier, I asked, "What was the story about you and Craig Forfar and the human skull?"

"We found that skull out in the woods near the Hyland River and brought it back to camp. We called it Skodini and put it on a stick right beside our tent. Well, when the police found out about it they were a little upset. One of them asked us, 'Are you guys killing people around here?' We assured him that we weren't and so they took the skull and had an investigation. When they finished, they told us that the skull was from an old Indian who had starved to death. His body had been placed in a tree for burial and eventually it fell down. But there was a funny side to this story, because we got some red reflectors from the Alaska Highway and put them inside the skull right behind the eyes. Man, I'm telling you that when the campfire reflected off those red eyes the Indians used to shudder. Several times they told us that we were going to be killed."

"How long did you stay out on that job?" I questioned.

"Until I got injured. One morning I went out to Logjam Creek at the highway to pick up a load of grub for the crew. While I was waiting for the truck, I decided to fix a bell on one of the horses. The wire I was attempting to use was not sharp enough to penetrate the material that supported the bell so I sharpened it up some with a file. Then I managed to get it part way through and it jammed. I fiddled with it for a while and then jerked it back out and the sharp end hit me in my left eye. The shock was such that I fell over onto my back. The cook came running over to assist me and when I took my hand away from my eye, it was covered with blood. The cook looked at it and said, 'You've got to get out of here somehow'."

"Did you think you were hurt bad, Frank?"

"You bet! And luckily, just then a US Army jeep came along. One of them happened to be a first aid attendant so he examined my eye and told me that I had to get to Whitehorse as soon as possible. I told him, 'I can't leave these horses here.' I was worried that Skook would be furious with me."

"Never mind the horses," he shouted. "You've got to get to a hospital."

"I told the cook to get word to Skook. I figured Michelle McCook—a little Native from Fort Ware—could handle the horses and he was with Skook at the time. Well, they loaded me in the jeep and started for Whitehorse. The road was rough and it took a long time to get there. After a couple hours my head got aching so bad I could barely stand it. Then the tall guy took out a bottle of whiskey and said, 'Here, drink this!'

"I took three stiff pulls of the whiskey and I guess because I hadn't drank much it really hit me. By the time we got to Whitehorse I was so loaded that I didn't want to go to the hospital, but the big guy just picked me up and carried me in. They put me in a bed and I stayed there for three days; all they did was put some salve in my eye. The fourth morning they put a gown on me and when I asked what they were going to do, one nurse said, 'Dr. Ross is going to take your eye out this morning.'

"I put up with that until they got me on the table and then I jumped off the table and shouted, 'Nobody is taking my eye out; I want to go to Vancouver!'

"Then the doctor and I went right at it. He was a big, fat guy with glasses who kept shouting at me to get back on the table so he could take my eye out, but I kept shouting that I wanted to go to Vancouver. The nurse was standing there with her eyes bugging out; I don't think she'd ever seen a performance like that before. I also told the doctor that I was working for the government surveys near Teslin Lake and that I should be on compensation. I insisted on going to Vancouver on the first flight. Finally he asked, 'How are you going to buy a ticket?'

"I gave him my dad's address in Kerrisdale and told him to call and he would get my ticket at once, which he did. It was a long, slow flight on that DC3 with four stops along the way; I was on a stretcher and the stewardess helped a lot by talking to me every chance she got. When we arrived in Vancouver, dad met the plane and took me to the Birks Building where he had an appointment with Dr. Elliot. After he examined the eye, the doctor told us that if I were an old man he would remove the eye, but because I was so young, he was going to attempt an operation."

"You must have went through hell during that time." I suggested.

"You bet I did, but I didn't want to lose my eye. Anyway, they operated at St. Joseph's Hospital and I stayed in bed with bandages over my eyes for a month and it is surprising how a person can get along. One night I got one of the guys to help me to the bathroom and the head nurse caught us; boy, did she give me hell. I wasn't supposed to be out of bed at all. Well, after 30 days they took off the bandage and I really freaked out. I said to the doctor, 'I'm blind, I can't see!'

"The doctor calmed me down by telling me that my eyes had to adjust. They made me wear tight, dark glasses that completely covered my eyes and after four or five days I realized that I had lost the vision in my left eye. But I still had the eye and that was important to me.

"When I left the hospital, I went to stay with my folks. I had never seen their new home so my first thought was, 'Wow! What a mansion.' It was obvious to me that dad had really done well in the mining business."

"So you found yourself back in Vancouver." I suggested.

"Yes, and an interesting thing happened while I was staying with my folks: I was out mowing the lawn when the neighbour came over to talk to me. He knew I was a stranger there so he asked where I was from and I told him about my travels up in the North. Then he asked if I had ever seen any Stone sheep up there. I assured him that I fed them to my dogs all the time. We talked for a while and he told me that he owned R. J. Pop's Taxidermy and that he would love to hire us to guide him and friends on Stone sheep hunts. I said I would talk to Skook about it and got his address, just in case. Then he invited me to his home and showed me lots of movies he had taken of bighorn sheep hunts he had been on. When I told him that the Stone sheep horns I had seen were much longer, he showed great interest. He also told me that he had the world record caribou, which he had taken up North."

"Did you stay long in Vancouver?" I asked.

"I was supposed to stay there for six weeks, but I got to thinking about Skook and how he could be short of help. I found myself missing the adventure of life in the North; it suddenly occurred to me that I was getting hooked on the wilderness. Well, I flew back to Whitehorse and caught a ride down the highway with a fellow in a Ford truck. He was a US Army guy and he talked with such a drawl that I could hardly understand him. He let me off and I walked three days back into the woods before I caught up with Skook. He put me back with the same horses as before so that Michelle could come back to work with him."

"Did you fellows have any humour back in there?" I asked.

"Yes, in fact that reminds me of a joke Skook pulled on a cook named Bill Anderson. Skook knew that Bill was terrified of bears and he got a chance to pull a good one on him. Skook had two mares— Big Lady and Little Lady—who often played and fought with each other. When they got going they would make the most hideous sounds. Late one evening they were going at it and the cook got all excited and wanted to know what animals were making those sounds. Skook told him it was two grizzlies fighting, and then he grabbed a big stick and went tearing out into the darkness. A minute later Skook's voice could be heard mingled with the animal sounds. After everything quieted down Skook came back to camp and said, 'God damn it! Those grizzlies were really raising hell out there.' The next day the cook let it be known that Skook was the bravest man he had ever met."

"So you did have a bit of humour out there in the woods." I suggested.

"Yes, but the trouble with humour is that it can backfire. I remember the night I played a joke on an Irishman in camp—he's dead now; he fell over a cliff. I was walking by his tent to go to my own tent when I started scratching his tent with my fingers. Boy did he ever holler. When the others came running I was in my tent, so they didn't suspect me. But afterwards it occurred to me that there were several rifles in camp and if he had been armed he darned well could have shot me. I scared the hell out of myself when I realized what I had done.

"I want to tell you another story that took place with that same crew. We had a real old guy for a cook, and if the men had seen him perform the way I did one day, they never would have eaten that food. He always had a big pipe in his mouth and he had no teeth. There were ashes flying off it and getting into the dough. Spit used to drip off the end of his pipe right into the food. When he came back from the toilet, he didn't even wash his hands. That wasn't my idea of roughing it, but that's the way it was, we ended up with some of the strangest characters on those surveys. It seems that we had to take whatever we could find.

"Anyway, when the job was finished we headed back toward Lower Post and I recall we were camped at the Rancheria [Indian Reserve] at Mile 10 when we got into an interesting conversation. Skook seemed concerned about something and finally said, 'You know, Kid, I don't know what we're going to do. This surveying is going to go to hell in a couple years and there will be no work for the horses. I don't know how we're going to make a living, Kid.'

"I then told Skook about meeting Mr. Pop and about him wanting to hire us to guide him and his friends for Stone sheep. Skook thought about it for a while and then said, 'God damn it, Kid, maybe it's a good idea.'

"The next morning when we went to gather the horses we found one of them dead. It was a colt that had traveled with us all summer.

The wolves had killed it only a few hundred yards from our camp. The wolves were to pay a terrible price for hurting Skook's horses, though, because Skook poisoned a lot of them. He got strychnine."

"Did Skook really go for the guiding idea?" I inquired.

"It took a while to sink in. I think he would have done almost anything to carry on with his way of life; his horses meant everything to him you know. Anyway, when we got to Lower Post I sent my dad a wire through the Hudson's Bay Store. I told him that I would come down to see Mr. Pop in mid-winter. So Skook got hold of the Game Department in Prince George and got a big game guiding licence for the next year. Inspector Walter Gill flew in to the Kechika and asked Skook what area he wanted. He brought out a map and Skook drew a huge circle on it, which he requested for a guiding area. It was accepted, as up until that time it had been considered just useless wilderness, and they didn't think it was good for anything else anyway. Man, when Skook got that area he smiled and said, 'Kid, I think we've got something going.'

"We went back into the Kechika, and in February I took one dog, Blackie, and walked out to Lower Post, a distance of about 120 miles (192 km). I left the dog with my friend Bob Kirk and then went to Watson Lake and flew to Vancouver. I met Rudy Pop and his friend George Reifel—a real nice fellow—and we discussed everything. They agreed to come up the following fall on a 30-day hunting trip.

Because I didn't want to walk back into the Kechika during the winter, I stayed with my folks in Vancouver until May when I flew back to Watson Lake. There was nobody to meet me, so I walked the eight miles into town. From there I went to Lower Post, bought some grub and walked back into the Kechika Valley. And don't forget when you walked in there in those days you had to ford a lot of water and build rafts. It was a rough trip. I used to make it in five and a half days if I was really traveling.

"When I got back to the cabin I told Skook the news and he said, 'That's good, Kid, how much are they going to pay?'

"When I told him that they were going to pay $100 a day for a 30-

day trip he was happier than hell. He hired some Indians: Jack George, old Jack Abou and John McCook to build a raft and cross the river, then they cut a trail up to what is now known as Colt Lake. Willard and I went with the horses to the Yukon Boundary survey, where I stayed until it was time to go and meet Mr. Pop and Mr Reifel. I took them down to the Cole River, which is called Fireside Inn now. Fred Forsberg met us there with a big boat Skook had bought from the US Army. Skook didn't like to run it so he hired Fred to run it for him. Well, Fred met us and took us by boat all the way to Skook's Ranch about 100 miles up the Kechika River, where we stayed for two days while preparing for the hunt. The hunters couldn't believe how beautiful the country was, and they spent hours talking with Skook about other areas they had hunted. Skook had been to most of the places and they had a delightful conversation."

"Were you optimistic about the hunt? I wondered.

"I was excited all right, and a little anxious; I really didn't know what to expect or if we would be successful. But we were determined to give it a good try, so we swam the horses across the river and Forsberg helped us move all our stuff with the boat. We took off and went up to Colt Lake where we spent the night, and I'll never forget what happened the next morning, because we woke up to find 30 rams right on the hill above camp. It's a funny thing, you know, 30 rams right beside camp and Mr. Reifel didn't care if he shot any or not. Mr. Pop was more interested in taking pictures. Darned if he didn't go close to them and takes pictures but he didn't shoot a ram. I thought it was really weird but that's because I didn't realize that they were just on an exploration trip. We went right through the whole country to the head of the Frog River and through Pop Lake, which we named after Rudy Pop, and then came back through Sifton Pass to the home place. It took us 33 days in total. I'll never forget what happened then, because they pulled out a wad of bills and paid Skook in cash. I was anxious to get paid, too, because I intended to go out with the boat, which was coming back for us. Skook was puzzled about my intent so he asked me, 'Are you going to go home and spend the winter with your mom and dad?'

"No," I answered, "I'm not going home; I think I'll go trapping on the Liard River for the winter.

"This seemed to irk Skook because he came back with, 'If you're not going to spend some time with your folks, then I'm not going to pay you.'

"I don't give a damn if you pay me or not, because I'm not going home; I want to learn something else.

"The two other men had heard the argument so Mr. Pop came over to me and asked, 'Do you mean to tell me that he's not going to pay you?'

"He's not going to pay me now, but he will someday, I'm sure.

"We were both upset by that time and the boat had arrived so I started walking toward it with my gear when suddenly Skook shouted, 'You really mean it, don't you?'

"I shouted back, 'You goddamned right I do.'

"Then a change came over him and he walked up to me and paid me $5 a day for the time I had worked. This made me happy as that was good money back then."

"What made you decide to leave Skook and go trapping?" I questioned.

"I had already spent three years with Skook so I figured it was time for a change. Besides, I always thought there was something romantic about trapping. You know, a man against the wilderness all by himself."

"I hear you, Frank, and I feel the same way."

At that point Frank and I discussed a poem written by poet Brian Salmond of Fort St. John, BC. Brian spent some years working as a trapper and guide and claims that he wrote the poem as a tribute to a trapper/outfitter named Wes Brown, who worked the Buckinghorse River area many years ago. Both Frank and I agree that it really speaks to the heart of trapping and the wilderness, so with Brian's permission I include it here:

Just dreamin'
The trapper kicked his snowshoes off beside the cabin door;
He stomped his feet and shed the heavy daypack that he bore.
Then flexed the tired old shoulders and squinted in the dusk,
And kindled up a fire in a cookstove clad in rust.

The fire took hold and soon the warmth had spread throughout
    the room;
Then he fired up his Coleman lamp to frighten off the gloom.
The lantern's hiss, the long, long day, a little nip of booze;
The old boy lay down on his bunk and soon began to snooze.

When to his head a dream appeared and played upon his mind;
Of a far-gone place in yesteryear; a mansion large and fine.
You see he was the guest of honour all dressed up in his best;
At a fancy table with a maid, and a butler with a vest.

The meal before him glittered from the light of chandeliers;
And silverware and crystal shone like none he'd seen in years.
There came a trolley loaded down with roasts of duck and quail;
Turkey and scalloped potatoes, things to make his hunger fail.

Dishes loaded down with seafood, fancy shrimp and clams;
Some Oriental dishes and a glass bowl filled with yams.
He ate his fill of choicest food, until he thought he'd bust;
When the butler poured a glass of wine; he lapped it up with lust.

And then desserts they brought him, to tantalize his taste;
He smelled of each and every one and gobbled them with haste.
Then from a box of cedar-wood, a big, old, fat cigar;
The finest from Havana, it had traveled very far.

But as the smoke assailed his nose, he woke up with a start;
He quickly took a look around to still his pounding heart.
For as he grabbed his forty winks, and dreamed the dream of
    dreams;
His old cook stove had got too hot and burned his pork and beans.

Brian's poem really got us into the proper mood, so Frank continued with his story:

"I went downriver with the others and once I got to Lower Post, I bought some new clothes. Then I happened to run into a man I will call Gus, to protect any living relatives of his. Anyway, we talked for a while and I told him that I was interested in going trapping for the winter. As it turned out, Gus had an excellent trapline not too far from Lower Post. He had 10 good dogs, ran a first class outfit, and knew what he was doing. He asked me to come with him and in return, he would teach me how to trap and we would split the fur sales in the spring. Believe me I didn't have to think very long before I jumped at the chance. I just figured if I was going to be in the woods anyway, then maybe it was time for a change and a chance to learn something new.

"So on November 1st, Gus and I left with his boat and 10 dogs. We went down the river to his main cabin, which we stocked with grub. We stayed about one week getting everything ready for trapping and then we returned home. When we left with the dogs again it didn't take long for me to see that Gus was very good with dogs. He treated them well and they obeyed him to the letter. He ran them like a good teamster runs his horses."

"Did you both travel the lines together?" I asked.

"At the start he went with me and showed me the eight-day line I would be trapping, while he was to trap a 6-day line. He set all the traps on that trip and showed me what to do and what not to do. Gus was a tough man, squarely built and known to carry a grudge. The Indians were afraid of him, and for that matter, so were the whites, but I got along with him all right.

"When we got enough snow to use the dog teams, I ran my line and he ran his. Sometimes when I got back to the home cabin he wouldn't be in. He was almost 60 years old at that time so I worried a bit about him out on the trail alone. I would wait a day and then if he didn't show up I would hook up my dog team and go looking for him.

I went in vain, though, because every time I met him on the trail. After a trip around our lines, we would spend a day or two together at the main cabin and then we would both take off around the lines again. We were both catching lots of furs and the prices were high then. This was the winter of 47/48 and the snow got deep that winter. We managed to keep the trails open, though, because we traveled them a lot. I used to go down as far as Cole River across from where Fireside is today. Some of the traps I was tending were up high near timberline, but I used care and always carried lots of grub in case of an emergency. Gus was a good provider that way; he always kept lots of grub and dog food on hand.

"I managed to get lots of mink and lynx, so everything really went well until the middle of March. We had a hell of a snowstorm and as I made my rounds up near timberline, the snow was deep and blowing something awful. I had a rough trip and when I got back to the cabin with only 7 or 8 skins, Gus was there. He looked at what furs I had and said, 'You didn't get many furs, did you?'

"He caught me by surprise but I defended myself by saying, 'No! It was really rough going up high.'

"Gus didn't seem to like my explanation, though, so he replied, 'My cousin trapped with me last winter and he stole furs from me.'

"I tried my best to convince him, and we argued a bit about it, but I learned from Skook that it is not a good idea to quarrel in the woods. Well, we kept on trapping until one day I was on my way back to the main cabin when he came looking for me. I had an excellent catch, so he had nothing to complain about. It was snapping cold when we got back to the cabin, and we just had a piece of canvas for a door. That evening Gus suggested that we sleep on the same bunk so we could share our body heat and keep warm. I didn't see a problem with that as I had slept beside Skook many times. Anyway, I was lying on the bunk trying to go to sleep while Gus was lying beside me smoking his pipe. All of a sudden he asked me, 'Do you want to f——?'

"I didn't hear him very well so I asked, 'What was that?'"

"He repeated the words so I heard him good and clear the second time. I leapt out of bed and almost crashed into the wall, because he scared the shit out of me. My rifle was hanging on the wall so I made sure I got between it and him and then I said, 'No! I don't want to f——!'

"That started a fight, so I grabbed my gun and said, 'You stay right there, Gus, or I'll blow your goddamned head off and I'm not bull-shitting.'

"I could see that he was really wild; his eyes bugged out like a bulldog ready for a fight. He glared at me and shouted, 'You slept with Skook; do you expect me to believe you didn't do anything?'

"My clothes were close to the door so I ordered him to stay in bed and then I got dressed. When I went out the door I took his rifle with me and made it plain what would happen to him if he followed me. Then I harnessed the dogs, left his rifle for him, and took off for Lower Post. It was about 9:30 p.m. when I left the cabin and I made the 45-mile trip into Lower Post arriving there the next after-noon."

"Perhaps you were lucky to get out of there at that time," I sug-gested. "If you had stayed he may have gone back to accusing you of stealing furs and shot you."

"Well, I should have been suspicious that there was something wrong because he had so many trapping partners. Anyway, the next day I met a friend named Jock Rattray and while we were talking, Gus came into town with his dogs. As soon as I noticed him coming I said to Jock, 'I'm going to have trouble with that guy, but I'm in town now and I don't give a damn. If he wants grief, he'll get lots of it.'

"Sure enough, Gus got into a bottle of rum and then came looking for me. Jock and I were talking in a US Army hut when he came in. He took one look at me and said, 'I'm going to get you.'

"He dove at me, but I swung and knocked him down, then I shout-ed to Jock to get outside. Jock dove out the door and then Gus got up and got me cornered. He was an exceptionally powerful man, who had worked in the woods for years on the Pacific coast—hand log-ging—so when he caught hold of me he dragged me right into him and I had a hell of a time getting away from him. He bit me on the

Clayton "Slim Pawnee packed for Skook for several years.

face and I kneed him in the crotch, so he let go of me and I managed to escape and dive out the door. Then he came at me again. I suppose it's nothing to be proud of, but I really went at him. I knocked him down seven times before he stayed down. When he came to, he sat up and then Jock said, 'We're in bad trouble because he's going to kill you.'

"I assured Jock that he wouldn't kill me; in fact, I guaranteed that he wouldn't. When Gus got up, he looked at me and made a statement I will never forget, 'Goddamn it, I can't lick ya.'

"I assured him that he couldn't lick me and made it very clear to him that he had better stay clear of me in the future or I would break his neck."

As Frank related his story to me a sudden thought came to mind so I asked, "Do you think he could have acted that way to drive you out of there and get the money for all the furs? Maybe he pulled that sort of thing on others and got all their work for free. There's always the possibility that he would have accused you of stealing furs again and drove you out, if that had been necessary."

"No! I don't think so; I heard a lot of stories about him later. Anyway Gus went down the river right after that, and although we became distant friends in the future, I never trusted him again. All told, I figure that I lost about $5,000 by leaving the trapline, because we had a great catch of furs. But I shouldn't regret it because I learned quite a bit from that man. And there was a bright side to my coming out from the trapline, because I met Hattie Fellers there. I was working for Jack Christie at the time and Hattie was a stranger to the area.

I hadn't been around too many white girls for a long time, so she looked like a million bucks to me."

"You were probably lucky that you met her," I offered, "because you could have got bushed if you had stayed in the woods any longer."

"Things just seemed to work out in my favour, because we started dating and it didn't take very long for things to get serious between us. Those were sure wonderful days, because after being alone so much I really appreciated her company. One day I asked her to marry me, and she accepted. The wedding was set for June 17, 1948. I contacted Skook and told him what was happening and he came to Lower Post. I took Hattie across the river to where his horses were and introduced her to him. Skook looked her over and then said, 'By God, Kid, you've got a good looking girl; you'd better marry her before someone else does.'

"There were several people at the wedding: Skook was best man and the policeman, Johnnie Betts, signed the wedding certificate. After the wedding we went to Watson Lake in Christies' taxi, took some pictures and returned to Lower Post. We had some drinks, and then we set up two tents face to face with a cook stove between them. Bob Kirk, the guy that made all the money out of Cassiar Asbestos was in the other tent. I knew Bob when he was broke and I knew Bob when he was rich, and

Frank Cooke and Hattie Fellers' wedding at Lower Post, 1948.

I knew him when he was poor again and he was a hell of a nice guy. But how Bob got rich, now that's a hell of a story of its own. When the government report came out about asbestos in the Cassiar area, Bob's brother Ron, Hiram Nelson and Richard Sittler asked Bob to be their partner. But Bob had news for them because he didn't like hard work. It was about an 80-mile walk back to the area they wanted to stake, so Bob came up with a great idea: he would let them use his dog team in return for an equal partner status, which the others agreed to. Well, the men staked the claims and each walked away with $1 million.

"I have so many funny stories I could tell you about Bob, such as the time he went to Las Vegas. One day he was telling some ladies about snowshoeing up North, but they didn't really understand what it was all about, so Bob decided to show them. He went and got an enormous load of cornflakes and spread them all over his hotel room; then he bought a pair of snowshoes and showed the ladies how it was done by snowshoeing all around his hotel room.

"But getting back to my wedding, we had a party that night up at old Hans Anderson's place. The Indians showed up and we had a great time. About 4:00 in the morning Albert Dick and I got into a fight and he damned near licked me because he was a wiry bugger. I was half-drunk—three-quarters drunk, really—and Albert was a real nice guy, but it was a booze fight and I had to fight like hell to beat him."

"Did you do quite a bit of scrapping, Frank?"

"Quite a bit. One thing about that fighting business, you just never know when you tackle a man what you're in for. Sometimes you'll get a licking from the person you least expect. I had a few of them. But it's the same old story you know: whiskey and fistfights. It's the same as whiskey and driving a car . . . they just don't mix. I never could handle my booze; it got me into the only grief I ever knew until I threw it away."

"I notice that you frequently mention Bob Kirk, Frank. I gather that he was a close friend of yours."

"Bob and I always were close friends; he was a special kind of guy, that's for sure. But getting back to the fights, after learning some things the easy way and learning other things the hard way, it seems to me that if you treat people right, most of the time it will come back to you."

Chapter 5

"Skook came to your wedding, were you pleased to see him again after all that time?"

"Yes, and wouldn't you know that he had a job to go to with an Army survey party; it was at the head of the Highland River and he wanted me to take the horses in for him. I told him, 'God, Skook, I don't know; I just got married and I don't know what to do. Let me figure this deal out. I don't want to leave my wife.'

"Anyway, I got talking to the head of the survey party and he coaxed me to come by telling me, 'I don't know you very well but I'd sure like to have you on this trip.'

"We talked for a while and he asked if my wife could cook. I told him that she couldn't when she got here but she had been cooking for Christies' since then. Suddenly he floored me by suggesting that I bring my wife along as cook so we could spend the summer together. I thought that sounded like a great deal so I asked Hattie and she assured me that she would love to go. The wages were $7.50 a day each, which was darned good money back then.

"We took off from Lower Post with 12 horses and Charlie Hogg in charge of the party. By God, Charlie sure could sing—"Danny Boy" and all those old-time songs—he sure could cut the mustard. Anyway, we went on that trip and spent the entire summer out there, Hattie and I. Just six of us in the party and everybody got along real well. I did the packing and Hattie did the cooking and we moved camp whenever they wanted us to.

"I recall the day I was putting a pack on a roan mare that had never been packed before. A Colonel by the name of Smith was on an inspection trip of the surveys and he was watching me intently. I had blindfolded the mare so I could load her, and then I intended to lead her until she got used to the pack. But the Colonel didn't seem to approve of what I was doing, so he ordered me to turn her loose. I tried to explain to him but he repeated the order so I took the blindfold off and she exploded out of there and across the airport at Watson Lake. By the time she hit the trees, cans of milk were flying in all directions. Well, that Colonel just stood there with a red face, while I managed to capture that horse and repack her. When Colonel Smith finished his tour with us he made it a point to come to me and congratulate me on my work. I have to admit that it made me feel good, but I knew that the credit should have gone to Skook because he was the person that taught me what I knew about packing.

Frank's pack train crossing a branch of Gataga River.

"Sometimes when I was alone out there, I tried to put some of my thoughts into words. Such as the poem I wrote called "Old Trails and Cowboys:"

You've finished your dickering with the Hudson's Bay,
The horses are packed and the train's underway.
We're four days out and we've forty to go
As the rain turns to sleet and the sleet turns to snow.

The horses bunch up and turn tail to the snow
And this damned old buckskin I got from Rowe
Is off his home range and the pack hurts his back
Look how he doubles and tries to head back.

Tom Willis is boss of this part of the train
And he wants to keep moving come sunshine or rain
But we're cold and we're wet and the going is slow
With a forty-horse string in a foot of wet snow.

Now April's turned to May and it's hot in the shade
And the boss is still grumbling 'bout the poor time we've made.
The mosquitoes and horseflies are making a show
But it sure as hell beats the rain and cold snow.

We're 20 days out and there's no turning back
And the wily lead mare keeps shifting her pack.
But that old buckskin pony that I got from Rowe
Settled down to business a long time ago.

We climb a steep hill and the Sikanni's in sight
And the boss says we're camping right here for the night.
Then Old Spook frightens and unloads her pack
And our gear is scattered to hell and back.

So we're cussing out loud and picking up gear
As that old mare shakes and cringes in fear.
Then we build a campfire and call it a day
Cause the cook has moose meat and beans underway.

Now we've come to the Fontas, with no time to spare
Where we've had to lie over and patch up our gear.
The boss is cranky and the cook has turned mean
While the rest of us boys are just honed down and lean.

"It must have been a tough operation to keep the crews supplied with food for months on end, wasn't it, Frank?"

"Dalziel had just started up BC-Yukon Airways, and he had his aircraft bring supplies to different lakes where I would meet them with the pack horses, so it worked out quite well. It was mostly army rations of dried food that we ate, but there were some exceptions. One exception was canned milk, which was craved by everyone."

"Finally we got to Tent Peak, where we were supposed to end up, and by that time it was getting toward fall. We traveled through a lot of great country—not very much game—but an abundance of wolf sign everywhere. I killed a big caribou at Tent Peak, one of the biggest I've ever seen. Hattie and I were sitting there talking about what a beautiful country it was when she pointed to something below us and there was this huge double-shovelled caribou. He was about 400 yards from us and I had a 250-3000 rifle that my dad had given me; it was a good flat-shooting rifle. I was craving fresh meat, which we hadn't had for a long time, and I could tell at a glance that this animal was hog fat. I told Hattie to keep motioning which direction it was from my position as I crept down through the thick underbrush, and that is what she did. Once when I looked up at her she was waving frantically, so I ran ahead and burst out into an opening just in time to see him disappear into the brush. I started to run after him and first thing I knew he was coming back on the dead run. He passed about 20 feet from me, and God, was he ever beautiful. I got down on one knee and fired and he dropped in his tracks. We dressed him out and took part of the meat back to camp. When Charlie, the boss, spotted the caribou he shuddered, 'My God, Frank, if the government finds out about this we will be in trouble.'

"I calmed him down by saying, 'They won't find out, but if they do I'll take the blame.'

"Everyone was sure happy to have some fresh meat, so I went back the next day and packed it all to camp."

"A short time later the work was finished, so Dalziel flew in to a lake and lifted the crew and their supplies back out. For Hattie and I, it meant another nine days on the trail bringing the horses back to Watson Lake."

"Was Skook still there in Watson Lake when you got back?" I asked.

"Yes, he was waiting for his horses so he could take them back to the Kechika for the winter. Over the next several days other parties kept arriving with horses, and when they all arrived, Skook left with all his horses and a couple Indian fellows for the Diamond J Ranch in the Kechika Valley.

"Hattie and I were really lucky because we had all our summer's pay and the survey parties gave all the excess food to us on orders from Dalziel. We had enough food to last us all winter so we were well away, except for a place to live. A fellow named Leo Cormier had an old house right on the riverbank at Lower Post. The roof and floor were shot but when I asked him about it he said, 'You can have the darned place if you want to fix it up and I'll just charge you $30 a month rent.'

"I went to visit a fellow named George Deserta—a Tahltan Indian with a large family. He had 19 children and they were all nice; the best family I've seen in a long, long time. I paid him to help me, so we went and bought lumber and fixed up the cabin. It wasn't long until we had it ready and moved in for the winter."

"So you spent the winter there?" I quizzed.

"No. We stayed until November and that was when I met Lynch Callison. He told me he was going to rent a sawmill from Jim Rose up on the Liard River. He asked me if I wanted to go to work for him and since I wasn't doing anything, I agreed to go. We packed up and moved to the Liard where Leonard Kefferd and I fell trees with a crosscut saw. What a bunch of characters worked there; some of them were in and out of jail and all that. When December came along we were looking for some extra money for presents when I got lucky and shot a wolf. I stretched it out intending to get the bounty money—I think it was about $20—but when I went get it behind the shack, it was gone. I guess I shouldn't have been surprised, though, knowing some of the people around there.

"One morning there was a knock on our door and it turned out to be Hattie's brother, Nibs, and his cousin, Dave Fellers. I had never met any of her family as they lived near Dawson Creek and I had never been there. Nibs told us that he was going to Whitehorse and that he wanted to pick us up on his return trip to take us to Dawson Creek for a visit with Hattie's family. I told him we were short of money but that I would try to get word to Skook, because he still owed me some money. Well it all worked out, and when we got to Dawson Creek we had a big party and I met everyone except Hattie's parents who were out at their ranch. The next day we rode out to the ranch and the road was terrible, with deep snowdrifts, which suggested they must have had a mean winter.

"When we got to the ranch, Hattie's folks came out to meet us and Nibs just said, 'Here he is if you can catch him,' and he walked into the house. I just stood there not knowing what to do. I was shy— probably from spending too damned much time in the bush. But they invited me into the house and it didn't take long for me to realize that they were wonderful people; I mean really down to earth people. We spent about two weeks there and during that time we cut wood and rode horses. Hattie's brother Herb was a great horseman and he showed me all over the area. They had good horses— some were half thoroughbred and half knothead [inbred], but they were great horses and tough as well. Herb and I raced horses and got along really great right from the start. We've had our fistfights and all that and Herb still drinks while I don't, but I'll buy him all the booze he wants as long as I can sit and listen to him talk. He is very interesting and has the best memory of any man I've ever known.

"When the two weeks were over, Hattie and I rented a house in Dawson Creek and I went to work for Mack McCallum who had a contract with the city putting in ditches, sewers and the like. Frankie was born in August and he was a big, strong baby. I was sure proud of him. Mom and dad came up for a visit and dad drove me all around Rolla. He asked me if I wanted to farm and told me to pick out any farm I wanted and he would buy it for me. It was obvious that dad was doing great in the mining business; in fact, some of the newspapers called him a mining expert. I told dad that I wanted to drive truck and he told me, 'You must be out of your mind!'

"Dad just couldn't understand that I wanted to be free; at least as free as a person can be when they have to support a family. Well, dad relented and bought me a truck for $1775. I put a box on it and went hauling slabs. That winter we hauled ties and firewood. We never did get paid for much of the wood we hauled."

Mining exploration trip. Frank Sr. on the right, 1947.

"You really did try a bit of everything. Were you ever sorry you didn't take a stab at farming?" I asked.

"No. I was raising hell in those days and I'm sure I would have gone broke. Instead, I put a van on the truck and started hauling fresh goods up the Alaska Highway. I tried that all summer but I couldn't make any money at it. The truck was worn out just as dad said it was—he always seemed to be right. Well, we gave that idea up and moved back to Lower Post. They were building a new Indian school there so I worked on that. My old friend Jack Christie hired me to drive truck for him. He and his wife were great people, you know, when he bought new trucks they had a tough time paying them off but they got the job done. As well as owning trucks, he ran a restaurant, sold gas and even acted as a fur trader, too."

"Somehow I just never seemed satisfied with the different jobs I worked at," Frank observed. "But the years went by and we had more children: Terry, Diane, Mac, Tammy, Gloria and Donna. During that time I spent several years cutting ties with the Feller boys near Dawson Creek. I drove truck and life was good, but I always kept getting pulled back north. I always wanted to own part of Skook's place—not the home place, as I felt that belonged to him—but I wanted something of my own. In 1951, I went on a 30-day hunt for Gordon Torkelson who was based in Dawson Creek. I started out with guide Frank Golata from Buckinghorse—Mile 175 on the Alaska Highway—and we went to the very head of the Muskwa River. We each had a hunter to take care of and I was getting $10 a day. We had a great trip and covered a lot of beautiful country; we also spotted a lot of game. I'll never forget Frank, because he taught me a lot on that trip. He was the guy who took out the hunter that got the world record Stone sheep—51 inches—and it is a record that may never be beaten. Frank was just a little guy, but he had been a boxer in his day, so he was pretty tough. Anyway, while we were back in there I went up the mountain with my hunter and on the way back, he played out. I got tired of waiting for him so I came back to camp. When Frank came back to camp he tied into me and told me that I should never leave a hunter, regardless. He told me, 'They're paying us and we have to stay with them and treat them right.'

"He told me that I would make an excellent guide but I had to change my style, and of course he was right. The trip was going great for me, though, because I got my hunter a ram, moose, caribou and bear. On the way back, we stopped at Keily Creek where we had taken the ram. While Frank and I were setting up camp, he told the two hunters to check out the ram carcass to see if there was anything feeding on it. I suggested that we shouldn't let the hunters go to the carcass alone but Frank disagreed. Well, it didn't take long before we heard the damnedest bombardment down at the carcass, and then Frank told me to rush down and find out what was going on. By the time I got there, a huge grizzly bear was lying on the sand-bar and one of the hunters was poking it with a big, long stick. The other hunter was busy taking pictures with a movie camera. I jumped across the creek and shouted, 'Look out! That bear is liable to get us.'

"One of the hunters thought I was joking so he started laughing. I had a cartridge in the barrel so I jumped across the creek and right away noticed that the bear was not dead. It was blinking its eyes and twisting so I shot it in the chest. I skinned the bear out and found that it had only been hit in the throat, and the bullet had just nicked a bone. I'm convinced that the bear was only dazed and that it would have got up in a minute. The men were sore but I had to act."

"When a bear's eyes are moving it is anything but dead." I interrupted.

"I know, and when I got back to camp I explained to Frank that the men had put their rifles down on the bar and were having a good time. They would have been helpless if the bear had jumped up. I learned a valuable lesson that day—don't let hunters go out alone. But there was more to this story. The hunters had agreed that they would count to three and both would shoot at the same time and that is what they did. Then, when we got the hide back to camp, they got into a hell of an argument over who should get the bear hide trophy. Finally the issue was settled when the biggest guy took it. We were a long way from the Alaska Highway and it was a strange trip out because those two men never spoke to each other again. Another lesson learned— keep the hunters apart while hunting. It got so bad that one of the hunters stayed alone and the other slept under our fly. But I've seen worse. At least these two people didn't have to see each other again, which is not the case when we take a man and his wife hunting together, because they can end up in a fight, too. I've seen that happen and it's really bad because they have to live together.

"Something else I want to mention concerns that big ram we got. The hunter wounded it and it took off up the mountain just as high as it could climb. We followed it, taking turns moving so that one of us could see where it was all the time. It got up high and then laid down on a boulder at the edge of a crevice. When we got up close to him it was a steep climb and we were walking about 12 feet apart with a ridge of rock between the hunter and I. Suddenly I stepped over a ridge of rock and there was the ram staring at me with his guts hanging out. He had been gut-shot. There was only one escape route for him and that was through me, so he lowered his head to attack. At the same instant, the hunter shot and I saw the bullet hole appear right at the base of his horns. The ram dropped and started to slide, but I dove and grabbed it to prevent it from sliding down the mountain. So don't let anyone convince you that they will not attack, because they will if they're trapped."

"I think almost any animal will attack if there is no means of escape, " I suggested. "Because I once had a large beaver run straight at me. It was chattering as it came at me, and I knew it meant business because I had it trapped in its runway. You don't have to guess which one of us gave ground."

"I agree. And I want to mention something else about Frank Golata—he was great with horses. He wouldn't let the hunters ride them up the mountains. When we got to the foot of a steep mountain we got off and walked, and that's the proper way to hunt as far as I'm concerned. The people that ride their horses up the mountains scare much of the game away.

"Another thing about that trip—when I was coming down the mountain with my hunter, we saw a lamb and the hunter said he would like to try the meat. I told him to shoot it, which he did. Then I dressed it out and carried it back to camp. Well, when Frank seen it, he fired me on the spot. I started getting my gear together to walk out when my hunter came to me and said, 'It's a 70-mile walk out of here. You are not going to walk 70 miles, are you?'

"I told him that I had walked a damned sight further than that, but he asked me to wait for a minute. He walked over to his partner and they talked; then they both discussed the situation with Frank. A minute later Frank approached me and asked me to stay on, which I did."

At that point Frank showed me a picture of Rita Oney and Lynn Ross with a fine Stone sheep. I think it is a must to mention that Lynn was the fellow who moved buffalo into the Pink Mountain country

Rita Oney and Lynn Ross with Stone sheep.

where they successfully multiplied to the point that there is an open hunting season in that area now.

"Anyway," Frank continued, "we came back down the highway that fall and Hattie and I moved into the old Haney homestead at Fellers Heights near Dawson Creek. We fixed up the cabin that Haney had raised his family in back in the Thirties. We had money and lots of grub so we had a great winter there.

"Then I went to work for Hattie's brothers who owned a tie mill. We worked hard and put out a lot of ties. I worked there all summer as well as the next winter, which was the winter of 53/54. In the spring of 55, I was sitting in the bar of the Dew Drop Inn with a fellow named Merle Moorman when the manager came in and told me there was a phone call. I went to answer it and it was my dad calling, asking me if I wanted to go to work at Ashcroft. He filled me in that he and Spud Hustus, Pat Reynolds and a few others had some good copper prospects there; they had put some money together and were going to stake the area. He then gave me an offer I couldn't refuse— $400 a month and all expenses. I talked it over with Hattie, suggesting that if it worked out we could end up moving to Vancouver. She agreed that I should give it a try so I flew to Vancouver and with my dad, drove back to Ashcroft. We worked for a couple months staking what is now Bethlehem Copper. Then I borrowed my dad's car and came back to Dawson Creek to get Hattie.

"While I was there the Doe River Stampede was in progress. We got into a big party there and I got in a row with a fairly tough guy called Frenchie. We had a fight and I got the best of him, so that called for more booze. I should have known better, but I decided to ride a bucking horse that we called Old 96. My friends told me not to, but that's booze for you, it gives you false hope or something. Anyway I got on that horse and I don't think it made two jumps before it sent me sailing through the air. When I hit the ground on my head I saw a million stars. The next thing I knew people were standing all around me and I heard someone say, 'I don't think there is any pulse.'

"For a minute I thought I was in heaven because I was aware of them even if they thought I was gone. Then I was aware of Claude Stubley who was holding my neck and saying, 'Don't move your neck, Frank, we think it's broken.'"

"What made them think it was broken?" I asked.

"They told me later that they heard a loud snap when I landed. But I managed to get off the ground and didn't feel too bad, maybe because I was full of booze. That night we went and stayed with Hattie's brother, Nibs, and I seemed to feel all right, but the next morning when I woke up I could hardly move. Hattie managed to get me dressed and we left for Vancouver because I had to return to work. Hattie didn't drive in those days, but I made it all right, so whatever happened to my neck seemed to right itself.

"When we got to my folks' place with the children we moved into their basement suite and I left for work at Ashcroft. One thing about mom and dad, they were great. Mom rented the house next door and then went shopping for furniture for us. I always paid her back later, though.

"When I got back to the mine everything was going great. The bulldozers were shoving copper out of the bedrock. One trench was pushed 60 feet deep and 1300 feet long. We had a little mill, so dad and I hauled ore to the mill with a jeep. Out of a 1-ton sample, we ended up with 30 pounds. At that time we were not sure if it would make a mine."

"Did you like mining?" I questioned, wondering if it could have fit in with his love of the wilds.

"I liked the money. I was earning good money working there. Was I ever surprised when I went home that first time; the house was fixed up so nice. On top of that, they kept me on the payroll all the winter of 55/56.

"We got a terrible shock that winter. Hattie's cousin's Betty got polio and ended up in the Pearson Hospital. I'll never forget the first time I went to visit her at the hospital. She was in an iron lung. I hid my emotions as best I could but it sure brings you to reality when you see something like that."

"How long did you stay in Vancouver?"

"About a year. I kept on working for Bethlehem Copper and even got a credit card. Anywhere they wanted me to go, I would go and stake claims for them. I went to Williams Lake, Clinton, Merritt and Kamloops; I staked claims all over that country. Finally we bought a house on Royal Oak in Burnaby and paid $7,500 for it. We got settled there and then Herb Fellers came and worked with me. We flew into the Chilcotin and staked claims in there. I loved it; there was so much adventure and so many places to see. We traveled to Whitehorse and Atlin, and then we went up the Liard River to Watson Lake. We staked claims all over that country and we were making good money—$50 a day plus expenses. We staked for many companies all over the North. I had a good car and got paid for it, so I used to drive it on the job. One day my dad contacted me with word that we were to go to Cannon Lake near Williams Lake because they found some molybdenum property there. They hired a man named Burt Goderich to stake the area because he was familiar with it. Dad asked me to go along, so I hired a man out of Vancouver and we went to Williams Lake. Burt Lloyd, a former school chum of mine, flew me up to the top of Boss Mountain in his Super Cub. It was late March so there wasn't much snow in Williams Lake but it sure was deep on Boss Mountain. Burt flew six of us in there and we staked 106 claims. Damned if it didn't turn out to be a mine."

"The next summer I went to Dawson Creek and bought some horses from Harold Fellers. I moved them back down and used them to pack supplies to Boss Mountain where they were diamond drilling. I worked there all summer. Anyway, I went through all that mining stuff and things started to quiet down so we moved back to Dawson Creek and settled on Dunc Irvine's place at Arras, about 12 miles from Dawson. I still had a dream about getting a guiding property in the North. I worked for Dick Bedell that winter out at Groundbirch cutting ties, but the pull of the wilderness was always there in the back of my mind. I plugged along working at odd jobs: I drove trucks on the highway, tanker for Trail Transport, logged and helped farmers. It was good education but it was tough at times. My wife stuck by me and her parents helped us a great deal. I will never forget their kindheartedness."

"You mentioned a story about a mule when we talked on the phone, Frank, do you care to elaborate on it?" I asked.

"That happened when I was living at Fellers Heights near Dawson Creek many years ago. My kids were quite young then and we had a bunch of horses at the time. Well, one day we brought in a bunch of horses and there was a mule and a young stud horse with them. My brother-in-law, Harold Fellers, helped me cut the stud, and then we realized that neither of them had been branded. I went into town and asked around, and I found out that an old man named Dalt Doonan owned them. I visited him and told him that his stock was at my place and that we had cut the stud. He said that was okay and then asked if I would keep them and winter them at my place. We agreed on a price and I thought everything was settled. After three years passed without any pay, I decided to sell the mule to an outfitter from Alaska who had brought two trucks to pick up 25 head of horses he had purchased from me. He offered me $50 for the mule so I sold it to him. As it turned out, he stopped and spent the night in Dawson Creek and darned if someone didn't recognize Dalt's mule. They told him about it and suddenly as I was walking down the street Dalt shouted at me that I had stolen his mule. He said he was going to report me to the police so I went with him. Next thing I knew the police agreed with him and told me that in the eyes of the law I had stolen the mule, regardless of how much money Dalt owed me. I didn't think it was fair, but I took the mule and led it back to Dalt's barn and the horse buyer came with me. Suddenly I got an idea, so I asked the buyer to offer to buy the mule, which he did. Dalt insisted it was a great animal and he wanted $40 for it. I got the buyer to give him the $40 on the understanding that I would return the $50 he had given me.

"Well, the end of the story was that when I went to give back the $50 to the buyer, he laughed and told me to keep it because it was worth every cent to see all the laughs everyone got out of it. I never did get paid for the feed, but I did get Dalt to come out and get the stud horse before I used it for bear bait. It was a standard joke in this country—the time I stole the old mule from Dalt Doonan—because everyone knows that I got the mule and it didn't cost me a penny."

After the story of the mule was finished with, I changed the subject and asked Frank, "You obviously got together with Skook again, how did that happen?"

"As a matter of fact I went on the odd hunting trip with Skook, and spent part of a summer with him. He hadn't been out of the North for years. Actually, on one occasion he spent five years at Terminus Mountain without coming out. Once I brought him down to Arras for a good feed of turkey, and he stayed with us for a while. This was about 1963, which was the last time I worked with him. I went on a hunting party with him and I said, 'Damn it, Skook, I'd sure like to buy a piece of this country.'

"He thought about that for a minute and replied, 'Why buy it when I'm going to give it to you anyway in the end?'

"'Yes, but I can't wait forever because I've got a family to take care of.'

"Skook pondered that and then said, 'I'll tell you what, if you can raise $5,000 I'll give you everything west of the Kechika River.'

"I was stunned. It was a dream come true except for one problem—I didn't have 5,000 cents. I didn't want to ask mom and dad for the money, yet I knew I had to find it somewhere. Anyway, the pilot who had flown me into the Kechika, Charlie Hamilton, had overheard my conversation with Skook. On the way out we were flying in his company plane, a Cessna 180, when I noticed that he appeared flabbergasted. As luck would have it, Charlie owned BC-Yukon Air Service at Watson Lake with his partner, Hal Comish. When we landed at Watson Lake, Charlie stepped into the office for a minute and then Hal called me in and asked, 'Is it true that you can buy everything west of the Kechika for $5,000?'

Skook with his trail cook Mabel Frank crossing Medula Creek at Diamond J Ranch.

"'Yes it is true.' I responded. And then before my eyes, Hal opened his desk drawer and pulled out $5,000 and handed it to me. Of course I was suspicious, so I asked Hal why they would give me the money."

"There is no catch, all we ask is that you let us do all your flying for you."

"We shook hands and then headed right back into the Kechika with the money. When we arrived Skook was already at the riverbank sitting in his old wagon. I handed him the brown envelope with the money in it and he just glanced at it—didn't even count it—and threw it under the seat. Charlie and I got into the wagon and we rode back to his cabin about a mile and a half, and then Skook said, 'I'm not going out to sign any papers, Kid.'

"Skook was a hard man to deal with and I knew that if we didn't get the deal done right away that he may change his mind, as he had already been offered $175,000 for the piece he was selling to me for $5,000. I made up a piece of paper as legal as possible to take to the Game Department, Skook read it and then said, 'I don't sign anything.'

"I reached over and pulled the money back from him and then I gave him a talking to, 'Skook, this is the last time I'm stopping here. I have a bunch of kids to raise and I'm having a hell of a time. I borrowed money from my friends because you said you were going to deal and then you don't deal. This has been going on for three years and this is the last time you are going to see me. It's either deal now or I'm taking this money back to the guy I borrowed it from.'

"Skook thought about it for a minute and then said, 'Give me that damned paper.'

"He signed it, and then Charlie, who didn't know Skook very well, told me, 'You can't do business that way.'

"I assured him that there was no other way because Skook refused to go out of the valley. I also told him that Skook's word was his bond and we didn't have to worry about him.

"Just before we left in the plane Skook told me, 'You stake that big flat at Scoop Lake for your headquarters and don't come back here and ask me for another thing.'

"I shook his hand and said, 'If I do come back it will just be to visit you, old timer'."

"So you finally got your own guiding area after all those years, that must have been a special moment." I offered.

"Yes, it was. And when I mailed that paper to the Game Department, it was accepted and they sent me a licence. Game was so plentiful in the valley by that time. Skook had managed an excellent wolf-poisoning program and it really paid off. Something I should mention is that when he lost all those horses to wolves in one winter, that's what got him going. If you messed around with Skook's horses you were walking on thin ice. On one occasion Skook got 16 wolves in one night.

"By the time I got the guiding area, the moose were getting thick and there were sheep everywhere. Skook wouldn't allow anyone to shoot game close to his place, and he wouldn't take hunting parties into the Moodie Lake area. By the time I got that area you might as well say that it was a green area because there were rams everywhere and big ones, too."

"What was the greatest number of sheep that you ever found together or close to each other?" I asked.

"The most rams I've ever seen in one bunch was in what we called The Burn, between the Turnagain and Colt Lake. Gordon Eastman, guide John Tibbetts, and a hunter named John Amber were with me on that trip. About 10:00 in the morning we came around a ridge above a big basin and there was a large dark spot that seemed out of place. I looked through the field glasses and there were rams, and I mean rams everywhere. We watched them for half an hour and counted 67, by far the most I've ever seen. Suddenly they got up and started moving out of the basin in groups of two through to one group of 16 and we realized that they had our scent. The most lambs and ewes I've ever seen together was a herd of 130. As for goats, one of the first times I went into the headwaters of the Frog River I counted 72 goats in one herd. We walked by not far from them and they just watched us. I'm sure they had never been hunted."

"Do you think the hunting pressure is thinning the game out in that area?" I asked.

"The game can stand a lot of hunting pressure if the wolf packs are controlled. But the game cannot stand both, so choices have to be made."

Chapter 6

MY INTERVIEW WITH FRANK COOKE CONTINUED WITH his acquisition of the west half of Skook's guideline, so I asked, "How did your family react to the news?"

"When I came home that fall and told my family about our new guiding area they were ecstatic. My first order of business was to write letters to prospective hunters that I had known through the years, and it didn't take long until the deposits started pouring in. I got enough money from the deposits to buy 20 horses. I built a corral and set about breaking them, and then in the spring of 65, I took them to Muncho Lake in preparation for moving them into the Kechika. This route was new to me, as I had always traveled in from the other direction of Lower Post.

"I waited at Muncho Lake for Oscar McDonald, an Indian guide, who was to come in and help me through the mountains. I had a helper with me named Joe Lithco, who didn't have any experience with horses, although he was a good worker. But I needed more help.

"Well, I waited for a few days but Oscar didn't show up, so I went to his camp and learned that he was out hunting, trying to get some meat for their elderly people. That did it; I decided that if he didn't show up by the following morning that we would head out, because I had to get the horses into the Kechika.

"Well, he never showed, so we loaded up and headed up the creek, me with a green man and green horses, and only a map to figure out which way to go. The first day out I was chasing horses in all directions. I had a mare that was hard to catch but I decided I was going to put a pack on her anyway.

"After seven days of traveling through the peaks, I instructed Joe to come behind with the horses while I scouted ahead, trying to figure out which way to go. So I scouted ahead and had a rough day until mid-afternoon when I hit a nice meadow. I decided it was a good place to camp, so I waited for Joe to show up with the horses. When he arrived, he had a surprise for me: he had lost the mare with our grub and some of our important supplies. This worried me because I thought she might follow the back-trail and go home. I jumped on a buckskin stud, took along another horse, and then went looking for her and was she ever hard to find. I got about three miles along the back-trail before I spotted her; she was standing in a buck brush meadow looking at me. I tied up the two horses and then took a piece of rope and tried to approach her. She was half-goofy anyway with her eyes bulging out and so she refused to go toward the other horses and headed back toward Muncho Lake. I fooled with her until it started to get dark, and many times I got right close to her but I couldn't get hold of her. At last I knew I had to do something in a hurry.

"In all my time with horses I had never had to shoot one because it couldn't be caught, but now I realized that I had no choice. The last time she tried to follow the back-trail, I got around her and hid. When she spotted me again, she took off wide open on the back-trail and I knew it was now or never. I fired and she dropped right on her nose going flat out. I had hit her right behind the ear with one of the best or luckiest shots of my life."

"I've heard it said that shooting a horse is one of the hardest things a person can do, and I found that to be true in my own experience. How did it affect you?" I asked.

"That's true. It is terribly hard to do, but I had no other options because she was carrying equipment we really needed. Anyway, I put the pack on the spare horse and went back to the meadow where Joe had a campfire going. I bawled him out a bit but finally realized it wasn't his fault—she was just a crazy horse. What really bothered me was the fact that I had lost a horse. Well, we went to bed but I didn't sleep very well so I got up in the middle of the night and built a fire to make tea. Then Joe got up and asked, 'We're lost, aren't we?'"

"'Yes, I guess we are.' I answered."

"What are we going to do—go back?"

"'I'm not going back. I've been seven days on the trail instead of the five days I thought it would take. You watch the horses because I'm going to climb that high peak after it gets daylight to see if I can figure out where to go.'

"Luckily, it was a clear day, so when I got up high I recognized Mt. Winston on the Kechika. I guessed it to be about 50 miles away, which meant I had gone too far to the south. I had been traveling toward the head of the Gataga River into real tough country. I didn't know what kind of country we had to go through, but I had been to Netson Lake before so we struck for it. We were out of grub but I knew Hattie would have a plane out looking for us. As it turned out, the pilot, Charlie Hamilton, was looking for us but when he would fly over we were always in the rough going and couldn't signal him. When we finally got to Netson Lake I shot a moose because we were right out of grub. Once I got to Netson, hell, I was in home country. We camped at one of Skook's camps there called Buckbrush. The next night we camped at another camp called Brokenbit, and the following day we made it to Skook's ranch at Terminus Mountain.

"As soon as we got to Skook's ranch he complained about my horses, saying that he was short of pasture feed. I responded by telling him that my horses had endured a rough trip because we had been lost half the time. Skook really laughed about that; he had fun rubbing it in to me. After Skook had enjoyed his laugh, I asked him to call out on his radio for an airplane, which he did. Then I told Joe to watch the horses until I returned in about three days. I flew into Watson Lake and let Hattie know that everything was fine and what my plans

Skook with Mabel and Tommy
Frank at Brokenbit Camp.

were, and then I returned to
Skook's place. He asked me
how I was going to cross the
river, and suggested that if I
used Rawhide that I would
have to pay him. Rawhide was
a Native named Ernest Frank
who had worked for Skook
many years, and he was one of
the best woodsmen I've ever
known. Well, I assured Skook
that I would pay him and after we had a little set-to and got it
straightened out, I took Rawhide and went to the horses.

"I explained to Rawhide that these broncos had never swam a big
river and that we might have trouble getting them to go in. Then I
chopped down a big tree that stood on the riverbank and when it
landed and stopped in the current, we had a place to swim the horses right below it so they would have some protection from the current. Skook and his cook, Mabel Frank, who was Rawhide's sister,
came down on the wagon to watch the crossing. Mabel was a great
camp cook, so you know Skook needed her for guiding. Well, when
we made our move, Rawhide—who had lots of guts and knew what
he was doing—went first with a big black horse and I attempted to
drive the others right behind him. Skook was about 73 at that time so
he couldn't help; it was a matter of us doing it or it wasn't going to get
done. So we made our move and then some of the horses tried to turn
back. I didn't let them, though, because I had Skook's old pistol and I
cut loose throwing lead all over hell. That did it by God—they followed Rawhide down and across the river. Then Rawhide and I swam
back to see Skook. When Skook saw that we had made it, he came up
to me and said, 'You did it, eh, Kid?'"

"You damned right I did. I haven't forgotten all the things you taught me.' That seemed to please him, but when I tried to borrow Rawhide from him, he refused, saying he needed him. That was all right, I paid Rawhide and then swam the two horses back across the river. Joe was there and a short time later Charlie Hamilton arrived with the Beaver airplane. He had a message for me that Warren Page, field editor of *Field and Stream Magazine*, had been trying to contact me. I left Joe in charge of the horses and got Charlie to fly me to Watson Lake. Two days later Charlie flew me back into the Kechika in a Super Cub. As soon as we landed on the river I sensed something was wrong because Joe didn't come out to meet us. We tied up the airplane and walked up to the camp and there was Joe with his foot cut half off. The accident had occurred right after we left when he had tried splitting wood, and he had been lying there for two days. Anyway, we put him in the airplane and Charlie flew him out. I also asked Charlie to get me another man from Lower Post, especially John Tibbetts, a good young Indian lad who had worked for Skook for several years, and could shoe horses, pack, hunt or do anything you asked. Meanwhile, I went and gathered up the horses. The next day Charlie returned with John Tibbetts and a boy named Eddie Miller."

"You must have been glad to see them arrive; you would have been toast without them, wouldn't you?" I wondered.

"I would have been in a fix all right so I was glad to see John, that's for sure. Well, we headed up toward Colt Lake with me bringing up the rear, and we were going up through very thick, steep going when . . . now I'm going to tell a story about something that happened to me that should not have happened: I was riding a big horse called Ranger, trying to drive the bunched-up horses up the hill, when I pulled out my revolver and went to fire some shots in the air to get the horses moving. But the gun had a hair trigger so it fired before I got it raised high enough and damned if I didn't shoot one of the colts right in the rump. I didn't know I had shot it until I spotted the blood pumping out of it. I'm telling you that I felt like hell. I knew it was my fault—that I was too over-anxious. We kept going for another two miles and reached Colt Lake where the horse laid down and I figured he would stiffen up. We let him stay down for a while and then we forced him to get up and I couldn't believe it—he started to eat. Well, that horse dragged his leg around there until the first hunters arrived and one of them was a doctor named Cook. I explained to him about the accident and told him that I figured I would have to shoot the horse because I couldn't get the bullet out. Then he informed me that it was common to leave the bullet in if it wasn't bothering a nerve. Sure enough, about a week later the wound broke open and drained and the horse was fine. Slicker, I called him, and that horse turned out to be a great horse and was still alive at Scoop Lake many years later. I put my own brand on him, which was the Diamond 9C. That was because there were seven children plus Hattie and I, which totalled 9 Cookes."

"So were you satisfied with your first guiding season?" I asked.

"I took out nine hunters including writer Warren Page. Also Russ Cutter who wrote for the same paper, so, yes, I was very pleased. Also I had Al Lamont who was as good a camp cook as a man can get and that is so important on long trips.

"We had a rather strange experience at Colt Lake when I took another hunter out for sheep. I can't remember his name but I do recall that he was a polo player. When we got up high we spotted some fine rams, and one of them was the biggest based ram I've ever seen, and I've looked at a lot of rams. He was facing away from me so I couldn't see all of his body, and he wouldn't get up. We started up and got fairly close when the ram turned his head so I could get a clear look at him. One horn protruded out of his head, twisted right around and went into his mouth. The other horn had been broken off. I knew that the ram was in bad shape so I told the hunter to shoot it but he refused. I took his rifle and shot it, and when we approached it we saw that it was blind in one eye, had a running sore on its face and was very thin. The horn was growing into his mouth just like a spear. It was not broken off; it just grew that way. I think the other horn had grown the same way but he had managed to break it off. I caped it out and we brought the head and horns out with us after the hunt. The next day I took that same hunter out and got him a big ram. When we came out after all the hunts were completed, I took that ram into Dawson Creek and gave it to the Game Department on the condition that it would be sent to Victoria. The next year when I was in their office I spotted the same head under a desk, so I took it home."

"Well, Frank, I guess your first hunting season on your own guide line was a success."

"Yes, and I enjoyed being my own boss rather than taking orders from someone else."

"Did you have many guides working for you?" I questioned.

"At one period when I was going at it pretty hard I had about 15 guides going. I eventually got many members of my family involved. My wife Hattie was cook and hostess. My sons, Frankie, Terry and Mac were pilots and guides. My daughters, Diane, Tammy, Gloria and Donna were cooks. My son's wives, Judy, Carleen and DeeDee were also cooks. My brother Dave was a fishing guide and riverman. Brother-in-law Bud Fellers was a pilot, brother-in-law Herb Fellers was a guide, and Uncle Pat was caretaker and cowboy."

"So you had a big operation going at Scoop Lake?

"Yes. Also, my dad came up and helped as well. Believe me it was a lot of work, but it seemed to us to be play because we loved it so much.

"I also had some of the best Indian guides ever. There was Ernest Frank who was always known as Rawhide—my daughter Tammy used to refer to him by saying 'he's not an Indian; he's my brother.' Pound for pound I would put Rawhide up against any guide on the planet. Skook trained him, as well as many of my best Indian guides. Rawhide could take care of a horse by shoeing him and fixing his teeth. He was really good in the woods and had loads of patience, which is so important in sheep hunting. I also had a guide named Jack George, Eagle Eye we called him, because he spotted game before any of us. He was good with dogs but didn't know much about horses. We have to remember, though, that these people were raised around dogs and dog teams, they didn't work with horses until Skook trained them. Then they became some of the best with horses and trail packing. John Tibbetts was another that was worth his weight in gold. It is such an asset to have reliable and knowledgeable guides. Without them it is almost impossible to keep your hunters happy."

I noticed that Frank was really into his outfitting/guiding memories so I asked. "There's quite a lot to learn about guiding, isn't there?"

"There's a lot to take care of, but I want to tell you about what Scoop Lake was like when I first went in there. It was heavy spruce country and you couldn't walk through it. Big trees were lying down everywhere. It was hellish tough going. You would never know it was the same place when you see it now. Anyway, the next year I took a hunter from Norway—his name was Pete—to Scoop Lake and he shot a moose at the next lake down from Scoop. I had a horrible time packing that moose's head and cape out to Scoop Lake where an airplane could pick it up.

"On that same trip, I recall, we were walking around Scoop Lake toward dusk when I stepped over a log and there was a big grizzly walking right ahead of me. I stepped aside and pointed at it so Pete could get a shot, and then I stood there waiting for the explosion. But none came and the bear was moving away from us at a good clip. I turned around and told him to shoot but he refused. I couldn't figure what he was thinking until he blurted out, 'In my country we do not shoot an animal in the ass.'

"I responded by saying, 'In this country we shoot a big bear anywhere we can hit him because we may not see another for a long time.' Well the bear got away and by the time we got back to the lake it was too dark for pilot Ernie Harrison to fly so we were forced to camp out for the night."

"Did that hunter ever get his big bear?" I asked

"No, and I didn't feel sorry for him either. When you get set up on a huge grizzly like that and don't take advantage of it, you may never get another chance. But I want to tell you about the trips in 1966. First off, when I checked the horses I found that they were in good shape after spending the winter in the Kechika, with the exception of a palomino mare. She had got bogged down in a spring and was dead when I found her. I couldn't afford to be flying all the time to keep track of them properly, and it really bothered me to lose her. But life goes on and I was glad that I was booked up solid for 1966. I decided to put up some tents at Scoop Lake to handle the pressure, and a big tent camp at Moodie Lake as well. My wife and all my children came to Moodie Lake with me and we had a busy year, cleaning the area like a park. We had it rigged out good, and that was the start of the boys' education with the woods and horses. Craig Forfar, my old school chum from Fort St. James, came up and worked for me. Several friends and their children came and we had a great summer out there in the mountains."

"What a summer that must been for the children." I commented.

"It sure was, and I remember something that happened then: A hunter decided to line up his rifle so he set out a target and then knelt down and fired right beside a tent. Unknown to him a man named George Jackson was fast asleep in that tent. When the gun roared there was another roar and George came out of that tent ready for action, because that rifle blast had scared the hell out of him. I just got there in time to prevent a fistfight. When you have a group of people back in the woods like that, you never know what's coming next. But all told, we had a hell of a year out there. When the hunts were over we took all the horses back to Scoop Lake for the winter. By this time my sons Frankie and Terry were working for me. And Rawhide—I don't know what I would have done without him—he taught my boys everything they know about hunting and guiding and he taught them right.

"There's another story I have to tell you about Rawhide. He came into Lower Post and got involved with a woman. They got into the booze in a big way and then got a hotel room. During the night, and

Left to right Constable Frank Cooke, Jerry Affey, Frank Cooke and Skook Davidson at McMCorkall Ranch, circa 1938.

Skook Davidson, Frank Cooke at Skook's ranch at Terminus Mountain. First hunting party, 1947.

Back row: Frankie,
Mac and Terry.
Centre: Gloria, Donna
Dianne and Tammy.
Seated: Frank and
Hattie.

John Porter to the left, Jack George, Skook in the middle and John Tibbetts and Ed
Ball to the right, 1955.

Above: Skook on wagon at Kechika River, 1955.

Frank Cooke and his son Terry.

siar

Aeroplane L.

Liard R.

Graveyard L.

Fort Nelson R.

Muncho
Lake

Kechika R.

Terminus
A Mtn

Fort
Nelson

Above: Frank Cooke's
Twin Beach aircraft
used to move hunters
from place to place.

Moodie Lake.

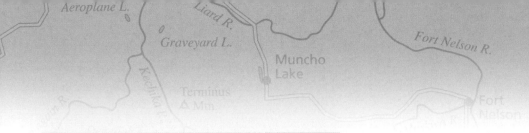

Charlie Boya, guide and trapper. Galaga Forks.

Crossing the Galaga River in low water.

Martin Benchoff and guide John Tibbetts.

Below: Four of Frank's hunters in 1970. Left to right: Bill Cain, Jack Segal, Galen Carlson and Leland Speakes.

Aeroplane L.
Liard R.
Graveyard L.
Fort Nelson R.
Kechika R.
Muncho Lake
Terminus Mtn
Fort Nelson

Bottom left Wrangler Jackie Williams. *Upper left* Guide Ernest Frank (Rawhide), Skook Davidson, Guide Jack George (Eagle Eye) and Cook Mabel Frank, 1970.

Elephant Ridge near Scoop Lake.

Frank Cooke
and partner
Joy McNeely.

Sharon Buck guiding at the head of the Findley River, 1995.

just for a joke, the woman at the hotel snuck into their room and took their clothes away and hid them. The next day we waited until noon and then I went and knocked on their door. When Rawhide answered I asked, 'When are you going to come out and join us?'

"In a kind of squeaky voice he answered, 'Cookie (he always called me Cookie), we can't come out because a weasel took our clothes.' We finally had mercy on them so we returned their clothes, and I never did find out if he really believed a weasel was responsible for taking their clothes."

A few memories stirred in my mind so I asked, "Didn't you have a photographer come into your area? I seem to recall seeing a movie that you were involved with."

"That would have been Gordon Eastman. He wanted to make a movie in there and like many of the other writers and photographers he didn't want to pay. I told him that I could not afford to take him for free because we were just getting started and had enormous expenses. We finally agreed on a price and he was very fair. Gordon paid me for everything I ever did for him and I respect him for that. Anyway, he spent two years in my area making a movie. I supplied the horses, men and equipment for him and he worked hard to make that film. He was a professional photographer you know, and when his

movie *High, Wild and Free* hit the market it made me as far as hunting goes. I just couldn't keep people away. Gordon brought his wife and family in with him the last summer he came up. They moved over to Dall Lake and had six or seven head of horses there. My son Terry worked with him for a

Gordon Eastman with 44″ Stone sheep.

while and I took turns as well. They built a raft and his children used
to fish the lake."

"I envy them; what splendid adventure it must have been for all
the children to spend their summer in that glorious wilderness."

"We thought it was so great that we decided to build a main lodge
on Scoop Lake and we started it that year. I had some damned good
men working for me. Besides the guiding, we cut and peeled logs and
constructed a cookhouse. I remember that we moved into the cookhouse on September 9th, 1967. For Hattie, it was just like moving
into the Waldorf Astoria after living so long in tents. The children
helped; my father came up and helped; everybody helped to make our
dreams come true. I had told Hattie so much about the area and by
then her and the children were all learning to love it there. We were
going to build a hunting outfit to equal anything in the guiding business and it looked like we were well on our way. When we came home
late that fall we were just so happy. Frankie and Terry, along with
Rawhide, went back and spent the winter there taking care of the

---

Three generations named Frank Cooke.

horses. It was tough for them but they were just as enthused as we were. I told them that we were going to burn all the dead wood out of the area because there were no green trees there anyway. I flew back in a few times to check on them, but on a couple occasions they were in there for two months without seeing another soul."

"So there was three generations of Frank Cooke at Scoop Lake at the same time I gather."

"Yes, and we sure needed the help; there was just so much to do around there."

"Ernie Harrison had some airplanes at Watson Lake then, and he didn't have enough work at the time so he asked if Jim Thibideau, one of his pilots, could come in and work for me. I would board him and only have to pay for the hours that the Super Cub airplane flew. I agreed, so Jim flew me in and we started working on the cabins at Moodie Lake. One day I said to Jim, 'Let's go down to Scoop Lake; I'm going to burn that flat down there.' Jim got extremely excited and tried to talk me out of it, but I insisted. The wind was blowing strong that day so I took 10 gallons of gasoline and spread it between the lake and the meadow and then I lit it. I'm telling you that old dry timber there, it burnt and it burnt like you wouldn't believe. Of course the Forest Service flew in and wanted to know who caused the fire and everything. I denied it, but at the same time I asked them what it could hurt because there wasn't a green tree in the area, only dead ones. I could tell he kind of agreed with me, but he couldn't say anything because he had his boss from Prince George with him. Anyway, while we were talking, this forestry guy asked if I knew where there were any big sheep, because he wanted one in the worst way. Ernie Harrison was their pilot so I described to him exactly where the sheep were from Highland Lake. They took off and sure enough, they were back in three hours with a 45-inch ram. He agreed not to press the issue of the burn, so I got the burn and he got the big ram and everyone was happy."

"I notice you didn't mention any names, Frank, did you know them? "

"Oh sure, I knew them, but what was the sense of making an issue out of nothing, because in reality they should have paid me for that burn. Anyway, I cleared that area and started seeding and I'm telling you that before I got done I had seeded more ground in the Kechika than most farmers do on 10 sections of land. Eventually it started to grow, so I put up a tent camp in there, built corrals and fenced the valley. Before I sold out, I took over $1 million out of the Kechika. I spent about half of it buying and feeding my horses and buying all the other equipment we needed. There are just so many expenses when you have to fly everything in and out all the time. I had to raise seven kids and fly them back and forth to Dawson Creek for school, but I loved it and my family loved it and that made it all worthwhile. I used to start flying things into the area in July when the planes were available. Things like oats and hay, so that I was prepared in case of a real tough winter. I never let the planes fly in empty—they took a load both ways.

"When you look at Scoop Lake today and compare it to what it was like when I first visited the area, you would not believe the transformation. I kept at it and then started moving stud horses in there and eventually my dream came true. I had a horse ranch at Scoop Lake. It was unique in the sense that the horses were free to go wherever they liked, and there are not too many places where that is possible anymore. You could run 45,000 head of stock in the Kechika and hardly ever find them. But don't tell that to some people, because I had a young fellow come in to Scoop Lake to collect samples of the vegetation and he told me that horses couldn't survive in the Kechika. Well, I told him to rush over and advise Skook Davidson right away because he had raised hundreds of them already. Some of these people are rather humorous, such as the biologist who told me we didn't have a wolf problem in the Kechika. Again, I told him to rush over and tell Skook Davidson right away, because he had lost 18 horses to wolves in one winter. Another thing while I'm on this subject, I read Farley Mowat's book *Never Cry Wolf* and I just couldn't believe that people could believe such garbage. What he knows about wolves I can carry in my back pocket."

"I'm sure in agreement with you there, Frank, when I read that book I just shuddered; it simply blew me away that the public and so many in government were gullible enough to believe it. Just the story of the so-called flight into the North was 'only for idiots to believe' as one pilot put it. But I would like to get back to guiding. Tell me more about some of the hunters you guided."

"As far as different types of people, we had them all: from Billy Graham's crusaders to the head of the mafia; from the Prince of Iran to General Franco's nephew. We had several millionaires and multi-millionaires—people with more money than they could ever possibly spend. Frankie had the pleasure of carrying a New York model across a slippery talus slope and another time he had to hang onto a cliff while a photographer climbed over his body to get pictures of a mountain goat. I imagine every person remembers Senator Connelly of Texas—the man who was with Kennedy when he got shot. Well, we guided his brother, Wayne Connelly, and when that hunt was over, we flew him to Watson Lake where he missed the only flight of the day by 20 minutes. I took him to a phone and he called some big company in Texas. When he hung up the phone he told me that a Learjet was leaving Texas and would arrive in less than four hours. Jack O'Connor was there at the time, so the jet dropped him off at Lewiston, Idaho on the way by. So that's how some people live.

"On the other hand, some people have been so pampered that they hardly know how to go to the bathroom. Hattie had a hunter come into the cookhouse and ask for a bottle of pop, so she got out two bottles and placed them on the table. She went back to making supper and he finally asked, 'What do I do with them?' Hattie pointed to the can opener and he stared at it and came back with, 'I have a maid.' Apparently that guy had never opened a bottle of pop before."

"That's hard to believe, Frank, but in all the years that you spent around Scoop Lake, did you ever spend part of a winter there?" I wondered.

"For a few years there, I chartered a DC-3 to take a large group of people in to Scoop Lake for the Christmas holidays and we stayed right through New Years. We took husbands, wives, kids and friends, as well as the turkey, booze and presents and had a hell of a good time in there. When the holidays were over, the DC-3 came back and hauled us all to Fort Nelson 175 miles distant. It is hard to describe the feelings we had in there—just so carefree in such a beautiful place."

One of Frank's guides for many years was a chap named Bill Eckert, who is now a horse rancher in Dawson Creek, BC. Bill and I spent a day reminiscing about the 10+ years he spent guiding for Frank Cooke and he certainly shared some wonderful memories, such as the following:

"When I first went guiding for Frank, we took a trip over to Skook's ranch for a visit. It was the first time I had met him and after we talked for a while he asked us into his cabin for lunch. I'll never forget that experience because Skook sliced some bread and then gave me a slice. I took it and there was a big fly right in the bread, right where I was going to put the butter. I didn't want to embarrass Skook, but I didn't want to eat the fly either. Finally I took my knife and pried the fly out of there, and Skook just watched with a big smile on his face. I think he really enjoyed it."

"Would you class yourself as a good guide?" I asked.

"I think you should ask Frank about that," Bill responded. "He used to call me 37-inch Bill. That was his way of saying that I never got my hunters very many big sheep."

"You guided quite a lot with Rawhide, what was your opinion of him?"

"I can give you a good example of Rawhide's ability: we went on a long trip together through the mountains and sometimes I didn't know where the hell we were; but Rawhide knew, though, and he took us right through miles of strange country without a problem."

"Did you ever get lost in that country, Bill?"

"Twice, and the second time was the worst. I left Pop Lake with a hunter and went toward Denetiah Lake where we climbed the mountain and got into really rough country. We got our ram and then decided to go along the other side of the mountain to our horse trail, which we wanted to follow back to Pop Lake. When we hit Denetiah Lake we ran into a cliff that stretched down into the Lake. This meant we had the choice of going all the way back around or else we had to swim the horses by the cliff. The hunters were able to climb around above the cliff, while we set about swimming the horses with their packs on. The other guide that was with me—Larry Bedell—tried riding his horse across and it stepped in a hole and went down. Larry couldn't swim so he gave up and climbed with the hunters. This meant that I had to swim and hold the bridle of each horse as I took it around the cliff.

"One of the horses was called Kechika—a real miserable bugger— and he laid down on me while we were in shallow water. I held his head up for a while until I had enough, and then I pushed his head under the water. Man, you should have seen him come up out of there. I guess he decided he didn't want to die after all."

"Why did he lie down, Bill, was he tired?"

"Maybe he was tired or maybe the cinch was too tight. He used to lie down in the muskegs sometimes; when he got to where he wasn't sure, he'd lie down. But when I pushed his head under the water he woke up. You can bet that I was cold and tired when I got those horses across the lake.

"Another time Frank Cooke brought a bunch of horses into the Kechika and one of them was a quarter horse stud; a good one that he had bought in Dawson. He had paid more for it than any of his other horses. When they got to Fort Nelson garbage dump on their way up, they picked up an old, black stud horse that the town had given to Frank. It had wintered near the dump, so Frank brought him in. Well, Herb Fellers and Frank got lost on the way in and wandered around in the windfalls for about a week. Terry and I flew over them and spotted them a couple different times and knew they were going to make it, finally, but it took them about a week longer than it should have."

"But Frank has a story about him and a different guy getting lost on their way in; they came in from the Muncho Lake side. Is that the same time?" I asked.

"That's one of the times. Every time they went through there they got lost. There were no trails; they just wandered around until they found something they recognized. Sometimes we would hit blow-down areas where you would have to cut your way through; then maybe you'd only make a mile a day. Larry Kennedy and I went through there one time with Frank's son, Frankie leading the way. We spent three days in there and once we could see the Kechika in the distance, but we ended up back an hour from the highway. That night when we went to bed Frankie said, 'I think I can hear a truck in the distance.'

"I told him, 'You'd better not be able to hear a truck.' We listened and sure enough we all heard a truck. The next day we found out that we were only an hour's ride from the highway. We started over again and that time we got through. And then when we were coming back out that time, we got lost again. We were riding along when Frankie jumped off his horse and picked up an old pair of chaps and shouted, 'I know where we are; these are Everett Haney's chaps—he lost them when we were lost in here the last time.' Sure enough he led us out of there."

"Didn't you guys use a compass?" I asked.

"No! I didn't even know how to read a compass. We just gave it our best shot and one way or another we got through."

"There sure were a lot of strange happenings in there by the sound of it." I offered.

"One time we were building fence when we heard some foxes yelping across the lake. We went around to a spot we called the Sand Dunes, where the foxes had dug in to make their dens. About ten of us worked all night trying to dig and smoke them out. Sometimes there was smoke coming out all the holes. Believe it or not we never got one fox. There was just a maze of tunnels all over under that hill. About ten years later I visited that same place and the foxes were still using the den.

"Another time we were hunting at Island Lake where we often seen a big black wolf with a white bitch and pups. While we were there we shot several of the pups in an effort to control the wolf population in the area. The next day we went back and the pup's bodies were missing. We checked the den and found the pup's feet; the adults had eaten their own young. We also found one big room-sized den a couple feet high that was packed with horns and antlers that had been dragged in there."

"I've had several of the old-time trappers tell me about wolves eating their own young during periods of starvation, so this doesn't surprise me, Bill. Any other stories of getting lost?" I wondered.

"Yes. This happened near the main camp on the Turnagain River when I had a hunter out looking for a mountain goat. We left the horses and climbed up high where we spotted a nice billy. We watched it for about three hours before the hunter got a shot. The goat slid down the mountain and when we got to it, we skinned it out and packed it back down to the horses. By the time we got moving again it was raining and the fog rolled in so that we couldn't tell which way to go. We moved along for a while and came to a horse trail that I was unaware of. We followed it for a couple hours and realized we were going the wrong direction, so we stopped and tried to build a campfire. What a hell of a time we had trying to get a fire going in that stunted balsam. My lighter was wet and the wind was blowing so it took some time to get a little fire going that didn't amount to anything. During that sleepless night the hunter informed me that he had left instructions with Mac Cooke that if he went missing, a search party was to be flown in from Switzerland right away. Now that put the pressure on me, I'll tell you. When daylight arrived I followed the trail for a couple hours and then realized that the trail led around the mountain and back to Frank's camp. I returned for the hunter and then the two of us carried on to the camp where we arrived exhausted and soaking wet, with a wet goat hide that must have weighed 200 pounds. On top of that, we were badly in need of some sleep. The guide there,

Stanley Stewart, took mercy on me and fleshed out the goat hide for me.

"There was a funny side to this story because when the hunter told Frank that we had been lost, Frank laughed and replied, 'Bill wasn't lost; he knew he was somewhere between the Kechika and the Pacific Ocean and that's not lost!'"

"Any memories of humorous events?" I wondered.

"Frank's son Terry could tell you a good one. One day he was flying to the Kechika when he spotted two animals mating on a flat rock on the mountaintop. He circled and came in low for another look but by that time the two animals had turned into people and they were back in their saddles pretending they were hunting. Finally Terry realized that the two people he had seen were brother Frankie and a good-looking woman he was supposed to be guiding. But that was Frankie—he would do anything to please his hunters.

"Another story that started out as a joke sure didn't end that way. Terry and I flew into Scoop Lake and at that same time, Rawhide and a guide named Paul Moe were working in there, cutting a trail up toward Moodie Lake. We took a bunch of booze in there with us, so it didn't take long for us to settle down to some serious drinking. Then Paul came along on snowshoes and told us that Rawhide was just a few minutes behind him. Rawhide didn't know we were there so I decided to play a joke on him. I knew he was ticklish, so I hid behind the door. Rawhide took his snowshoes off and when he entered, I grabbed him by the ribs and started tickling him. He let out a howl and kicked back and his heel hit the axe blade, which cut his heel in half. It was a terrible cut. Well, all we had to work with was some horse liniment so we filled him full of booze and then we wrestled him down and poured that liniment in there and he screamed something terrible. We kept him liquored up for a few days until the plane came in to get him, and then we flew him out.

"But there is more to the story because when Hattie was taking him to the hospital she stopped at a stop sign and just as she started out again, Rawhide jumped out of the car and broke the same leg that the cut was in. Well, Rawhide ended up in a cast and just a few weeks later the hunts started so we needed him. You wouldn't believe how funny he looked going through the woods on his horse with that cast sticking out to the side.

"We left Pop Lake on horseback with a hunter, and wouldn't you know that Rawhide's horse went down in a muskeg, and darned if it wasn't lying on his cast. Rawhide was kicking her with his good leg and hollering for her to get off his leg. Well, we got him out of there but by the time the hunts were over there was nothing left of that cast except a little piece at the top; he wore it right out. He sure was a tough bugger; I have to say that. His favourite name for me was, 'Billy, Billy Bayou.' Another thing about Rawhide, no matter how early you got up he already had the campfire going and the coffee brewing. He would say, 'Coffee on a stick—five cents a lick.' He was some kind of a guy, I'll tell you.

"Some of the adventures we had were not fun, such as the time a hunter named Tom Martell got sick on us. We were two day's ride from Island Lake when we realized we had to get him out to medical attention, and somehow he managed to ride out on his own. He was flown out of there and had to undergo an emergency operation for appendicitis."

"Any other unusual memories to share from your guiding years?"

"One that comes to mind was the time Rawhide and I watched a mother grizzly with four cubs. Now that's something you seldom see."

"I agree, Bill, I've seen

Rawhide and friend.

countless hundreds of grizzlies during my lifetime but I've never seen a family of five. I know other people who have, though. But getting back to guiding, are there any particular trips you would like to talk about."

'There was one trip that I will never forget. I think it was the second year I was there. Frank brought a Canadian hunter in for us to guide and this fellow was looking for a record book ram to add to his other three species of sheep. If he succeeded in his quest of the 'Grand Slam', his trip would have been paid for by some hunting society. So Rawhide took him out and showed him a big ram with ten inches of one horn busted off, but even at that it would have made the records. With the broken horn in place, that sheep would have gone number three or four in the world. Anyway, the hunter refused the sheep so Frankie and I were elected to take him on the next hunt. We flew from Pop Lake over to Island Lake where we started up the mountain with backpacks and it didn't take long for us to realize that this hunter was a complete asshole. But you have to do your best, so we headed up the mountain, the hunter carrying his rifle, and Frankie and I each loaded down with over 100-pound packs. When we got up near timberline, I headed back down to get another load because Frankie and I didn't have sleeping bags—all the gear belonged to the hunter.

"The next day I climbed the mountain again and when I got up to their camp I found out that Frankie had already got the hunter a sheep. But it was about one point short of a record and the hunter was in a foul mood. He wanted to shoot another sheep but I told him he had his sheep and he would have to live with it. That night Frankie and I sat in the snow by a little campfire made from stunted subalpine fir trees so you know what kind of night we had. The hunter wouldn't let us sit in his tent. When daylight came I said that I was going back down the mountain so I loaded up my pack and headed down. Frankie was worried that his dad would be upset because the hunter still had ten days left on his hunt, so he stayed on the mountain with him, perhaps to help him get a goat.

"I went back down to Island Lake and fixed up a nice camp for myself and decided to wait for them to come out. About five days later Frankie arrived in camp with another 100-pound load on his back, while the hunter trailed behind carrying his rifle and jacket. Frankie was carrying at least three of his guns as well as four pairs of his boots. So the hunt was over and that guy gave Frank a check for the hunt and left camp. When Frank went to the bank he learned that the cheque was bad. We supplied that entire hunt, aircraft and all, for nothing. To make matters even worse, Frankie told me that when I was getting ready to leave camp on the mountain, that this same hunter had a 357 Magnum pistol pointed at my back. I asked Frankie what he was doing and he replied, 'I was standing behind him with an axe; if he would have shot you I would have hit him with the axe'.

"I couldn't help but answer him with, 'Gee thanks, but I don't think that would have helped me any.' Anyway that shows just what kind of assholes you have to deal with out there sometimes."

"My God that must have been discouraging. Any more stories like that one?" I mused.

"We had another guy come in from Alaska, and he was a real nice guy who got along with everyone. When he left he gave each of us guides a cheque for $500 and when we got out to town we found that they were all rubber, too. In fact, we found out later that he was one of America's ten most-wanted criminals."

"So you guys got beat several times."

"You bet. If Frank had all the money due to him he would be a wealthy man."

"Anymore memories of unusual events?"

"Well I just remembered that when we shut the camp down at Pop Lake, a Native guide named Scrawny Johnny and I took two hunters and the horses back toward Moodie Lake and when we got to Dall Lake, we headed into the Sharktooth Range. It snowed in there and everything was soaked, so we put up a lean-to and made a big fire in front of it. Then we put our clothes and boots on sticks around the fire to dry them out. I fell asleep for a while and when I woke up my boots were burnt to a crisp. Now that's a fun day, I'll tell you—caught in the mountains without boots."

"What did you use for a substitute?" I asked.

"I didn't have much choice so I wrapped my feet with tarps and tried to stick close to the saddle until we got out of there."

"Frank mentioned a horse called Jughead, were you familiar with him, Bill?"

"That was a part-Percheron horse and a weird horse for sure. I tried riding him but he wouldn't go ahead. He would lay his ears back and then back up and you couldn't get very far that way. But he would carry twice as big a load as the other horses. At the start he wouldn't work at all but we pulled him around with the tractor for a while and got him started. When we were packing through the woods and came to even a tiny creek, he might refuse to cross. We just kept on going, though, and eventually we would hear him breaking brush as he found his own way around."

"Did he ever become a good pack horse?" I questioned.

"Oh, he was always a good pack horse."

"I mean did he ever get to where he would obey?"

"No! He just did things his own way. If we went through the woods in one spot and he didn't like it, he would go a different way, then we would hear brush breaking and trees falling and he would catch up to us in time. We built a big barn out of dry snags at Scoop Lake and we hauled those snags a couple miles. We just hooked a couple of them behind Jughead and he always took them over to the barn. He never took the same trail twice, though, for some reason he had to go a different way. We would hear brush breaking as he bulled his way through so you can imagine that he broke a lot of harness. He was a powerful horse but ornery as could be."

"Did you like working with horses, Bill?"

"I fell in love with horses as a kid, so when Frank asked me to go guiding for him I jumped at the chance. I was making about $200 a day working at the dam [Peace River Dam] at the time but I left it to

Frank and Hattie Cooke.

work for Frank at $20 a day. They were the best years of my life, that's for sure."

"I hear you, Bill. It is just one adventure after another and that builds a life filled with memories that never die."

"Some of the airplane trips were scary but I really enjoyed them. Terry Cooke started flying when he was about 17 and I flew with him quite a bit. I remember the time we built an airstrip at Moodie Lake and the next spring Terry and I flew in there. Just as we were touching down I shouted to Terry that it looked soft so he gave it the power and we went back to Scoop Lake. When we touched down, the plane veered to the left and we went into the willows. We got out of the plane and found the problem—we had a flat tire. If we had touched down at Moodie on that narrow runway we would have had a wreck for sure. Another time Terry flipped the plane on its nose at Skook's hay meadow. He didn't get hurt but he sure twisted the prop all to hell. Then there was the time Terry crash-landed Gary Moore's Super Cub up the Liard River when the engine failed. Billy Franks was with him and it took them a couple days to walk out to Fort Liard. Don't get me wrong because I'm not knocking Terry's flying ability. He was an excellent pilot, that's for sure.

"Any other stories about hunting tragedies?" I queried.

"I've got one about a German hunter that we took out in 1986. We had been out hunting sheep and when we got back to camp on the Turnagain River, Kevin Tuft, one of our guides, had a hunter that wanted to get a moose. We glassed the area and spotted a big bull on the mountain right above camp, so Kevin headed up there with the

Mac Cooke with moose.

hunter. I was watching their progress through the spotting scope and telling Frank and the others how they were doing, when I saw Kevin point at the moose and then the hunter lifted his rifle to shoot. Just as I expected him to fire, he fell face forward on the mountain. I told Frank that the hunter had just had a heart attack but he thought I was joking so he said, 'Okay, you guys go up there and if he's dead, just bury him.' But when Frank looked for himself he knew it was the real thing. So Dale Crowder and Mac Cooke and I headed up the mountain as fast as we could go. When we got close Mac hollered to Kevin, 'Is he dead?'

"Kevin shouted back, 'I think so.'

"So Mac yelled, 'I want his binoculars.'

"Then Dale got into the act by shouting, 'I want his boots.'

"We joked a little more and then went down to the camp and told Frank, who notified the police. I looked through the spotting scope again and spotted some ravens. They were in the process of pulling the jacket off the face of the corpse. It took them only a few minutes to find it. So Mac and I climbed the mountain again. Shortly after we got up there, the plane arrived with the police, so I said to Mac, 'If we're going to rob this guy we had better get at it because here come the police.'

"Mac quickly let me know that he didn't see any humour in my joke, so I kept quiet. After about an hour the others arrived with a doctor and a policeman. The doctor just rolled him over with his boot and didn't touch him, except to pull out his wallet and as he thumbed through it, it was obvious that it was loaded with $100 bills. He threw the wallet to the policeman, who crammed it in his pocket, then we put the body in a body bag, tied it on a saddle horse, and went back down to camp. When we checked the hunter's suitcase it was full of money—probably about $20,000 worth. So some of those people sure live well.

"There is more to this story, though, because after hunting season we had to go to the police station to sign papers concerning what had happened on the mountain. When I went to leave, the policeman

Doctor, Bill Eckert and Mac Cooke with German hunter's body.

thanked me for coming in and also for not taking the money off the corpse. Just as I was going out the door I winked at him and asked him how he knew there wasn't another $10,000."

"You fellows managed to mix the humorous and the morbid together quite nicely I notice."

"No doubt we always had lots of humour, but I've got a similar story about Terry Cooke and a deer hunter he took out. They found a deer on the power line and the hunter wounded it, so it took off. Terry knew that the hunter had heart trouble, so he left him at the truck and followed the deer tracks in the snow for a couple miles. He didn't find it, though, so he ended up coming back to the truck from a different direction. When he reached the truck, the hunter was not there. He looked around and hollered but there was no sign of the hunter. At that point Terry phoned the police but they wouldn't come to search until a certain amount of time had passed. It was snowing and blowing and getting dark by that time but Terry did his best to follow the man's tracks in the snow. Finally he realized that the hunter had followed his original tracks, so he went after him and found him dead in the snow. This took place about two years after the German hunter died on the mountain."

"Got any other good memories for me, Bill?"

"I'm thinking of the time Terry and I flew into Pop Lake with the mail and some horseshoes. We landed and met the guide and his hunter. That guide was on his first hunt and only about 16 years old. Apparently they saw a bear and the guide said, 'You better shoot that bear because it is the biggest black bear I've ever seen.' Well, we looked at that bear hide tied on the horse and knew that it was a huge grizzly bear. But the hunter didn't know either, so he told us that he was really pleased that he had taken the biggest black bear the young guide had ever seen. The best part of the story was that the hunter had gut-shot the bear and they had followed it into thick brush where they found it still alive. That story could have had a sad ending because it was a case of the blind leading the blind."

"You worked with young Frankie quite a bit I understand."

"I sure did, and believe it or not I was the guy who killed him."

"I never knew that, Bill, how did that happen?"

"We were supposed to haul a load of horses from my place at Groundbirch out to Frankie's place at Arras near Dawson Creek, and then we were going to go on a hunting trip together and stay out in the bush for a while. So we hauled one load of horses over there and then went to town for something or other. We got in the bar and started drinking and then Frankie took off with a woman to my place. When he got back we had words in the bar and the bartenders chased us outside because we had already wrecked the bar several times. Well we went outside and right away Frankie took a run at me and I punched him on the jaw and down he went. When he hit the ground he struck his head and got knocked cold. His sister was there, so we loaded him in the car and went to an all-night party. After the party we went to my place and Frankie said he had a headache, so he stayed in bed all day. The next day he went home and still had a headache. By the following day I found out that he was in the hospital so I went to see him there. He told me he was set up for a brain scan in a month, and then he checked himself out and went home. The next day he went into a coma and was flown to Vancouver where he died."

"What a terrible turn of events. How did Frank and Hattie deal with it?"

"The police wanted to charge me with manslaughter but Frankie had protected me by telling folks at the hospital that he fell off a horse and banged his head. Frank and Hattie both said it was a fair fight and that the death was a result of an accident, which it was."

"I gather you're still friends, Bill."

"We've always been friends. They were just like my mom and dad because I lived at their place for years. In fact, Hattie told me that it could just as easily have been me because I was always drunk and fighting. But just like many other fights, it was the result of too much booze. I could tell you about many fights: such as Frank's nephew, Pat

Cooke, who ran the fishing end of things at Scoop Lake for Frank. He got killed in a fight, too. We were a haywire bunch of bastards, riding bucking horses and bulls. It's a wonder we weren't all killed one way or another."

"So I gather there was a lot of fighting went on."

"There was. You wouldn't believe some of the things that went on. One day a bunch of us got fighting in the Dawson Hotel. When they went to phone the police, Frank tore the phone off the wall. Then when the police arrived Frank went and hid in the cooler. They shut the hotel down and Frank was locked in there all night. When the cleaning lady arrived at 6 a.m. he was almost frozen to death. Then he came and woke me up and he was shivering and complaining that there had been nothing to drink in the cooler except beer and who wants a cold beer when he's freezing?"

"You fellows certainly raised a lot of hell by the sounds of it."

"We did, but I wouldn't change it for anything. They were by far the best years of my life."

I thanked Bill for his stories, many of which were extraordinary. But none were as strange as the time in Houston BC, when he was shot through the shoulder with a 30.06 rifle. Not only did he survive the deliberate attack, but through a prolonged period of weight-lifting, his shoulder and arm are even stronger than they were before the attack.

Chapter 7

FRANK AND I GOT INTO A DISCUSSION ABOUT FLYING, SO I pointed out, "I notice you refer to bush pilots as rough terrain pilots, Frank, somehow that seems rather appropriate."

"It is. There are many kinds of flying, such as over flat land covered with bush, and there is the type of flying in mountainous country known for strong winds, downdrafts and foggy weather. I recall talking to an airline pilot when I suggested to him that it must be something to fly one of those big planes. The pilot surprised me by saying, 'Any person who can go to the bathroom can fly one of these planes, but I admire the pilots that fly low through those fogged-in mountains, because that requires skill.'

"Well I can tell you that he got it right. I've known many of these rough terrain pilots and a lot of them are dead. There just isn't much margin for error. When my son Terry started flying he took unnecessary chances. I talked to him about it and after a good bit of training he became a good, careful pilot. He went out and got his twin-engine licence and got endorsements on many different planes. One time Terry was flying a group of Mexicans from Dawson Creek to Scoop Lake in our Beach 18 and about 80 miles north of the Peace River Dam he lost an engine. He was carrying a heavy load so he couldn't maintain altitude. He knew he wouldn't be able to make Dawson Creek, so he tried instead for the Hudson Hope Airport. As he approached the airport, there was a hill in the way and he knew he couldn't clear it, so in a desperate move he brought the Beach down on the highway right close to the dam. It was a narrow road, but he put it in there and no one was hurt. Terry was wise that way. He used to listen to Ernie Harrison and Stan Bridcutt and the other experienced pilots and he used to pick their brains.

"One of the most important rules for a pilot is to use your best judgement and don't let people pressure you into flying when you know it's not safe. We had that problem many times with hunters. They would get their game and suddenly decide that they had to get to Watson Lake at once, to catch a plane back to the States. Even if it was socked in they still wanted to go. A pilot must not give in to this type of pressure. I recall one time when Terry went on a flight with Sheldon Luck. When he got back he said, 'My God he's a strict old bugger.' I assured Terry that he had just discovered the reason why Russ had survived for so long."

In an effort to get a better picture of Terry's flying experiences, I

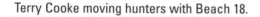

Terry Cooke moving hunters with Beach 18.

met with him and questioned him about any other odd adventures he had experienced during his years of flying in the North. In response he told me about a strange adventure with a wild cat:

"I flew to Scoop Lake early one year and while I was there I heard something up in our food cache. I climbed up expecting to find a marten, but when I opened the door there was a beautiful Siamese coloured cat, and it was just as wild as an animal can be. It took me completely by surprise because I never expected to find a cat over 100 miles from nowhere. Anyway, I set a trap for it with a box and caught it, and then decided to take it back to Dawson Creek. That was a bad idea, though, because while I was flying along that cat managed to get out of the box and then it went absolutely crazy. It tore around the plane tearing up everything it touched. It even landed on my head once and scratched me up with its claws. I couldn't do a thing about it because I had to fly the airplane. When I landed at Dawson Creek, I opened the door and the cat went out like a flash. We never did see it again.

"I have another story about animals in planes. This happened when Gordon Eastman was filming for his movie *High, Wild and Free*. He had two dogs that used to fly with us and they absolutely loved it. They couldn't wait to get into an airplane. Then Gordon thought it would be a good idea to film the two dogs parachuting out of an airplane. We set it all up and dropped them over Scoop Lake and Gordon got his pictures. But it was all a waste, because he never used them in the movie—probably because he thought animal rights' people would raise hell. The end result of that fiasco was that we were never able to get those dogs back into an airplane again. I guess it scared the hell out of them."

"Besides flying, did you guide as well?" I asked.

"Yes, I guided quite a lot, but not as much as my brothers."

"I have another question for you, Terry. Your father and some of the hunters I've talked with seemed mightily impressed with Rawhide (Ernest Frank) as a guide, how would you define his ability?"

"After they made Rawhide, they threw away the mould; he was in a class all by himself as far as I'm concerned. I remember a forest fire we were on with Rawhide near Scoop Lake when a funny thing happened. We had a Native cook named Jack Abou who was about 80 years old at that time. He was a good cook except that he only made tea for breakfast because he didn't like coffee. One evening Rawhide told him to make coffee for breakfast because 'white guys like coffee.' The next morning Jack compromised—he made a big pot full of coffee and tea mixed. The end result was that it tasted like hell so no one touched it and it all went to waste."

"I understand that Rawhide got killed in a vehicle accident. Are you familiar with the story?"

"Yes, it was a vehicle accident. There were four people riding in the pick-up when it went off the road. Rawhide was asleep at the time and he died from a broken neck. No one else was even hurt in the accident."

After I talked with Terry Cooke, I quizzed his father, Frank about other aircraft accidents that occurred in the North.

"Even the best pilots have their accidents and I recall an accident that happened to Russ Baker and an engineer named Danny Driscoll back about 1939. They crashed on take-off only about a mile from Lower Post. Apparently the river was clear of fog and they thought they could get through the other layers of fog but they got fooled and flew into a hill. Both of them survived the crash but their dog got killed when the battery broke loose and crushed it. Well, after they got away from the plane Danny started walking downstream and eventually arrived at Angus McDonald's cabin. I've heard that when Angus opened the door, there was Danny in white coveralls all covered with blood, and I guess he freaked out a bit. He gave Danny a ride back to Lower Post by riverboat and by that time Russ was already there. The plane they were flying in was a twin-Fleet, and as far as I know there were only a few of them manufactured and then they were given up as failures. But it shows that even the best of pilots can have their bad days.

"I think you are right on the money with that observation, Frank, perhaps you recall the terrible tragedy at Sovereign Lakes in 1957 when four people lost their lives. A man named Cooper was the pilot, and along with his co-pilot and engineer, was ace bush pilot Ian Watt who had gone along as an observer. They were on a salvage mission to recover the floats of a Beaver that had crashed at the lake earlier. When they attempted to take off with the floats of the Beaver strapped to the twin-engine Stranraer aircraft, they crashed. Some people who attended the crash scene believed that the float that had been strapped to the left under-wing interfered with the lift, which caused the plane to veer left clipping the tops off trees before it crashed. Whatever the cause, the result showed once again the hazards involved in flying in and out of small lakes in mountainous terrain where there is precious little margin for error."

"That was a terrible tragedy, and I know of so many more just like it. While I was guiding I flew with some great pilots. Ernie Harrison was one; he accumulated so many hours flying in the North. He suggested to me once that he figured planes would get him someday, but he was a careful pilot. I flew many miles with him in all kinds of weather. I recall the day one of my hunters shot a moose at a lake near Colt Lake. Ernie helped us drag the moose onto one of the floats of his Beaver and he flew it back to our camp at Moodie Lake. Several times he flew deep freezes into our camps by just strapping them on the floats. He was a great pilot flying a great airplane.

"Jim Thibideau that I mentioned before, he crashed a Beach 18 on floats about 48 miles up the Trench from Lower Post. He was coming out of Johnnie Drift's place on the Turnagain River with some hunters on board. Maybe the plane had been overloaded, as it was common to do back then. I remember it was late fall and I had already pulled my guides out for the winter. It can fog in so quickly at that time of year. Anyway, they were all killed on impact—just some more victims of wilderness flying. I can tell you one thing for certain: out of all the bush crashes that have occurred in that country, at least 90% were not because of engine failure, instead they were caused by pilots bucking bad weather. The bad weather will kill you no matter how good a pilot you think you are."

In the late seventies, Frank leased a Beaver aircraft from a Vancouver firm to carry hunters and supplies back and forth to his various camps. On one of these flights there was a horrible accident. I asked Frank to relate the story as best he remembered it.

"The pilot took off from my camp at Colt Lake heading toward the Kechika with a passenger and his supplies. When he came around the mountain the valley was full of fog. He attempted to pull the plane around in a tight circle but it stalled out on him and down they came. It wasn't a complete stall, so they were not killed, but they were terribly injured. For some reason they could not get out on the radio from Colt Lake so my son Frankie helped get the injured to camp and then he and Robert Napoleon rode all night through the mountains. It was

This Beaver airplane crashed with Ed Reiner and Ted Long on board; both survived.

40 miles to Scoop Lake and it rained and snowed all night, but they made it in 12 hours. When they arrived, they were soaked and cold. As soon as the weather lifted a bit Terry took off with the Cessna 185 and flew up to an elevation where he managed to contact Watson Lake Airport. He reported the accident and a short time later help arrived by helicopter. The two men were flown to hospital and both survived."

"There are many types of flying, Frank, I understand you used to fly high at party time. There is a story about you swimming under the wharf; is it true?" I asked.

"Yes, it's true all right. I went on a three-day party in Watson Lake years ago and finally decided it was time to get back to camp. Ernie Harrison loaded John Tibbets and I into his Beaver and flew us back to Moodie Lake and when I tried to get out of the plane, I fell into the lake. I was swimming underwater for all I was worth but it seemed I wasn't getting anywhere. The reason for that was because I was only in three feet of water. I had swum under the wharf and I was trying to move the end of the lake. Good old John saved my life that time; he grabbed my feet and pulled me out of there. Ernie sure must have got a kick out of it because he was still laughing an hour later."

When Larry Whitesitt flew Beavers around the North, he frequently flew into Frank's guiding camps. In his book *Flight Of The Red Beaver*, Larry describes one such trip:

"One late evening in September, just before dark, I managed to fly into Colt Lake to spend the night. I knew there were some young ladies in camp who were excellent cooks. Besides a good meal and fresh pie, I knew I could spend a few hours talking to these attractive young ladies. Frank's camps were known for their good food, and I always tried to fly in, if possible, around dinnertime, so it was no accident that I landed here on this particular evening. I had been flying for Gary Moore, near Skook's old ranch south of here. After a good feed, the boys, Frank Jr. and some other guides started to tell what I thought were tall tales. They spoke of flying saucers and swore they visited the camp after dark, flying nearby. I listened tongue-in-cheek, trying not to laugh, and told them, 'Oh sure, what else is new?' As it got dark, the stars stood out sharply in the clean mountain air, and sure enough, up high overhead, I could see moving objects, which I was sure were satellites. But in a short time, a pinpoint of light many miles east of the Kechika River and beyond the distant Rocky Mountains appeared. Within a few seconds the light became a rather large pulsating object, hovering over the Kechika River. It must have gone 50 miles in a couple seconds. The hunters in camp were looking through a spotting scope on a stand, which I also used, and we saw a pulsating light beam emitted from this stationary object, hovering maybe a mile high and seven miles away. It soon disappeared in a few seconds to the east over the Rocky Mountains, and then a little later reappeared the same way, at the same terrific speed. I was stone sober and have no explanation for what we saw."

When I asked Frank's sons about the UFO's, they replied that they were constant visitors to the area and were seen by many of the hunters.

After we finished discussing the UFO's, I brought the subject back to airplanes. As I knew that many of the pioneer woodsmen didn't care for airplanes, I asked Frank, "Did Skook do any amount of flying?"

"Sure he did. I remember one evening when he, Rawhide and I were flying back from Island Lake with Ernie Harrison. It was getting dark as we approached Moodie Lake so we were all concerned. Skook was sitting up front with Ernie and just as we were coming in to land, Skook turned to me and shouted, 'It looks like we'll be eating loon-shit for breakfast, Kid.'

"Rawhide appeared puzzled so he asked me, 'Cookie, what does he mean?'

"I couldn't help but laugh as I told him, 'He means that there's a lot of loon-shit in the bottom of this lake and if we make a bad landing, that's what we will be eating for breakfast'."

"Aside from the trip you just mentioned, Frank, did you ever have any scares in aircraft?"

"Well, I got into a pickle with my son Terry just when he was learning to fly. We were flying between Mile 232 and Fort Nelson and we got into fog. We headed to Fort Nelson and almost hit the smoke stack of the gas plant. I think Terry learned a lot that day. I also had a bit of a scare riding with a guy I'll just call Ted. When we took off he ran into some willows. That was bad enough, but then he told me that he had an awful time landing airplanes. I think I held my breath until we got down, and I didn't go up with that guy again.

"I did get the hell scared out of me once, though, when I was coming out of Quesnel with my son Terry and Gary Moore—the guy who bought Skook's place—in a Beach 18. Terry had checked the weather and the fog layer was only supposed to be 300 feet thick, but when we climbed out it proved to be much thicker. We got up to about 9000 feet before we broke out of it, and when we did, we couldn't see any-

Gary Moore and his Super Cub.

thing. We flew for a couple hours and the plane was iced up when we finally found a hole. That's the worst situation I've ever been in as far as airplanes are concerned. When we did come down through a hole we found the Fraser River and followed it to Prince George. Once we were on the ground I told the others that I was taking the airlines home and that is what we all did. About a week later Terry brought the Beach on home. It was a good thing Terry had his instrument rating or we would have got it that day.

"I got another bit of a scare when I was flying from Prince George to Dawson Creek with one of Bob Keen's pilots in a Beach Baron. We got into solid fog and that's when the radios quit working. We flew for quite a while and ended up in Prince George again. The weather was better by then so we got the radios working and carried on. I remember the pilot begging me not to tell Bob about it because he was afraid he would lose his job. I kept my peace.

"Probably the dumbest thing I ever did in an airplane was the time I flew horses into Scoop Lake in a DC3. We took two loads of three and we had them in chutes made from two by fours. Well, we got into some rough weather up around 8000 feet and one of the stallions started acting up. Make no mistake about it, I would never do that again unless the horses were tranquilized.

"As I said before, the weather will kill you if you don't respect it. I've flown in some rough weather in the Kechika. Once I was with Ernie Harrison when the Beaver got turned right upside down. We shouldn't have been flying then but you get pressed for time and you push things. In 1980 I was in the Kechika when we had powerful winds. It took the roofs off two cabins and then blew them down. So that shows you why the Indians named it Kechika, which means Windy Valley."

Frank's story about the strong winds reminded me of another story so I told him, "A friend of mine told me that he was watching some horses eating on a mountainside during high winds, when he noticed that their tails were sticking straight out from the force of the wind. After he watched them for a while he realized that the horses weren't eating—they were holding the grass in their teeth to prevent themselves from being blown away."

Frank didn't respond to my humour, in fact I think I heard him groan, so I changed the subject and asked, "How many aircraft did you have altogether?"

"We had the Super Cub, which in my opinion had the poorest heating system ever devised, and then we got a Cessna 185 and a Beach 18. Later we had two Aero Commanders and a Cessna 401. We also leased a Beaver for two years. So you see I spent a lot of time in the right seat of different aircraft and got to the point where I knew whether we should be flying or not. For instance, I could look at a river and tell if there was enough water to safely land there. That is a must, because many pilots have been killed trying to land on shallow lakes and rivers. To tell the truth, I hate landing on rivers in the late fall because they get shallow and can fool the best pilots, such as the most famous Canadian pilot, Wop May. He got killed landing on the river at Fort Nelson when he hit a deadhead and drowned. He was just one of several pilots that got it on shallow rivers.

"The North has produced many great pilots such as Sheldon Luck and Stan Bridcutt who for my money were some of the best and safest pilots I ever flew with. And Jimmy Anderson—everybody knows Jimmy—he put a few airplanes in the bush while he was learning to fly. But I'm telling you that many of the stories about Jimmy are just plain bullshit. I've sat and talked to him on many occasions and he told me as much. Once while we were waiting for the weather to lift he came to my house and we talked for seven hours. That man had a lot of experience and knowledge. He was much smarter than he got credit for being. No doubt he did take chances, such as the time he flew live caribou out of the mountains for Al Oeming in his Super Cub. But we have to remember that what may appear dangerous to one person may not be dangerous at all to someone else who is familiar with the procedure. I also knew Jimmy's father, Jim. He sold about 40 horses to Skook back about 1944."

Frank handed me another picture of an airplane crash so I ask him to fill me in on it.

"This was another terrible accident that was caused by the weather. It happened at Birches Bay in 1986 when pilot Coyne Callison and his passenger died in the crash of his Beaver. Birches Bay was in Coyne's guiding area on the Turnagain River in Northern BC. He was only 37 years old at the time and was considered an excellent pilot.

"Coyne came from a family of ranchers, guides and trappers, so you know his first love was the mountains and the bush life he grew up with. He was involved in logging and trucking but it seemed that guiding was his chosen profession. Anyway, both men were killed and the plane burned to a cinder. That was just another example of the dangers involved in flying around the mountains.

"I can tell you about a terribly tough flight that was well documented in the newspapers back about 1962. That was the Ralph Flores and Helen Klaben flight. They were flying from Whitehorse to Fort St. John when they got lost in cloud and crashed just four miles east of my leased land at Aeroplane Lake. Everyone was amazed when they were found alive after spending 49 days outdoors in temperatures down to –50 degrees. I know the pilot that found them, Chuck Hamilton, and he brought them out of the woods. One of the saddest parts of their ordeal was that Chuck had seen Helen while he was flying a guide named Jack George—Eagle Eye we called him—as well as mail and supplies out to Skook's Ranch. They circled and both men agreed that it was a Native woman standing by the fire. Ralph had stomped out an SOS in the snow, but they thought Indian trappers had placed it there, as they often left messages in the snow when they needed food or supplies. Anyway, on the way back from Skook's ranch, Chuck circled the woman [Helen] again and saw the registration number of the airplane and they were rescued. But can you imagine how Helen felt when she saw them circle her and leave?"

"It's odd that you should mention that story, Frank, because I just finished reading it. The title of it is *Hey, I'm Alive*, and I would recommend it to anyone interested in wilderness survival. They only had enough emergency rations to last a couple days, so the fact that they survived seems to defy logic. I doubt that they could have lasted much longer as Ralph had lost 58 pounds—from 178 to 120—and was traveling on will power alone. Helen lost 40 pounds—from 140 to 100—yet believed she could have lasted a while longer. That was a remarkable survival story by any standards. Apparently the government spent about $1.5 million on the search, which was undertaken during some of the worst weather conditions imaginable."

"That rescue shocked everyone; we just couldn't believe they were still alive. But I want to tell you about another scare I had when I was at Skook's Ranch. I was waiting for a ride out with a commercial pilot when a fellow—I don't want to name him—came in with his Taylorcraft airplane. He told me he was going back out again in the afternoon so I should catch a ride with him and save the fare. That sounded good to me, so when the Beaver landed I went with Skook and his horses to pick up the supplies at the river. While we were unloading, I told the pilot that I was going to fly out with the Taylorcraft. The pilot got a strange look on his face and suggested that I was making a mistake. Then he flew away, and left me wondering if perhaps he knew something I didn't know. That afternoon we went to take off in the small plane and found it had a flat tire. We went to Skook to see if he had any tire-patching repair, but he didn't. Skook called for another plane because he wanted more supplies anyway, so the tire went out for repair. When the tire came back with another load, it was too late in the day so we stayed overnight and decided to leave the next morning.

"The next morning we climbed into the old Taylorcraft and started across the meadow. He gave it full power and as we traveled along the meadow I shouted to him that there was a big ditch ahead and that he had better stop or take off, one or the other. The ditch was about six feet deep so we would have had a terrible crash. Well, this pilot managed to get off the ground but I guess he didn't have enough flying speed because he swung to the right and came down and we bounced pretty hard. Then he got up again and we swerved to the left and went through the tops of some willows. This was enough to scare the hell out of anyone, and he wasn't done yet. He just managed to clear the trees at the end of the meadow and I could tell that the plane didn't have the right attitude; the tail was hanging down too much. Then to really scare me, he looked down and said, 'If we had to, we could land in that meadow covered with fireweed.'

"Man, did that give me a jolt. I had walked through that so-called meadow and there were hundreds of trees lying down under those fireweeds. That's when I realized that the pilot didn't have a clue about flying.

"When we got down on the airport at Watson Lake I was so damned happy to be out of that plane. We went to the bar and had a few drinks, and believe me we needed them. I can also tell you that I never got into that airplane with him again. About a year later I ran into that same pilot and he admitted that we almost got killed that day. From what I was told, he quit flying just a short time later and probably some lives were saved because of it."

In looking through Frank's pictures I noticed a photo of a large four-engine plane almost out of sight in what appeared to be a lake. I asked him to explain.

"That picture was taken at Watson Lake during the war when they were freighting all those bombers and other aircraft overseas. That plane took off from the Watson Lake Airport and for some reason went down in the lake. Everyone managed to get out except the tail-gunner who drowned. As far as I know, they never found out what went wrong with the plane and I believe it is still in the bottom of Watson Lake. But I have another picture here of a terrible crash that took the lives of Charlie Elliot and Dan Miner. These are just a sampling of the crashes that have occurred in the North, so you know you have to take your hat off to these brave individuals who put there lives on the line when they fly in bad weather conditions."

Most bush pilots will admit that the only reason they survive is because of good luck. Ernie Harrison of Fort St. James is a retired bush pilot with close to 20,000 hours who often flew for Frank Cooke and Skook Davidson. In fact, he spent one summer flying a Beaver aircraft out of Scoop Lake. Ernie is quick to point out that there is no substitute for luck when flying in the mountains. For proof, he cites the day he flew barrels of fuel to Chukachida Lake. When the job was finished he took off and flew just a short distance when his engine failed. Because of an error made during an overhaul, he was forced to dead-stick land the Beaver in a small lake where he hit the bank at the end of the lake. Ernie makes no bones about it—if the engine had quit when he was carrying the full drums of fuel, he would have ended up just another statistic.

A memory that still brings a smile to Ernie's face concerns the time he was flying a husband and wife to some remote area when her cat went crazy. Ernie had been against the idea of flying a cat without a proper cage, but the woman insisted that her cat never got excited. They lifted off and everything went along fine until they ran into some turbulence over Takla Lake and then the cat came out of the box it had been held in. On its first pass around the cabin, it left a trail of droppings, especially on the owner's sweater. On its second pass around the cabin Ernie grabbed it and fired it out the window. Although this event took place many years ago, Ernie considers it a possibility that the cat could still be swimming out there somewhere in Takla Lake. His dry sense of humour led him say, "I've heard it said that a cat always lands on its feet, but I'll be damned if I can figure out how a cat can land on its feet if it hits the ground backwards at 120 miles an hour."

Ernie has a picture in his scrapbook of the airplane he landed on Tachie Road near Fort St. James. As he came down through the trees to make an emergency landing, he noticed a power pole on either side of the road and realized that he could not escape hitting them. He braced for an impact that surely would have taken the wings off the

Pilot Ernie Harrison.

airplane, but to his surprise, he sailed safely by. After he emerged from the plane he walked back and checked the distance between the two poles and found that he had 18 inches of clearance on either side. By some miracle and a substantial amount of luck, he had passed dead centre between them. Perhaps he is right when he states "skill is good but luck is even better."

Probably the biggest threat he faced in forty years of flying was the time a trapper met him with a cocked 30-30 rifle and pointed it at his chest. Ernie had been delivering mail to Fort Grahame, Germanson Landing and Manson Creek when he decided to assist a lonely trapper along the Liard River. He had told the trapper to wait until there was five inches of solid ice on the river, at which point he was to tramp a trail in the snow so Ernie could land the Beaver safely. When Ernie spotted the tramped trail he would drop off the mail and other necessary provisions. But no trail was tramped in the snow, so after a few weeks passed Ernie decided to try landing and check to see if the trapper was in trouble. He landed the plane successfully and walked to the cabin where he came face to face with the trapper who pointed a cocked rifle at him and shouted, "What took you so long? I've waited weeks for you."

At a glance Ernie realized that the trapper had gone bush crazy, so he stepped into him, grabbed his rifle, hit him across the head and watched him drop to the snow. Then he threw the rifle far away into the snow. When the trapper came around he got up as calm as could be and said, "You finally got here; it's good to see you."

Some time later Ernie mentioned this episode to his doctor and was told that he had done the proper thing: he had shocked the man and brought him back to reality. Ernie also makes the point that he is certain the trapper never remembered being struck by the gun, and on ensuing visits it was never mentioned. He also suggests that the trapper must have wondered how his rifle got into the snow-bank when he found it the next spring.

Ernie was first inspired to get his flying licence after he and a friend named Frank Hoy were left and forgotten at a remote lake. It took a week of tough slugging before they reached civilization and it was at that point that Ernie decided he would rely only on himself in the future. But not entirely on himself, because he feels that he owes his life to Peter Deck—the man who taught him to fly. Peter taught him how to escape from a dead-end canyon by pulling a plane up sharply and then going wing over to fly back in the opposite direction. Several years later he was caught in a storm and flew into a dead-end canyon. The fact that he is alive proves that the technique worked successfully.

After perusing Ernie's pictures, I asked him, "What happened to the airplane that crashed on the ice?"

"Oh, that's just an example of the hazards of winter flying. I guess I hit too hard and the thing broke through. But that's nothing because I walked away from it without a scratch."

Ernie had another story about the time 50 years ago when he and a game warden were supposed to be poisoning wolves in the

Chilcotin when in fact they were on a long, drawn-out party in the Yukon. "How did you get away with it?" I asked.

Ernie's answer was a lesson in simplicity, "No one knew where we were, so we just figured it was time for a party."

I listened to Ernie's stories for a few hours and then asked, "Was there ever a time when you regretted flying for a living?"

"No! How else could I have had so much adventure and seen so much beautiful country? I wouldn't have missed it for the world."

"You used to fly for Skook at times; got any stories about him?" I asked.

"Everybody who knew Skook had to have stories about him because he was one kind of a guy. I always took a bottle of Crown Royal with me when I flew into Terminus Mountain. Sometimes I would unload and pretend I was getting ready to leave when Skook would shout, 'Didn't you bring me a bottle?'

"After I teased him for a minute I would whip out a bottle of Crown Royal and hand it to him, and then he would take off the cap and make his famous toast:

'Here's to the land of diamond hitches, packers and cooks, the sons of bitches.'

"I remember another story about Skook. Back before 1940, Skook was a close friend to Const. Frank Cooke, but they went their separate ways and it was about 25 years later when Frank Sr. came to Scoop Lake to help his son, Frank, build some cabins. One day I suggested to Frank Sr. that we should fly over and visit Skook. He went for the idea and while we were flying to the ranch we decided to play a joke. I knew that people had been flying into his ranch for years trying to buy his guideline from him, but the answer was always a definite no. Well, we circled the ranch and a few minutes later Skook arrived at the river with his horses and wagon. We pulled into shore and then I walked ahead, while Frank pulled his hat down over his eyes and lagged behind. Suddenly Skook hollered, 'Who's that with you?'

"I walked up to him and said, 'this fellow has a pocket full of money and he wants to buy you out.'

"Well, right away Skook hollered, 'Get that son of a bitch out of here; the place is not for sale. Put him back in the plane and get him to hell out of here.'

"When Frank Senior got right up to Skook he tipped his hat back and said, 'Skook, you're getting meaner every year.'

"Well you should have seen the performance when Skook recognized him; he hugged him and then almost shook his hand off. It was really something to see."

"Anymore flying stories, Ernie?" I questioned.

"Well there was the time near Mackenzie when I had a Ministry of Transport guy with me and the Otter engine quit. I had been having trouble with it for a while and I knew by the sound of it that things were not quite right. When I survived that venture I said to my boss, Jack Philpot, 'I quit!'

"Right away he answered, 'No you don't; the Otter's going to quit.' He meant what he said, because in a few days the Otter was sold and gone.

"Another memory concerns the time I flew several dignitaries to Anchorage to celebrate when Alaska became a state. I recall one of them stood up and said, 'Well, Texas, we don't have take your bull anymore because we're the biggest state now.' I never did get those fellows back out of there. They got on such a bender that I eventually had to leave to pick up some prospectors who were waiting for me back in the mountains. I never did find out how they got home."

"Any memorable rescue missions?"

"Oh sure. I can tell you about the time there was a motor vehicle accident at Watson Lake. Four people were badly injured and needed emergency transport to Whitehorse Hospital. It was dark night out when I was asked to help fly them out. The police got special clearance for us so another pilot and I flew them out in two Beavers. The airport lights were on when we arrived in Whitehorse and they were a pretty sight after two hours of flying in the dark."

During my visit to Fort St. James, I took time to visit the memorial that had been placed at the edge of Stuart Lake on July 13, 1991. A replica of a Junkers W34 airplane sits atop a pole where a commemorative plaque spells out a tribute to the many bush pilots who have served the North so faithfully throughout the years. The message is clear:

"Dedicated this date in honour of the bush pilots who flew out of Fort St. James to points north and their contributions to aviation history."

Ernie Harrison, Pat Carey and Sheldon Luck were among the guests of honour in attendance that day.

While I'm on the subject of mountain flying, I want to bring in pilot Stan Simpson, who is an outfitter/flyer in the Far North. Stan is another flier who has had his anxious moment in the air. Just to give an idea of the problems they face while flying in the far North, I want to tell about the time it snowed and his plane became frozen in the ice of the river near O'Grady Lake in the Northwest Territories.

The guide that was with Stan on this trip sure earned his salt. He spent three days chopping a trail through the ice on the river, a distance of about 300 yards, so that they could get the plane into the open water of the lake for takeoff. On another hunt, he and his hunters were trapped for ten days because of bad weather. Stranded in a small shack, there was so little room that they had to take turns eating, and the last three days they were down to eating moose meat and pancakes. By the time the weather changed, the hunters had enough of the wilderness and were more than a bit anxious to get home.

Another memorable event occurred when Stan's hunters stumbled onto a wolf attacking a caribou calf. By the time the men got close enough to shoot, the calf was fatally injured. The hunters gave the wolf some of its own medicine that day, and one of them went home with a wolf pelt.

Stan's worst experience by far occurred just a month after his wedding in 1983, in the remote Keele River area of his guiding territory.

He was flying a Super Cub at the time of the accident, which took place after he turned the plane into receding air. The air was receding faster than his rate of climb so he was unable to escape the inevitable. The plane came through the trees and crashed, tearing the wings off in the process. So great was the impact, that the guide in the rear seat broke his seatbelt and plunged into Stan from behind. The force drove Stan's head right through the windshield. At the same instant, his shoulders struck the two support rods resulting in the fracturing of both scapulas and clavicles. His left leg took the brunt of the crash, though, which resulted in a fractured tibia and fibula just above his ankle, as well as the main femur bone a short distance below his hip. Stan was in such an injured state that he could not assist himself, so he pleaded with the guide to get him out of the aircraft and into a sleeping bag. When that was accomplished, the guide built a shelter and started a fire in the hopes that a rescue helicopter would soon arrive.

As Stan told it, "Immediately after the crash, a Russian satellite picked up the emergency location transmitter signal from my airplane and a short time later two Hercules aircraft were circling our position. By some freak mistake, the wrong co-ordinates were forwarded to the rescue helicopter in Norman Wells, 45 miles from the crash site. We were forced to spend the night there, and during the night while I was lying in the sleeping bag a wolverine came and started tugging on the sheepskin cape, trying to pull it out from under my head. Now that was a bit of a surprise I'll tell you."

"I'll bet it smelled the blood and that's what brought it to you. Did it hang around for a while?" I wondered.

"No, it didn't. Anyway, the next day the chopper came to the general area and began its search, but it couldn't locate our position. Finally, by flying in and out behind mountains, it narrowed the search and spotted the campfire the guide had built. It was 24 hours after the crash when the chopper arrived. But we weren't out of the woods yet, because when they were packing me to the chopper, they dropped me into a swamp and got me a little bit wet. All told, it was a total of 36 hours from the time of the accident until I arrived at the hospital in

Edmonton. During that time I didn't suffer any terrible pain, it was more of an aching."

"I suspect you were in extreme shock, and that could explain your lack of pain. Did you have many flying hours to your credit at the time of the accident?" I asked.

"I had about 200 hours at that time; now I have 8000 hours, so a lot of mountains have passed under my wingtips since then."

"How long were you in the hospital?"

"I was in the hospital for one month and during that time they put a steel pin in my femur. I wasn't surprised when they told me that I would have bled to death if the femur bone had broken through the skin and caused a compound fracture. I know I was really lucky that it didn't. The end result of it all is that my left leg is five-eights of an inch shorter than my other leg."

"Did you think you had reached the end of the trail at any time during that long ordeal?"

"Not once. I just felt positive that I would make it and I did."

Before I close this chapter on bush flying, there is one more story that simply must be told. It concerned the well-known bush pilot Bill

Harvey, who flew both fixed wing and helicopters throughout the North for many years. This story began the day that Bill and his assistant, George Fleiger, decided to take the Forest Service staff in Fort St. James out for a familiarization flight in a Beaver aircraft. As they flew along, Bill pretended he was getting sick, and then faked barfing into a bag carried on the aircraft for that purpose.

Hunter Tim Senty at Keele River.

When he finished barfing, he went to throw the bag out the window but George stopped him with the words, "Give it here, I haven't had a thing to eat yet today."

Bill handed the bag to George, who grabbed a spoon and began eating the stew that had been placed in the bag just prior to the flight. Within minutes all the forestry staff were busy using the other barf bags and they weren't faking it.

Chapter 8

AFTER SO MANY YEARS OF GUIDING, FRANK COOKE HAS numerous tales to tell. I decided to get him going on the subject by asking, "Did you ever take any unusual people out on hunts with you?"

"I sure have. I've taken doctors, lawyers, surgeons, psychiatrists, an FBI agent, and a member of the mafia, as well as two Japanese that were polite to a fault. I have to tell you that you never know what to expect. There was the time we took an FBI agent out on a sheep hunt and that was something else. He got set up on a big ram and fired 27 shots without getting it. I decided to tease him so I said, 'Now I understand why you guys couldn't protect Kennedy.' Man, did he ever take offence. The kids at camp really got a kick out of that story, but he turned out to be a good egg, so by the time the hunt was over, all was forgiven. But just to show you, I also guided one of the kingpins of the mafia and he was one of the best shots and best hunters I've ever seen."

I just couldn't resist coming back with, "He probably got more practice than the others."

After perusing Frank's pictures, I noticed a picture of a hunter named John Caputo with a huge moose, so I asked, "Where did he get that magnificent animal?"

"That was taken at Pop Lake and I was guiding him at the time.

But I have to tell you about when I had the mafia guy in there, because I also had a DA in there from the Southern States. I sat there most of the night and listened to them talk. Each knew what the other did for a living so it was an interesting conversation. They got into the over-proof rum and they sure talked. These guys were okay, but I had one party in there that taught me that people are not equal no matter what we want to believe. These two guys called us right at the end of the season and were desperate for a hunt. They kept calling until I agreed to guide them. When they arrived in camp they were loaded down with booze and settled right into some serious drinking. The cookhouse was spotless when they arrived but a short time later, things started going downhill. Suddenly one of the men spit on the floor so I went over and cleaned it up just to show my disapproval. He spit on the floor again, so I told him we didn't do that indoors. Well this idiot laughed and spit again. That really got to me so I told him, 'We are not a bunch of tramps around here; if you spit on the floor again you are going to find yourself down there cleaning it up.'

"Well, he gave me a look and then they both went to their cabin where they continued drinking. Herb Fellers and I were tired so we went to bed, but only a few hours later we were awakened when these guys came for something to eat. I got up and made them coffee and one of them spit on the floor again. That did it. I grabbed him and fired him out the door, and then I ordered him to get a pail of water from the lake and scrub the floor. Well, he did it, and we got things understood around camp. The next day we took them out and they both got their game.

"I used to tell my sons Terry, Frankie and Mac that we were bound to get some assholes but we had to do our best to put up with them because they were only around for a few weeks. It is so important to have good guides. Skook trained several young Native guides and they turned out to be the best in the business. I used several of them after Skook stopped guiding and I can't say enough about them. I had a trick I used to play on them—I would go to them and tell them that my white guides were the best guides I had ever seen—then I would tell the white guides that the Natives were by far the best guides. Man, that really made them dig deep."

"You must have had some strange hunts out there at times." I suggested.

"I recall when I first started guiding on my own territory. I had an American hunter named Anderson from Arizona and we went to Scoop Lake. He was after bear, and right away I got him set up on a large boar grizzly. As we watched, a lone wolf came along and suddenly that bear took off on the run. I was surprised that the bear was so afraid of the wolf. Well, the hunter got the bear and he was overjoyed."

"Are you sure that the bear ran from the wolf?" I asked. "Maybe it got the scent of you and the hunter. They have an outstanding sense of smell you know."

"I figured it ran from the wolf, but anyway, that afternoon the hunter wanted to go fishing so I got out an old boat that was there and we headed out on the lake. The boat we were using had two air compartments, which should have made it unsinkable, but we sure put it to the test that day. As soon as we got fishing, he hooked into a big one and got all excited. Just as I went to shut the motor off, he stood up and the little boat flipped upside down. The ice had gone off the lake just a short time earlier, so you know the water was unbearably cold. We didn't have life jackets with us so the only thing we could do was grab hold of the boat. At once it started to sink and at the same time the hunter started yelling that he couldn't swim. I got him to hold on to the opposite side of the boat from me, while I attempted to get the motor off the boat so it would float higher, but each time I moved to the back, his side of the boat went under and he screamed bloody murder. At the same time I was hollering to get the attention of the others on shore. Finally I noticed someone run out of a tent and then I heard a chainsaw running. Several times I tried to get my boots off and succeeded in removing one of them.

"We were about 600 yards offshore, and while I could have made it on my own, the hunter would have drowned it I had left him. Well it seemed like forever until Frankie and Rawhide reached us with a raft, and another long time until we reached shore. All told, it must have been close to an hour until we got on the bank and stripped and forced ourselves to run to the cabins. I couldn't help laughing at Dan, because he looked so funny. I asked him, 'What do you think your stenographer would say if she could see you now?' He let me know that he didn't give a damn what she would say because he was just so happy to be alive.

"When we got into the cabin, we each had a couple stiff drinks and after we warmed up, I summed up Dan's trip for him by saying, 'Well Dan, you had quite a day. First you had a row with a grizzly bear and then you almost drowned. I've got a feeling you will not forget this day for a long time.' Dan assured me that he would never forget it.

"Another thing I have to tell you, it was weird that while I was in the water I kept thinking how crazy it would be if I drowned in the lake after all the dangerous rivers I had crossed."

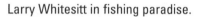

Larry Whitesitt in fishing paradise.

"While we are on the subject of grizzlies, Frank, perhaps this would be a good time to quote from Larry Whitesitt's book, *Flight Of The Red Beaver*:

"Shortly after arriving in Watson Lake, Ernie Harrison said, 'Larry, you have a trip to Moodie Lake, a hundred miles south in the Rocky Mountain Trench, for Frank Cooke.' I was to take BC-Yukon's Beaver CF-JBP and fly some freight to Moodie Lake."

"It was August 10th, 1969, and this was to be my first trip to the area, so I had my sectional maps on my lap. The weather was lousy after take-off, and I had to climb up over the cloud cover, but I could see holes in the layers. I was flying, feeling good and following a river when I noticed the river was running the wrong direction, according to the map. I discovered I was not sure of my location. In other words, I was lost. A short time later, I saw a lake through a hole in the clouds and thought I spotted a couple of pack dogs by a cabin. This made me feel better; I could land and ask directions. Upon landing, I taxied the Beaver to shore, tied up, and started to climb up the bank, intending to walk over to the cabin.

"As I topped the bank, I met a large mass of fur coming toward me only 15 feet away. I froze. The grizzly didn't like my looks any better than I did his. I walked slowly backward to the plane, and he went in the other direction, much to my relief. Looking at my map, I figured I was probably at Scoop Lake; Moodie Lake was about 15 miles southwest.

"I flew on to Moodie Lake and met Frank Cooke for the first time. Frank, a lean six-footer who looked like a cowboy—which he was— had wrangled horses since his childhood. He was a nice-looking, intelligent individual, friendly, well organized, and seemed completely in charge of every situation. I explained my encounter with the bears and asked, 'Frank are there any pack dogs by the cabin?'"

"He replied, 'No, but I'll bet they were bears, and they probably wrecked my cabin.' Frank rounded up a hunter and we flew back to Scoop Lake to deal with the grizzlies . . .'"

Rather than carry on with the quotation, I asked Frank if he recalled what happened there and he took over:

"When we tied up at Scoop Lake, I remember looking out the window of the Beaver, and sure enough, there was one grizzly in the yard. I wasn't going to let the hunter shoot him, but I looked over at the cookhouse door and saw that it was open and all the windows were knocked out, so I knew there would be a mess in the cabin. The bear started to run so I said, 'Shoot him!' He did and killed him.

"The gun had no sooner gone off, though, when out the door came another grizzly, and then out the window came another. I hated to shoot them, but I knew that I had to, as they would keep coming back and destroy the place. Well, one started running along the lake, and the other bear started toward us at the plane, so I shouted to the hunter, 'You take the one going down the lake and I'll get this one coming toward us.' I dropped my bear, and damned if the hunter didn't wound the other one. He was wildly excited because he had never been involved with grizzlies before that encounter. Well, I finished off the other bear and that took care of the problem."

"What was the damage to the cabin?" I wanted to know.

"It was a total wreck. They took it apart like you wouldn't believe."

I recalled from Larry Whitesitt's book that there had been another mix-up with a group of grizzlies, so I asked Frank to elaborate.

"That would be the one at Moodie Lake," he recalled, "where about 20 of us were having a barbecue near the cabins. It was just starting to get dark when my big dog, Zero, growled and the hair stood up on his back. Even though we were singing and making a hell of an amount of noise, it was obvious something was coming. I sent the women and children into the cookhouse and told the men to grab their rifles. Then right away five grizzlies came out into the clearing just as if they owned the entire area.

"When they spotted us the biggest bear came straight at me and I shot it in the mouth. It dropped and the rest of the bears came straight at us. I yelled to the others to shoot and then heard Mac, who was 15 at the time, warn me that a bear was coming at me from the side. I

Frank's dog Zero.

hadn't seen it, so it was right up to me when I fired and it dropped right beside me. Another one ran at Mac, who protected himself by running out into the lake. It was over in a minute and then the women came out to see the bears. Everyone laughed at Mac out in the lake, but he had made a clever move to protect himself. It seemed strange that the bears came to us when there was so much noise going on. Perhaps they had never been around people before.

"In my opinion bears are the most dangerous when you surprise them on a carcass, because many of them will attack you then. You have to use good judgement when you're guiding hunters so that you don't put them in a dangerous position around bears. I always tried to get above a bear if possible. Another thing I want to mention about bears is that the best grizzly habitat in BC is between Dawson Creek and the CNR Railroad between Prince George and McBride. There are more bears in that area than in the Yukon or anywhere else I've traveled, and some big ones too. But that reminds me of something I've wanted to ask you. I read your book *Grizzly Bear Mountain* and I notice that you believe bears pick up sound through the ground."

"Yes, I'm positive they do. That is why bears are such a threat to two people walking together. Since bears have padded feet, they know that it is not another bear approaching. Therefore four feet hitting the ground suggests it is an ungulate. Twice I have had grizzlies come out from behind a tree right in front of me when I was walking with another hiker. I feel certain that they only realized what we were at the last instant, which made them decide to leave. In many cases they may attack before they find out it is humans they are dealing with. This would explain why some bears attack humans and then leave the area in high gear when they realize what they have tangled with. But getting back to your bear problems at your camps, did you always keep dogs around?"

"Yes, when we were there. That's something I want to mention about dogs. There should be at least one around every guiding camp.

Guides Robert Napaleon, Billy Franks, Frankie Cooke and Larry Bedell with two wolf-killed Stone rams. Horns were put together to form the all-time world record.

They earn their feed by guarding the place and by giving a warning when danger approaches.

"We watched a funny performance between my dog and a small bear. First we heard the dog barking and then the garbage can went upside down. We shone the flashlight out the door and there was the dog and the little bear nose to nose. The dog was doing his best but he couldn't bluff the bear out at all. Maybe the bear sensed that the dog was old and arthritic and not much of a threat. After a while the bear left and we cleaned up what was left."

"I noticed the joke about the picture of the world-record-plus sheep horns, Frank, care to explain them?"

"Some of my guides found two wolf-killed Stone rams so they put the two sets together to form the new all-time world record—move over Frank Golata!"

"I also noticed several different animals killed by wolves in your pictures, Frank, did you find very many carcasses?"

"We sure did. I remember when John Caputo and Rawhide found two large rams that had been killed by wolves. It was in a muskeg area where the wolves took them down and the men brought the horns back to camp to show everyone.

"You've spent a lot of years in the woods, Frank, so I assume you must have some moose stories to tell, haven't you?" I asked.

"I recall one story that my dad was involved in when I was just a kid back about 1937. An Indian named Portage Pius shot a bull moose just before dark about 16 miles from Stuart Lake. He left the animal overnight and when he came back the next morning, he attempted to dress it out. The moose wasn't dead, though, so it got up and threw Portage with its antlers. One prong of the antlers penetrated his guts and he was critically injured. My dad was involved in the rescue and they had to carry him 16 miles by stretcher. It took three days to get him out to the lake and down to Fort St. James by canoe. Then dad drove him to the hospital in Prince George. It was too late by then; they operated but there was serious infection so they couldn't save him.

John Caputo and Rawhide with wolf-killed rams.

"There was another case up the Middle River where another Native was attacked by a moose. His name was Lizar Tomi and from the story I heard, he had a 10-year-old boy with him at the time. Apparently he was thrown about 15 feet in the air and was terribly injured. They were taking him to the hospital when he died. So moose will attack people, especially when they are in the rut.

"I had an interesting experience with a bull moose near Teslin Lake when I was working for Skook. I had stopped and unpacked my 12 head of horses, and was chopping wood to make a campfire when I heard a grunt. I looked up and spotted a big bull moose about 100 yards away. My dog Rex also saw it so he gave chase and it ran across a swamp meadow out of sight. The dog returned and I carried on chopping wood. A while later I heard another grunt, so I looked up and there was the rutting bull behind a big broken tree about 10 feet from me. By this time the horses were really fussing so I ran and got my rifle. Rex took after the moose again, but not for long, because the moose turned and it was Rex's turn to run. The moose looked crazy; it was thrashing the brush and grunting. A couple of the horses got all excited and were ready to scatter. I finally realized I couldn't drive it away so I shot it.

"I know of another case on the upper Liard River where an elderly Indian man named Stewart wounded a moose and it ran into the trees. He followed it by walking along the edge of the trees. Well, it attacked him and apparently he didn't see the attack coming because it hit him in the back and dumped him right on the Alaska Highway.

Paul Loiselle was the guy who picked him up and drove him to the hospital. He died a short time later."

"I want to get back to guiding, Frank, so just offhand, who would you say was the worst hunter you ever guided?"

"Well, I can tell you about one hunter that I never wanted to see again. He was a lawyer who came with another lawyer. Anyway, one evening they were having a drink and talking when one of them said, 'I almost didn't make it on this trip.'

"The other one asked him why, and he answered, 'I had a last minute court case; I had to defend this nigger. But I just went in and told him to plead guilty and managed to get right out of there. That poor bastard is probably still trying to figure out what happened to him.' I was absolutely furious; the hunting trip meant more to him than a man's life and freedom."

"Did Skook do much guiding?" I asked, because I had heard rumours that he didn't.

"Most of the Americans thought he did, but I think he only guided for a few years. He hired guides—most of them Natives. I'm telling you that he hated killing animals, except the wolves that bothered his horses, and eventually he would not allow anyone to shoot sheep near the ranch. He ran the outfit, paid the bills and wages and made sure everything was done right.

"He got shot through the hips during the war and suffered terribly from it. In later years he was in such terrible shape that he rode sidesaddle on his horse, Poison, and he had to have help to get off. There was no give-up in that man, though, and I never in my entire life saw a man that could rope as good as Skook. Even in a corral, he could pick any horse out of the bunch and lasso it. He had a record of every colt that had been born on the ranch and he let the old horses die a natural death. Another thing, when Poison died it really took a piece out of Skook because they were together for a long time."

"I have read that over 100 miles of trails were cut around Skook's ranch. Is that true?"

"There was at least that much, probably even more. One year there was a big burn on the lower Kechika and the next year Craig Forfar and I cut 40 miles of trail through it. The following year, Skook, Craig and I were backpacking through there and when we hit the Red River, Craig tried to ford it but the water was too high. Skook decided we would wait until 4:00 in the morning because the water would drop a bit by then. In the morning Craig and I crossed the dogs' packs; we made five trips across. Then it was Skook's turn. He made it fine until he got to a deep spot, and then he couldn't seem to go ahead or back. I went to his assistance and helped him downstream a little and we made it across. Then we made a big fire and got dried out. Skook couldn't swim a stroke, you know, yet he spent all those years around rivers."

"Did you ever have any scares because of hunters doing stupid things, Frank?"

"I recall the day I was crawling along trying to sneak up on some game when I got a surprise. A hunter was crawling along behind me when I heard a metallic sound, so I asked what he was doing. He whispered that he has just put a cartridge in the barrel of his rifle. Try to imagine how I felt—that rifle was pointed right at my butt. I moved over and let him go ahead, and told him in no uncertain terms not to do that again. You learn as you go along, though, and if it isn't one thing, then it's another. One of the worst scares I ever got happened right at Moodie Lake camp. We were in the cookhouse when someone fired a rifle outside. I rushed out to where my three-year-old daughter Donna was playing. I checked in the tent and there was a red-faced hunter. He apologized all over the place and then admitted that he had been cleaning his rifle when it fired. Once again, and against our policy, he had been carrying a cartridge in the firing chamber. The bullet had gone out the doorway of the tent and from what we could figure it must have missed Donna by just a small margin."

"After so many years in semi-open country, you must have had some interesting observations of wildlife." I suggested.

"It was common to see the rams fighting, but there were other

times, such as the day John Tibbitts and I watched a wolverine and a couple two-year-old grizzly bears above timberline. I checked a previous kill with the glasses and spotted a wolverine eating on it and while we watched, the two grizzlies came along.

"The bears took turns running at the wolverine and each time they moved in, the wolverine would lunge at them. For a while it appeared to be a stalemate, and then the bears tried to attack it again. We watched for at least half an hour and the wolverine was still on the carcass when we left, so we went back to camp and told the others about it. Well, the next day we went back through the same area and found the two bears feeding. They must have succeeded in driving the wolverine away."

"I find that interesting, Frank, from all the years I spent watching wildlife above timberline, I've arrived at the conclusion that not everything is as obvious as it first appears. For instance, I've seen grizzlies chase other grizzlies in what appeared to be serious combat, yet a short time later they bedded down or began to feed just a short distance apart, seemingly unconcerned."

"Yes, there is a lot to learn from watching wildlife, but the most important thing I learned about hunting is that you must have an abundance of patience. When stalking a big ram, sometimes you may have to wait days to get him in the proper position. If he is bedded down on a ridgetop with a good view of the area and you try to sneak up on him there, you will just drive him away. Sheep have outstanding eyesight, as many unlucky hunters have learned the hard way."

"I imagine there is quite a lot to learn about overseeing a group of guides. Did you ever have to fire any of them?" I asked.

"I learned from Skook that you have to get rid of the bad ones. With him you didn't get many chances, especially if you mistreated his horses. You may get one warning and that would be it. But yes, there is a lot to being a successful outfitter because you have to keep tabs on everything and it is a full-time job. I always made a habit of checking the boats and airplanes, making certain they were well tied in case a storm came up. I would go and check the cookhouse to make sure there were no cigarette butts still burning.

"That reminds me of a friend we had at the lodge on the Turnagain River. She had a young daughter that would repeatedly play with the propane stove in the cookhouse. When told to leave it alone, she would back off and then start again. One night there was a terrible explosion in the lodge. A man who was staying upstairs was

Lodge burning at the Turnagain River.

blown clean out through the window and by a miracle, landed on the ground, unhurt. We lost the lodge, which was valued at over $100,000 and about $10,000 worth of food and other things besides. There was no way to prove it, but I suspect that the child turned the valve on and when the propane hit the pilot light it was all over."

"So you built another lodge on the Turnagain, is that correct?"

'Yes, but it wasn't as big as the first lodge. We gathered all the rock necessary for the new lodge right out of the river, and believe me that was a big job. Mac sure put in a lot of time on that."

"I understand that the Turnagain River area is an incredibly beautiful place?"

"It is, and you wouldn't believe the fishing in that country. I've seen some happy fishermen come out of that area."

I studied a picture of the new Turnagain Lodge and then asked, "That must have been a monstrous job because a huge amount of rock went into that building."

"There was a lot of time went into it but that was one thing we had lots of. We enjoyed being out there, in fact, we would always find reasons to be there as there was always work to be done."

"Any other observations about hunters, Frank?"

"Something I learned the hard way is that you have to listen to them. Some of the hunters have hunted all over the world and they know a lot. If you keep your ears open it's surprising how much you can learn from other people, even some that may appear to be greenhorns. But most important of all, I learned to treat the hunters right. I made certain that the horses were there early in the morning and ready to go. If the hunter doesn't want to go, that's his business. But I did everything possible to make their trips successful. I used to hire young lads to keep the camps shipshape. They would have the fires going in the tents so that when the hunters came in cold and wet, they could get dried out in a hurry. These lads would keep a good supply of wood and kindling by each stove and the gas lamps full of fuel. Young Gord McNeely was a horse wrangler for me when he was 15 and 16 years old. He remembers the time he went out early in the morning to bring in the horses, and while he was riding along bareback, a rutting bull moose attacked him and his horse. The horse took off with Gord clinging desperately to its withers, and all he could think about was the hell he would get from me if he was late. He got the horses in on time.

"But there are so many things to think about, such as making certain that all the capes, horns, feet and all animal parts are put up in a cache so that dogs or other animals can't get them. Imagine how a hunter would feel if he got up in the morning to find a dog chewing on his expensive goat or sheep head. It would be a ruined trip, that's for sure."

After that conversation with Frank, I received a phone call from a woman named Lucille Isfeld, who was a trail cook for Frank's guides for several years. She explained that a special closeness develops between people who spend time together in the wilderness. As she put it, "It causes you to re-evaluate your life and what is really important." When I asked her if she would do it over again, she answered, "In a minute. Without a doubt those were the best years of my life."

As Frank had told me in our phone conversations about some of the different types of people he had guided, I asked him to elaborate.

"I think that the most memorable person I ever guided was Von Fleck, who owned Mercedes Benz at the time. This man had all his staff arrive at Scoop Lake ahead of him. There were 11 servants, including his own cook, all of whom he had brought from Germany. When everything was ready, Von Fleck came to Watson Lake by Learjet, where we met him with a Beaver and flew him to our camp. This was a performance unlike anything I have ever seen before or since. He had about 23 suitcases full of clothing, and each morning the staff would have his clothes all laid out for his choice of the day. Von Fleck never hunted while he was there; he used to go up in the Beaver for hours just looking the country over. Several times we flew him and some of his associates to Watson Lake, where they would board the Lear jet and go to Whitehorse for lunch. Von Fleck didn't spend much time talking to people. Usually he spoke directly to an expediter that he had brought from New York, and that led to the cap-per of the trip. One day this expediter—Ralph Edsold was his name, if I remember right—told me to go to Watson Lake and take the Learjet to Jasper, Alberta. The purpose for the trip was to pick up some wine they had left in storage in the hotel on an earlier trip. We flew the Beaver to Watson Lake, and then I took the pilot with me and we accomplished the mission, but only after a heated debate with the hotel manager who was reluctant to surrender the wine. At last he was convinced that his job could be in peril if we returned empty-handed, so down we went, to the wine cellar where we found only three bot-tles of this special wine left in the case. I brought it back, but it seemed so ridiculous to me that thousands of dollars had been spent for three bottles of wine.

"When we arrived back at Scoop Lake, I told Ralph, the expediter, that I was worried about the bills that were accumulating, such as the continued use of aircraft. In response to my concern he asked if I had heard of the super wealthy. When I admitted I had, he asked, 'Have you ever heard of the super, super, super wealthy? Well that's one of them right there.'

"When I persisted about my concerns, the expediter told me to follow him, which I did. He led me into his cabin where he pulled a large valise from under the bed and opened it. So help me I didn't know there was that much money in existence. He pulled out enough money to satisfy me and I think it was $59,000. He could tell I was surprised so he said, 'Money is no object to that man.'

"That was quite an experience; I got a glimpse of how some peo-ple live. And another thing, when those people left, there was still a shed full of Heineken beer that they left behind."

"I understand that you and the Game Department didn't get along very well, but how did the hunters feel about your operation?"

"I have hundreds of letters of appreciation from hunters, many of which were forwarded to the Game Department. But that didn't seem to interest them. I can show you some of these letters."

After I perused several of the letters it became apparent that Frank

had done his best to please his hunters. There are letters of appreciation from airline captains and people from all walks of life. Wildlife
photographer Gordon Eastman wrote an excellent letter of approval
of his years spent in Frank's area. He acknowledged that Frank's
guides had acquired seven ratings in the Boone and Crockett records
in one season for goats, sheep and grizzlies. The largest of the sheep
had a measurement of 45 inches with 50 inches at the base. In
another year, Frank had five of the top 20 Stone sheep taken from
the entire Cassiar Range. John Amber, who was the editor of *Gun
Digest* many years ago, related how the party watched a memorable
scene:

"Between two ridges in a broad treeless valley we saw 49 rams
grazing quietly together, unaware that they were being watched
through a spotting scope a mile distant."

During the 1967 hunting season, Frank's hunters took the first
three awards for Stone sheep, and the first award for mountain goats.
Hal Ward, a district attorney from North Carolina was one of the
lucky sheep hunters, and Richard Bickell of Maryland was another.
According to Frank "one of the charges levelled against me was over-
hunting. Is it any wonder that there was over-hunting when we realize that guides were competing with resident hunters? Perhaps quo-
tas should have been introduced many years earlier."

I dwelt on Frank's words for a minute and then replied, "There is
probably enough blame to go around, because the former policies
have not worked. Regardless of where the blame should lie, I think
that people who have known freedom—such as you and Skook—simply cannot fit in with bureaucracy. It's like trying to mix gasoline and
water. "Any more stories about hunters, Frank?"

"Well, never mind the hunters, we had one of our guides that sure
had us wondering when he came into camp after a session of heavy
drinking. One day he went outside and fell in love with a propane

tank. He sat there telling her how much he loved her and that there could never be anyone else for him since he met her. I walked out to where he was sitting and tried to talk to him but he told me to bugger off. That love affair ended when he sobered up. It's not easy to stop people when they are determined to party. I mean it's their money, but they sure must feel stupid later when they find out the trouble they've caused.

"I did my best to keep booze out of the camps, but there is only so much you can do. It was a tough job running such a big operation. My worst fear was that the hunters would get my guides drunk, because some of them could not handle booze at all. I recall one guide I had serious trouble with—one of the best guides you could ever find. But when he got on the booze, my God Almighty, he would go berserk. One time he was out with a hunter at Island Lake and they came in early after a day's hunt. The hunter got him started on booze and then he got into the extracts and went nuts. When my son Frankie and I stopped to check, the hunter was hiding out in the woods. When he seen us, he came over and told us that the guide was crazy, so we went looking for him. We found him sitting in the cookhouse completely out of his mind. He had spread a bag of sugar all over the floor and when he seen us, he grabbed a knife and came at us. Frankie stepped aside and laid him cold with one punch and that settled it. Well, I had to make a point for everyone to understand, so I fired that guide and flew him out to Watson Lake. As for the hunter, we moved him to our main camp where he had an enjoyable and successful hunt. People may think I was a bit harsh to fire the guide, but believe me I did not want stories like that to get spread around or it would have ruined the reputation of our entire outfit.

"I did hire that same guide back a few years later, but I made him work out of the main camp where I had control and could keep a close watch on what was happening. I had another guide that thought he was a jet plane when he drank. He used to go through the bush howling like a jet motor. I never saw or heard anything like it in my life.

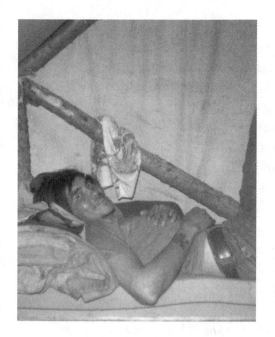

Ernie Abou, lost near Tucho Lake and never found.

"There was another guide that went snaky on us and ran away into the forest near Tucho Lake. Now that was a tragedy because Ernie Abou was another of our first-class guides. One of the other guides tried to talk him into coming back to camp but Ernie just kept on playing hide-and-seek with him. He would stick his head out from behind a tree and make a noise like 'hoo' and then run away and do the same thing over and over again. Finally he disappeared and was never seen again."

"Do you have any other stories like that?" I asked.

"Probably the worst case I ever witnessed happened when we flew a guide I will call Al back home for a break between hunts. A week later my son Terry flew him back to camp at Scoop Lake and he was still drunk. I decided he needed watching, so I kept him in the cabin with me that night. The next morning he seemed to be okay, but I noticed that he was following me wherever I went. That night he went to bed in my cabin again and about midnight I woke up and by the light from the power plant, I saw that he was standing above my grandson holding something in his hand. I quietly got up and flipped the light switch and then realized he was holding a machete in his hand. I hollered at him, and when he turned, I hit him and knocked him down. When I looked into his eyes I realized that he was right out of it; that he was crazy as a wild animal. I took him to the cabin of another guide named John and told him to watch him and call me if he needed any assistance. About five in the morning I woke up and walked over to the other cabin to see if everything was all right. When I opened the door I saw John sitting on the floor with a rock beside him. I asked him what happened and he explained, 'That crazy Al went outside for a leak and when he came back in, he struck me on the head with that rock and knocked me out.

"The guide was gone, so I went looking for him. Out on the airport I found his shirt, shoes and then his socks. I followed his tracks until he went into the woods and then I gave up because I lost the sign. By that time it was daylight, so I went back to camp and got Terry to go up in the plane and look for him. A few minutes later I noticed Terry was circling at the end of the lake so I got the tractor and went over there. When I got close to Al, he started to run for the woods. I cut him off with the tractor and then he ran out into the lake and stood in the water right up to his shoulders. All he had on was his overalls and it was cold out. I shouted to him to come out of the water but he just stood there staring at me. Then I told him to come out and we would go have a drink up at the cocktail lounge.

Caribou airplane at Turnagain River.

"That brought him out and so he got into the cart and I started driving back to camp. Suddenly he hollered and started pointing at two big, burnt stumps. I shut the tractor off and asked him what was wrong, and he shouted, 'Those two guys over there are Rawhide and Jack George [two other guides] and I want to give them a drink, too.'

"I told Al that Frank Cooke had told them to find the horses so they couldn't drink. That was okay with him because he didn't even know who I was, that's how snaky he was. When we got back to camp, my cook, Gerry Loiselle, told me to put him in the root cellar, which I did. There was an air vent and lots of food, so I wasn't worried about him being in there alone. So I put him in the cellar, and Al looked around for a minute and then said, 'Gee, this sure is a funny cocktail lounge.'

"We locked him in, and then went back to the cookhouse to decide what to do. After we thought about it for a while, Gerry decided to try a different technique so he went out to the root cellar and called down the air vent, 'This is God calling. You have to quit drinking, Al, or you will be in darkness forever.'

"It didn't take very long and back came the answer, 'Okay God, if you let me out of here I will never take another drink.'

"Terry had to take the 185 to Watson Lake with three German hunters, but the Beaver was available to transport the guide. The Beaver pilot was terrified of the crazy guide, though, and refused to fly him out. Finally we decided on a course of action: Gerry would open the door and if Al came out on the fight, I would rope him and we would tie him up and fly him out. So Gerry opened the door and Al walked out as calm as could be and said, 'Gee, it's sure a nice day, Frank.'

"I gave him some clothes to put on and then said, 'Get in the plane because we're going to go to Watson Lake for more booze.' So he got in and sat on some bedroll and began talking to someone who wasn't there.

"The pilot, Ed Myers, was worried about him losing it again so I told him, 'If the guide goes nuts again just tip the plane on its side and I will open the door and dump him.'

"Ed got all excited and told me that would be the same as murder, but I suggested it was better him than us, and then I said, 'If Al starts choking you I'm going to dump him fast and then we can tell the police he jumped out.' But we never had a problem with him, and the strange part of this crazy episode is that the guide quit drinking that very day. He kept his promise to God and never touched another drop. So that's some of our experiences with booze out in the mountains. Maybe now you understand that when I talk about the problems of booze in the North, I'm serious. It has caused more grief than anyone can imagine. One of my closest friends, Craig Forfar, committed suicide. I'm telling you that his death took a chunk out of me because we shared so many great adventures together."

Chapter 9

FRANK COOKE SPENT MANY YEARS IN THE NORTH AND knew a great deal about the area. This led me to ask him questions about his early years in that area, "Did the Natives have many chances for employment during your early years in that area?"

"It was mostly only trapping and things like that until Skook started hiring them as guides. He taught a lot of them and created opportunities for them."

"Did you and Skook mostly use Native Indian guides?"

"We preferred them because they didn't mind staying out in the woods. Some of them were tough and they were not complainers. If Skook trained them then you knew they were some of the best. He helped a lot of them and they helped him in return. Some of his guides took famous people out for sheep and they always got their game. Prince Abdareeza of Iran was one of the most famous and I'll think of others as we go along.

"You must know about many tough trips traveling through the wilderness with horses, tell me more about that." I suggested.

"There was a young lad that went out on one of the survey parties, I can't remember his name now, but he was trying so hard to do a good job. His outfit met another survey outfit at the McMillan River, where they stopped for dinner. While they were eating, one of the horses swam the river and of course they had to get it back. That

Prince Abdareeza of Iran and his guide Jack George

lad was the first to volunteer, and so he decided to cross on a cable that spanned the river there. He did fine until he got out near the middle of the river, but there was too much slack in the line so it put him in the water. Well, the current tugged at him until he let go and went down the river. His body was never found. Looking back at it, it was a crazy thing to do. They had other options—for instance they could have built a raft. That was a sad and unnecessary death.

"Another time there was a young Indian fellow at Lower Post that had seen Skook swim horses across the river many times. One day he jumped on a horse and went charging across the river. When he got about halfway across, the horse appeared to be having trouble, so the lad bailed off and tried to swim for it. He didn't make it; instead they found his body on Six-mile Bar. If he had stayed on the horse he would have made it because the horse survived. In my opinion you should not quit your horse, because they usually make it fine. An exception, of course, is if you drift into rough water with big boulders, because that can really bugger a horse. Probably the worst danger in crossing horses is driftwood. We used to put a spotter upriver when we crossed in high water, because if a horse gets mixed up with driftwood it will surely drown. I learned how to cross horses from Skook who was the best in the business. When we came to a river he would walk along the bank for a few miles. Then he would explain to us where we were going to put the horses in the water, and most important of all, where they would come out of the water. If you just push the horses in anywhere they will drift downriver and perhaps run into steep banks where they are unable to get out of the water. Many horses have been lost because of thoughtless acts. I've been in some damned fast water with horses, such as the Fox and Finlay Rivers."

"I have another question for you, Frank, a friend of mine—who claims to know lots about horses—told me that a person cannot ride a horse across a river or it will drown. Is that correct?"

"You can tell your friend that he should have told me that at least 60 years ago, because that is how long we've been riding horses across rivers. We crossed lots of rivers on our horses and we have movies we've taken which show us riding them across streams. I'm not saying I would ride one across a big river like the Fraser River, but we ride them across these northern rivers all the time. You have to use common sense though, because you have to make sure that the horse has a decent place to climb out of the water. You don't just push them in anywhere."

"Did you ever have any experience with using horses on ice?" I asked.

'I recall in Fort St. James when they used horses to haul

Riding horses across the Gataga.

heavy loads on the ice. They used to have a wire that went down to the kingpin that held the doubletrees to the load. If the load went through the ice, then the wire was used to pull the kingpin out and set the horses free from the load. Otherwise they would drown for sure."

"What was the technique used for getting horses out of the water if they dropped through the ice?" I questioned.

"The Indians had a method that worked quite well—they would throw a rope around the horses neck and float it while they pulled it out with other horses. It worked like a charm. But the best method is to check the ice beforehand and not put a horse in a position like that in the first place.

"I want to mention another thing about the Indians; in some respects they were far ahead of the environmentalists. Old man McCook, for instance, he burned off a big area to create moose pasture and it worked. Sometimes their people starved because they couldn't find game. Is it any wonder they set fires? Well, McCook had a wife and many children and they traveled around the area a lot. They would go to Gataga Forks and all through that area hunting sheep, which they would dry and then haul back to Fort Ware. They trapped a big piece of country and didn't even have real cabins. They camped out in tents and it was a tough life; damned tough.

"I recall the time John McCook went with Skook up the Kechika in Skook's boat. They got way up in there and on the way back they ran out of gas. John walked out and got some gas and I helped him pack it back in. We went through the brush in places where I didn't know where in hell we were. John kept saying it wasn't far, but it sure seemed far to me. We took turns carrying the five- and ten-gallon cans and when it got dark we had to camp for the night. The next day we were walking along and we ran into four grizzlies. We were unarmed so John told me to light the grass on fire because he thought the bears would run away. I did what he said but they didn't run; instead they walked around the fire and kept on going. I just followed John and damned if he didn't come right out at the boat, and there was Skook lying on the rocks by a campfire without a worry in the world. I think that man could sleep anywhere. Anyway, we took off with the boat and we were back at the landing in less than two hours.

"Got some more of those stories, Frank?"

"I remember the time I was walking out to Lower Post from the Kechika and when I got to Fish Creek, Louie Boya and Amos Alec were trapping beaver there with their families. On the walk out, I had been walking through a lot of sand, and since one of my moccasins had come apart, the sand had got in and my toes were worn raw. I was short of food so they gave me some beaver meat, which I started chewing on. Suddenly one of the wives noticed my moccasin and said, 'Sonny, you got no moccasins'. Then she added, 'You wait awhile'. She disappeared for a short time and then out she came with another pair of moccasins. These people were sure good-hearted. I remember another time I was sharing a campfire with an elderly Indian called Jack Abou. Just to make conversation I asked him, 'Do you still like women or are you too old?'

"He looked at me real seriously and then answered, 'Oh no gee whiz just stiff like stick me yet.' I couldn't help laughing; it sounded so funny. One of his favourite sayings was, 'I've been all over the world to Wrangell and Prince Rupert'."

"It seems to me that there was a lot of humour mixed in with some of those tough trips, Frank."

"There sure was. I'll never forget the time a man and his wife stopped and because the weather was bad, Skook let them stay in the cabin with us. When it came time to go to bed, they just spread a couple eiderdowns on the floor and we called it a day. I didn't get much sleep, though, because all night I heard what sounded like spitting or hissing and now and then a 'ping' sound. The next morning after they left I asked Skook what the hell had made that noise. More than a little disgusted he replied, 'That woman was chewing snoose and spitting in a can all night. Lord lifting Christ! How can a man sleep with a woman that is chewing snoose and spitting all night?' I couldn't answer that question for him so we just dropped the subject."

Skook, 80 years old, at home at
Terminus Mountain.

I studied Frank's picture of
Skook at the river with his
wagon and horses and this
forced me to ask, "When Skook
was getting equipped for guiding season he had to be serv-
iced by airplanes. It seems to
me that it must have been a
hassle for him to have to hook
up the horses and take the
wagon over one mile to the
river to meet the planes, wasn't
it?"

"Well, we always knew
about when they were coming,
and the planes would circle the
ranch before landing anyway,
so by the time they landed we
would be at the river in a few minutes. I recall one day when the
Beaver came and circled about five times before it landed. I asked
Skook why the pilot was doing that and he hollered, 'He's rounding it
off to an even $300 for the trip.' Skook was probably right. The pilot
was trying to get a few extra dollars out of that trip."

In one of our telephone conversations Frank had mentioned the
curse of booze in the North; I asked him to elaborate.

"The problems caused by booze are beyond belief. There's just
something about living up there that drives people to booze. Some of
the nicest people I've known up there either committed suicide or else
had their lives buggered up because of booze. I recall a writer named
John that I flew into Island Lake. He was going to do a story on the
area. There was no money involved, but he was supposed to write a

good story about my area. Well it turned out that he came for nothing, because he got drunk every day. Finally I flew in to the lake and told him he had to get out in the mountains and do something because I was paying a crew to assist him. He got upset and told me that he would write a story about me but I wouldn't like it very much. He was a good writer, but I had no choice so I sent him home. That was my idea of a tough trip because it cost a lot of money and we had nothing to show for it."

"Did you see much serious trouble result from drinking?" I asked.

"Yes, I did. In 1944 a fellow made a big batch of home brew at Fort Ware and then took a bunch of it, or sold a bunch of it to the Indians on the Reserve. It was about 4 a.m. when Skook hollered at me to get up and bring the rifle because they were fighting at the Reserve. He was a Special Constable then, so I guess he figured it was his duty to break it up. I followed Skook on the run to the Reserve and when we got there, one Indian had his rifle pointed against the head of another Indian who was lying on the ground, while two others were kicking him. Skook drew his gun and ran right up to the man holding the rifle and struck him across the head. He dropped and then Skook emptied his pistol into the air and all the others took off. Something I didn't mention was that when Skook and I were running up the hill, I checked to see if there were any cartridges in the rifle, and the damned thing fired right beside Skook and blew some gravel on him. That's the only time I ever had anything like that happen to me and Skook sure gave me a talking to about it, believe you me.

"When I talk about tough trips, I don't want to give the impression that all hunters were that way. In fact, I had some of the best. Jack O'Connor was one. He was field editor for *Outdoor Life Magazine* and because of that position he had hunted all over the world and was very knowledgeable.

"He was well up in years when I met him; in fact, he was 69 when he came on that hunt. His wife came as far as Vancouver with him and tried to talk him out of the trip. She told him that a man of his age—

a grandfather—had no business hunting sheep. She told him, 'If you drop dead up there, you can stay there for all of me. I will not come after you. If they send you back express collect, I'll refuse payment.' But he came on three hunts with me and described my area as some of the best Stone sheep country in the world. I spent a lot of time with Jack in a tent at Colt Lake and we talked a lot. He had hunted with Frank Golata, a guide I had worked for years earlier. When I guided for Frank I got a 44-inch ram for my hunter, so Jack and I had a lot to talk about.

"Anyway, my son Frankie guided Jack on his successful sheep hunt and later Jack wrote it up under the title of "Last Sheep Hunt"."

Frank gave me the story of Jack's sheep hunt, a portion of which follows: (Courtesy of *Outdoor Life Magazine*);

" . . . The moose season was not open, but we saw moose almost every other day. Some were enormously sleek and fat and looked as if their velvet-covered antlers would go 60 inches or better. The highlight of the day was running into a pack of wolves, the first I had seen for many years. Jim [hunting partner] had never seen one before. We saw no sheep until late in the afternoon when we were headed back to camp. On a lofty pasture of green and tender grass across a deep canyon about half a mile away, we saw a bunch of eight rams, the largest of which might have had a curl of 36 or 37 inches.

" . . . . The next day we went out to case the rams and the basin. It was a sight to gladden and sadden the sheep hunter's heart. The basin must have been a half-mile in width and nearly a mile long, and the whole thing was dotted with rams. Some were in little bunches, others were alone—big old rams, middle aged rams, young rams, rams almost white enough to be Dalls, rams with white heads and necks and saddles almost black, rams with grey heads and necks and dark bodies. Rams, rams everywhere—but try to get a shot. Stalking was impossible, driving exceedingly doubtful. About all we could do was look at them through the spotting scope and drool."

A few days later they spotted two rams on a ridge about three miles distant. Jim, who was much younger than Jack, took after them with his guide, Larry, while Frank and Jack watched the unfolding drama through the spotting scope. The article when on to say:

"After some time, we saw Jim and Larry [Bedell] begin the climb up a big, grey limestone cliff so they could get above and behind the rams. Even through the powerful spotting scope, they were tiny dots. Where we were, the cliff looked straight up and down, but of course it wasn't or they couldn't have made it. Larry made the climb in cowboy boots. Finally we saw guide and hunter top out, rest for a minute and then disappear on the other side of the ridge. The rams were dozing, probably savouring their cuds. About half an hour later, Frank, who had made exactly the same stalk the year before, went back to the spotting scope. 'It's about time we should see a little action.' He said. A moment later he turned. 'Take a look for a moment,' he said. 'You can see them all.'

"I could see sheep and hunters, tiny and fuzzy with mirage at three miles. As I moved away from the scope so that Frank could look, I heard a shot, then another. 'The ram's down.' Frank said. 'The other's running like hell. Jim and Larry are looking at him now. Larry's measuring him. I can't tell too much, but I think it's pretty good.' Afterwards Jim told us that he fired the second shot because he was afraid the ram would fall off a cliff."

On the last day of the hunt Jack got his chance. They had been spotted by the three rams, which watched their every move. Frank left the horses so the sheep would watch them and then they started the stalk. Jack described it this way:

"At 300 yards I wanted to shoot but Frank shook his head, 'We can get closer,' he whispered.

"We struggled along in the grass and lichens. It was like crawling up a hill on your belly in a featherbed. At 200 yards I found a sweet place to shoot from prone. I could rest my hand on a soft hummock, and the fore-end of the old .270 on my hand. The rams had seen us. The grey one stood up and stared right at us. He was slightly quartering toward us. The cross-wires in the 4215 Leupold settled low on

Frankie with Jack's last ram.

the neck just forward of the right shoulder. I started the squeeze, and then the 130-grain bullet sped on its way."

Jack took the ram with one shot and thereby ended another successful and memorable hunt. When Frank questioned Jack about whether that really was his last sheep hunt, he answered, "I'll take it under advisement, but with a good mountain horse under him a man can successfully hunt into old age."

While describing Jack O'Connor to me, Frank mentioned a trip to Jack's hometown.

"My son Terry and I flew to Lewiston, Idaho to check some Beaver aircraft that were for sale there. When we got finished with that, I phoned Jack and he told us to drop in for a visit. He was well up in years then, but we enjoyed our visit. He and his wife showed us their considerable trophies, and we sure got a kick out of the two of them. They could not agree on where the different animals had been taken or under what circumstances. But I sure liked Jack; he was a knowledgeable and likable fellow. When my son Frankie guided him, Frankie's wife cooked for them and Jack thought the world of her. He certainly gave us some good advertising.

"I want to tell you about another trip my son Frankie made. He was guiding two women, Joan Leeds and her daughter Barbara, when they came upon a grizzly eating on the remains of a sheep taken on an earlier hunt. As they watched through the binoculars, they noticed a bigger grizzly approaching the carcass. Suddenly the two bears went at it and they were lucky enough to witness a roaring blood and guts fight between two grizzly bears. But it didn't take very long for the bigger bear to put the run on the other, and he succeeded in driving it down into a draw that Frankie's group had to pass through on their way back to camp. Sure enough, when they came through that draw, the bear, already in a foul mood, stood up right beside them and scared the hell out of them and the horses. Frankie had a time trying to steady his horse enough to get a shot, but he finally did. Then the horses took off and ran some distance before they were able to calm them down. It took a while, but they did manage to get back to the site where they found the bear dead. The next day they went out again and Joan got her ram. Believe me, when she left after the trip was over she was positive that Frankie was the best guide in BC.

"I have to tell you another story about a grizzly and its sense of smell. One day we were looking through the spotting scope when we spotted a big grizzly making its way across the mountain. Every so often it would stop and scent the air and then continue on in the same

Barbara Leeds and Frankie Cooke with the grizzly that lost the bear fight.

direction. It took a while for us to realize that the bear was heading toward the remains of a moose we had taken several days earlier. It was at least two miles from the carcass when we spotted it so we could only guess how far it had been from the remains when it first smelled them."

I was most interested in stories about the pack trains so I asked Frank, "Did you ever lose any horses while crossing the rivers?"

"Not when Skook was in control, but I remember when Skook, Willard and I were distributing 80 head of horses one spring. When we got to the Dease River, Skook sent Willard ahead to start the horses across the river, only because Willard assured us that he knew where the crossing was. Skook was in the middle of the train and I was bringing up the rear, when I heard Skook holler at me to stop. I went as fast as I could up to where he was standing and there was Willard driving the horses into the water just a short distance above a whirlpool. The fellow that had crossed some of our supplies in his boat was just downriver from us, so I got him to bring his boat upriver. When we started into the whirlpool he must have got excited because he ran the big boat right over three of the horses. I managed to get ropes on the other three and we pulled them out of the whirlpool and so they crossed the river okay. But we lost three horses there and I'm telling you that Skook was steamed that day. We moved the rest of the horses up to the proper crossing and they made it fine. After that was over Willard never said a word for about a week, because it was his fault and he knew it.

"But getting back to tough trips that you asked me about, I've got another story about Skook while he was a special constable for the police. This episode started during the winter of 1943 when an Indian named Stephen Poole murdered his wife. The incident took place at Fort Ware, but they had no communication with the outside world at that time, so an Indian had to snowshoe the 80 miles to Finlay Forks. When he got the news, the Hudson's Bay man radioed his company at Hazelton, who then called Sergeant George Clark in Prince George. Anyway, three weeks passed before Sergeant Clark, Game Warden A.

Jank and Skook Davidson left Prince George in a Fairchild airplane piloted by Pat Carey. Shortly after takeoff, the weather socked in and the plane was forced down at Fort St. James for three days. When the weather broke they flew on to the Finlay River where they stopped for fuel. Then the weather socked in again and they finally reached Fort Ware on February 4th, 24 days after the wire had reached Prince George."

At that point in the conversation, Frank handed me some newspaper clippings taken from different papers, so I will make some direct quotes from the *Prince George Citizen*:

"Fort Ware consisted of a Hudson's Bay Store, a fur cache and warehouse, and a cabin for stopover trappers. Nearby, another cabin housed store Manager Jack Copeland, his wife and two children. As the police party clambered from the plane, Copeland greeted them with the warning that his latest weather report by radio didn't sound too good. He suggested they hurry their investigation if they didn't want to get snowed in. Taking the advice, Clark quickly got these facts. It seemed that Stephen Poole of the Beaver tribe, returning home over the river ice one night in early January in a drunken rage, had clubbed his wife to death with a rifle butt. Leaving her on the ice, he stumbled home to sleep. Next morning he retrieved her body, telling those around the post she had frozen to death. Viewing the body, they thought otherwise. Hence the message to the police. Poole's 10-year-old boy Tommy was apparently a witness to the crime.

"Meantime, Clark learned, the body had been buried and Poole was back out on his trapline. Checking over the Indian's cabin, Clark took possession of the bloodstained rifle, and then arranged for Skook Davidson to stay behind. He would collect the remaining witnesses and then detain Poole when he came in with his fur. Then, to beat the approaching storm front, they hurriedly boarded the plane and took off. But as events turned out, they would have been much better off had they stayed at Fort Ware. Their flight to the refuelling site at Finlay Forks was uneventful, and then came misfortune heaped upon misfortune. As they were fuelling, snow began to fall.

"Forced to stay the night, Clark shared a cabin with trapper Mort Teare, while Carey and Jank slept in another cabin. The next day the snow was flying thicker than ever. That afternoon, a tremendous wind arose that threatened to blow the airplane away. It took great effort on the part of all involved to secure the plane and get a canvas cover over it. For five more days the storm prevailed and when it let up, the men found the plane almost buried in drifts. It took a great deal of effort to get the plane out of the drifts, and when they did succeed in that, the engine wouldn't run. Another day was wasted before they discovered the engine had suffered a cracked cylinder head. They radioed Finlay Forks the news of their predicament and were assured a new cylinder head would be flown in shortly."

"Once again the weather turned bad and for three days they were trapped in their cabins. Then they received word that the rescue aircraft had been diverted to a search for a downed plane in the Peace

Wilderness camp.

River area. For 10 more days the men were prisoners before they got word that the plane would attempt to fly in the next day. Finally, on the following day, another Fairchild airplane brought in the cylinder head and took the officers back to Prince George.

"Back in Prince George 40 days after the first report, Clark was forming an inquest party to return to Fort Ware. On March 2nd, Skook radioed that he had arrested Poole. That set the wheels in motion and the next day the inquest party arrived at Fort Ware. The following day Margaret Poole's body was exhumed and Dr. Dawson performed a post mortem. All through the proceedings the accused sat watching with a puzzled expression his only sign of interest. A jury was selected and after all the evidence was heard, Poole was committed for trial. By this time it was almost midnight and Poole suggested that Margaret should be put back in the ground, 'so the wolves can't eat her.' The four men trudged back up the hill and lowered the coffin into the ground. When the coffin was covered, Skook drew his pistol and shouted, 'Let's give her a military funeral,' at which point he fired six shots into the air.

"The return trip to Prince George was eventful, in that the overloaded plane almost crashed on takeoff. But they did safely return and after a long drawn out trial it was 10 months after the crime when Poole was convicted and sentenced to life in prison."

"The most interesting part of the entire case was not mentioned at the trial," Frank advised me, "instead it took place at Fort Ware. Skook was responsible for Poole, so after the arrest he handcuffed him to a post and let him sleep on a mat in the bunkhouse there. But he looked so uncomfortable that Skook set him free because there was no place for him to go anyway. Well, just a short time later Poole disappeared. It wasn't long after that when another local Indian arrived and began snooping around. Skook knew there was a connection so he asked, 'Johnny, where's Poole?'

"In a not too convincing manner Johnny replied, 'I no see him Mr. Skook.'

"Skook studied him for a minute and then told him, 'That's too bad,

Johnny, because when the sun comes out a policeman is going to come in an airplane and I'm going to tell him that you killed that woman. Then the policeman is going to take you to Vancouver and put a rope around your neck and squeeze it until it is about like this.' For emphasis, Skook made a little circle with his thumb and forefinger.

"According to Skook, Johnny got the message because his eyes got real big and he took off on the run; about 20 minutes later he returned with his rifle in his hands and Poole marching in front of him. When he came to the door, he shouted, 'I catch him Mr. Skook.' Well, Poole was taken in an airplane to Prince George and then to Vancouver where he received his sentence."

"Getting back to pack trains, Frank, I wonder if Skook ever told you about Stan Hale's tough trip into the Far North when he packed for the Army Surveys?"

"Is that the one where the horses were shot?"

"Yes! Apparently Stan's group rented horses from Skook and when fall came they got trapped in the muskegs north of Watson Lake. It was in October when the muskegs froze and the party came to a standstill. The men were able to walk on the lightly frozen muskegs but when the horses tried to walk they broke through and cut their legs. They waited for a while, hoping the weather would change, but it didn't. Finally the men got word by radio to shoot the horses—which they did—and then they walked out to a lake where they were picked up by an airplane. Stan told me that the Army paid Skook for the horses."

"I remember when someone asked Skook to use his horses in a remote area and they told him they intended to shoot them when the trip was over. Skook told them straight out, 'You're not going to shoot my horses.' And that was that."

"I wonder if there could be a connection between the two trips. Perhaps it's possible that this was the same trip and the horses were shot to save having to take them countless miles through the wilderness? Maybe it was far simpler just to shoot the horses, although Stan certainly didn't tell me that." I offered.

"I can tell you some horrible stories about the misuse of horses in the North—such as times when the horses were just left to fend for themselves over winter and didn't survive."

"I know of a few similar cases, Frank. For instance, about 40 years ago I had an elderly guide tell me of a tragedy that his son—also a guide—experienced. He had his horses back in the mountains at a lake and he used to fly his hunters in to that lake where they would begin their hunts. But the snow came early one year and trapped his horses before he could take them out of those mountains, which was an area of heavy snowfall. He could not afford to fly feed in to the horses, so it was February before the snow settled enough for him to get feed in by snowmobile. When he did find the horses, he was shocked by what he found. A couple of them were dead and one of the surviving horses had attempted to eat devil clubs, several of which were protruding from its throat. This fellow told me that his son was so sickened by their condition that he lost interest in using horses after that terrible experience."

"I know of many cases of horse abuse in the North and there is no need for it. The authorities should make it plain that outfitters must have abundant feed and people to stay with the animals, or else move their horses out of the mountains. We spent a fortune looking after our horses and why not, when we ask so much of them in return."

After Frank and I discussed horses and tough trips, he changed the subject and talked about Native skills.

"When I look back at my adventures and the pictures of the old hunts, I know that I wouldn't have missed it for the world. And some of the Indian people—they knew things we didn't know. For instance, we needed a skin boat for the movie *High, Wild and Free*, so we got old Jack Abou and his family to build it. They went and got three moose and turned them into a boat. Just some spruce for ribs and the frame and the moose hides and they produced a 60-pound boat that could carry a good load. My God, you couldn't find people today who would know how to do that. I think Gordon Eastman gave that boat

Don Miller and Gordon Eastman in semi-transparent moose-hide boat.

to the museum in Victoria after he and Don Miller finished their trip down the Liard River."

"Tell me more stories about Skook and his partying. I've heard that he used to tie on some good binges in Watson Lake. Is that true?"

"I remember when Skook used to arrive in Watson Lake. Everyone knew it was party time for a few days. He was sure good-hearted and many people took advantage of him. But when he left the bar and got back to the woods it was all business again."

"Was he as tough as people claim he was?" I asked.

"Skook was the toughest man I've ever known. He had terrible arthritis and he suffered a great deal, probably because of when he was shot through the hips during the war. But he was not a quitter. He could sleep on rocks or anywhere else for that matter, and he sure paid for it when he got older. He didn't complain, though, he just kept on going. I remember when we used to camp out at night. Sometimes I would wake up and Skook would be holding his legs up in the air. He must have suffered like a bugger but he never complained."

"Do you have any other memories of stories Skook told about his youth?"

"Well, I don't think it is well known, but Skook was one of the original presidents of the Williams Lake stampede. He worked for a ranch somewhere around 158 mile for a few years and that's where he met the gal he called Lil."

"I notice from your pictures that Skook had a sawmill on his ranch, how did he manage to get that sawmill into the Kechika Valley, Frank?"

"That's quite a story in itself. Skook had a hunter that really thought the world of him and offered to move a mill up from Oregon. Well, believe it or not, he did what he promised: he had a sawmill trucked all the way up to Fort Ware and then had it flown into the Kechika. Then he took the motor out of his own car and had it flown in to power the mill. The car was left abandoned on the highway.

"We got a lot of good use out of that mill and it was sure nice to work with lumber instead of logs all the time."

"Do you have any more stories of tough trips?" I wanted to know.

"There's another type of trip that is tough, I'll tell you, and that's coming off the back of a horse and sailing 20 feet through the air. I'm talking about breaking horses and rodeos. Terry used to fly the boys to different rodeos and they got pretty good at it. Another thing I have to mention is that Terry is a judge at rodeos all over Western Canada now.

"Anyway, we used to have rodeos right at Scoop Lake because we broke a lot of horses there. At one time we had about 200 head. As a matter of fact, we even wrote a poem about Frankie trying to ride a real wild bronco there. I think it went something like this:

Out in Scoop Lake we had a hard one to tame,
A little pinto stud—Come Apart was his name.
We had a little rodeo on the Fourth of July,
No one would ride him till Frankie had a try.
He walked into the chute just as quiet as a lamb,
Frankie knew he could buck but he didn't give a damn.
We put on the saddle and screwed it down tight,
Then Frankie climbed on, such a fearless sight.

When he left the chute he went straight for the clouds,
Amid screaming and cheering from that noisy crowd.
He sailed so gracefully up through the air,
He was reaching for leather but there was no leather there.
He lost his stirrups and his saddle as well,
He was cussing or praying cause we heard him shout "hell."
Old Come Apart snorted and just seemed to say,
"Don't feel bad Frankie for losing today,
'Cause I'm the best bucker that's ever been known,
And I've made more widows than the Strawberry Roan."

"I can remember that happening; it was quite a day. It made me think of the times at Skook's Ranch when we were breaking horses. We just got on and hoped for the best. If I remember right there were quite a few horses that never were broke, or carried a pack for that matter. As for the bronco busting, I'm paying for it today with a lot of aches and pains, but even so, it was a lot of fun. We didn't realize it at the time, but we were living in heaven."

Chapter 10

THERE IS SOMETHING ABOUT ROAMING WILDERNESS mountains that seems to penetrate to the very depths of an individual. Some people use the experience of sheep or mountain goat hunting as an excuse to answer the call, while others may use prospecting or exploration. In his magnificent poem "The Spell Of The Yukon, " Robert Service told of the search for gold and wrote, "Yet somehow life's not what I thought it, and somehow that gold isn't all." Then he went on to say:

No! It's the land. (Have you seen it?)
It's the cussedest land that I know,
From the big, dizzy mountains that screen it
To the deep, deathlike valleys below . . .

Since the long-ago days when that poem was written, countless people have experienced the same feeling—the sense of being completely overwhelmed by the power and silence of the wilderness.

In an attempt to get the views of some of the hunters who were guided in the North and felt the call of nature, I interviewed several people—the first of whom was Martin Benchoff of Waynesboro, Pennsylvania. I knew that Martin had hunted the Kechika Mountains many times throughout his hunting career, and had been guided by Frank Cooke and Skook Davidson's guides.

Guides John Tibbetts and Leo Miller with Martin Benchoff's ram

But on my arrival at his home I was totally unprepared for what greeted me, because there were trophies from all around the world—more trophies than I had seen in my entire life. Among them was the Grand Slam, registered in 1991, which consists of a Stone sheep, a Dall sheep, a desert sheep and a bighorn, each with at least a full curl. Since Martin has hired guides and hunted all over the world, I was especially interested in his experiences and comparisons of guides here at home and abroad. Perhaps we should feel proud that he considered a Native named John Tibbetts—a protégé of Skook Davidson and Frank Cooke—the best guide he had ever been with. In his own words Martin stated, "John could look at a sheep through a spotting scope and tell you the size of its horns within half an inch and that is not easy to do."

"I understand that you had John Tibbetts as a guest at your home here in Pennsylvania; how did he adjust after leaving the wilderness of northern BC?"

"He did okay, but I was renting a ranch in Texas at the time so I sent him down there to do some guiding for me. Well, I soon got word that he was sick and unable to guide, so I went down there and as soon as I arrived he made a remarkable recovery and fit in well."

"I find that most interesting, Martin, because I would have guessed an extreme culture shock. But perhaps you can elaborate on the importance of John being able to judge the size of sheep horns so accurately."

"Yes, some people may wonder at the significance of it, but when you are allowed only one sheep, then you had better be certain beforehand that you will be satisfied with the choice you have made, because you will have to live with that decision. Often hunters are tempted to shoot the first decent trophy they come upon. Then, as better trophies present themselves, pressure is brought to bear on the guides to let them take a second, illegal animal."

During the four days that I spent with Martin, I listened to a man who was the most experienced and knowledgeable hunter I have ever met. He told stories of blunders and courageous acts from all around the world, as well as errant guides who gave bad instructions that resulted in failed trips. In his view of the guided trips in northern BC, Martin seemed pleased. If I understood him properly, he considers a hunt in the North the epitome of an excellent hunting experience.

The story of his hunt for a Kodiak bear on Kodiak Island in 1978 was certainly a tale of adventure. After 14 days of searching, they found a large bear at the mouth of its den, just waking from its winter sleep. The bear must have detected their movements, because suddenly it came straight at them on the run. Martin dropped to one knee and fired, the bullet taking the bear in the shoulder. It went down, but immediately rose and continued its attack. Martin fired six shots before the bear stayed down for keeps. On examination it was found that four bullets had penetrated its right shoulder, one of the bullets had taken it in the backside, and another had penetrated its left shoulder. Martin's experience only confirms what many other hunters have also noted: when a bear has its adrenaline going, it can be dead on its feet before it drops.

For several years Martin and Archie Lang owned the Watson Lake

Martin Benchoff with a grizzly
bear, 1971.

Hotel in Watson Lake, Yukon. During that time Martin witnessed many strange occurrences there. One of the more memorable concerned the night he was talking with Frank Cooke when a man came rushing up to their table and shouted at Frank, "The stories you've been telling about me not being able to pack a horse properly are going to stop and they are going to stop right now."

As soon as the words left this man's mouth, Martin heard a loud crack as Frank's fist came in contact with the man's jaw. Then the gentleman went back in the same direction he had arrived from. At the same moment both Frank and Martin noticed a policeman standing in the doorway watching with keen interest. Frank whispered to Martin, "Just keep on talking as if nothing has happened." Sure enough, after a few minutes the policeman continued on his routine. Perhaps he just considered it normal activity in that town. When I asked Frank if he had in fact stated that the man couldn't pack a horse, he answered, "Sure, but I just told the truth; that man couldn't pack a saw-horse properly."

Another evening Martin was sitting in the bar with Frank when a former employee of Franks rushed over to their table and ordered "Frank, I want $200 and I want it right now."

Frank tells the story this way, "I tried to tell the man to sober up and come back the next day when we could discuss it in a sensible manner. The man refused to reason, though, and again ordered me to loan him the money. Well, I learned a long time ago that some people only understand force so I talked to him by hand. He came to his senses right away and left the bar heading backwards. The next day when he returned he was in a more reasonable frame of mind."

While referring to the above incident, Martin stated, "I have to say that Frank Cooke had one of the best right hands I've ever seen in action."

Martin had another story I found interesting and it concerned wildlife photographer Gordon Eastman, a close personal friend of his. When Gordon finished filming a movie in the Kechika Mountains, he and Martin were having a drink in the Belvedere Hotel in Watson Lake when the subject of naming the film came up. Gordon asked Martin to assist in picking an appropriate title for his new film, and together they decided to name it *High, Wild and Free*. In my opinion they could have searched for a thousand years without coming up with a more fitting title.

Martin also recalls the time he was being guided by Henry Delmonico in the mountains near Dease Lake. There were three hunters in the group and it turned out to be an exceptionally successful hunt. Martin got a Stone sheep and a grizzly while the other

Martin Benchoff Jr. with giant moose at the Turnagain River.

two men got moose, sheep, caribou and a grizzly. There was also a hunt with Frank Cooke that will stay in his memory. As their pack train was making its way along, a grizzly bear suddenly emerged from some trees and came at a gallop straight toward the horses. Martin had his rifle handy and managed to bring the animal down with a close range shot. Their first suspicion was that she was protecting cubs, but she turned out to be a dry sow and no reason was established for her unusual behaviour.   Understandably, it also took a bit of time to get the frightened horses to calm down and get the pack train underway again.

I doubt that there can be a better hunting thrill than to suddenly be confronted by a giant northern moose such as the one that confronted Martin Benchoff Jr. along the Turnagain River. When it is sporting a huge set of antlers, it is truly a sight to remember. I recall a guide telling me about one of his hunters taking what was estimated to be an 1800-pound moose. While the creature was being cut up for transport and loaded on the pack horses, the hunter suddenly exclaimed, "Are you telling me we have to pack all this meat out of here? You've got to be kidding!" The guide assured me that the hunter was right on the money, because they were far back in the mountains and it was a major undertaking to get all that meat back to a lake where it could be flown out to the highway for transport.

During the time Martin spent in the Kechika Valley he became close friends with Skook Davidson. When I asked his opinion of the grand old man he replied, "I have met many good men during my lifetime but I can say for certain that I never met a better man than Skook Davidson." Somehow I find it rather surprising that a man like Skook—who spent so much of his life in isolation—commanded such respect from his peers. Martin also pointed out what several others have stated throughout the years—that Skook was one tough hombre. Proof was offered in 1972 when Skook's cabin burned down, because he just pulled a sleeping bag out of the cabin and slept beside the fire on the ground.

Herb Kline was another ardent hunter Martin knew very well.

Skook and Herb Kline 1959.

Herb started as a drill hand in the oilfields of Wyoming between Rawlings and Lander. A few years later he and a friend used the money they had saved to drill for oil in Texas. Their first hole was a hit and they made nothing but money from then on. Herb became a close friend to Skook and was taken on several successful hunts by Skook's guides.

"I notice you hunted sheep all over the world, Martin. Did you luck out most of the time?" I asked.

"I only failed on one sheep hunt and that was in Mongolia. I was getting into position on what must have been a 55-inch sheep when it jumped up and ran. It was too long and tough a shot to take on the run so I didn't shoot; instead I took a chance that we would find it again. After it disappeared from view I turned and noticed that the man looking after our horses had walked right into the open and scared it away. We never found that magnificent animal again, and while I could have taken smaller sheep, I refused. That was the only sheep hunt where I got skunked."

"It's obvious from your collection that you were a very successful sheep hunter." I stated. "If you were to go after another Stone sheep, what area would you choose?"

"I would go for the areas Frank and Skook guided, because if you check the records you will see that those areas produced a lot of fine sheep. In fact, all of the world's most noted sheep hunters, such as Elgin Gates, John Caputo, Warren Page and Jack O'Connor were guided by Frank's guides and that tells the story, doesn't it?"

"What do you consider your best all-time hunt?" I asked.

"Probably my hunt with Alex Davis out of Canyon Creek in the Yukon. I remember the day we spotted a grizzly and my guide told me to shoot it. I fired and hit it in the shoulder with my .270. It went down and immediately regained its feet and started running again. I fired a second shot and it went down to stay. That was sure a great trip because we got two grizzlies, two Dall sheep and our caribous as well. It doesn't get much better than that."

"To what do you attribute your hunting success throughout the years?"

"I think the main reason for successful hunts is shooting with regularity so you can hit what you aim at. Many people don't practice enough and therefore lose or wound game. Believe me when I say that I did my homework and knew where my rifles were hitting. I always bought the best rifles, too. I had several guns made by Paul Jaeger and while they cost a bit of money, they sure performed well. Another cause of failed hunts is only allowing a short period of time for the hunt. This means people are in a hurry and that often leads to bad decisions. I usually went on 21-day hunts and that gives time to do things the right way. I proved it time after time and I never lost a sheep that I shot at. I guess that says it, doesn't it?"

Another individual I conversed with was Stan Simpson of Ram Head Outfitters Ltd., whose guiding area lies in the Northwest Territories. Stan originally guided in Alberta, where he had guided Martin for whitetail deer many years earlier. As is often the case with hunters and guides, they have remained steadfast friends ever since.

Stan Simpson with record-sized cougar

Prodded into leaving his winter retreat in Phoenix, Arizona, Stan flew to Washington's Dulles Airport and spent four days with us in Pennsylvania. In recalling memorable events from his guiding years, Stan told us a story that horse lovers should find fascinating. It concerned a hunt where one of his guides and a hunter left their two horses tied to a small tree and went searching for game. When they returned from the hunt they found that the horses had left and taken the tree with them—probably terribly frightened by what must have been a bear or some wolves that came near them. The guide and hunter followed the trail of one of the horses and it led them back to their spike camp, but the other horse, Ginger, could not be located. Stan was notified and flew the area in his Pa. 18 Super Cub for a month off and on throughout the summer, but again no sign of the horse was found. Because the horse still had its saddle on, many possibilities were considered: perhaps it had become tangled in brush and was lying down in the sparse growth near the valley floor; or maybe the wolves had taken it down.

When the guiding season was over, the other horses were taken out of the area and the lost horse was given up for dead. But at Christmas time a strange story emerged from the wilderness. A fellow from France had been traveling through that area with a dog team when he took movies of a moose staying at Stan's isolated lodge on Godlin Lake. When he arrived in Norman Wells, this gentleman showed the film of his expedition and the audience quickly informed him that the creature in the film was not a moose, but was in fact the missing horse, Ginger. In response to the news, a helicopter pilot flew to the area and found the horse eating an abundance of grass that had been seeded along the landing strip. He also noted that a wolf pack had a caribou down out on the lake and that several more caribou were hanging around the camp. Because it is not normal for the caribou to winter in that locale, Stan suggested the possibility that they had befriended his horse and that had tempted them to stay around for the winter.

The idea of moving the horse out of the area was considered and abandoned, since it was a near-impossibility to get the horse out, anyway. At last a decision was made to leave the horse for the rest of the winter and keep an occasional eye on it to be certain it had an abundant food supply.

When the pack train headed back in for the next years' hunt, everyone wondered just how well Ginger had fared. Well, when they arrived at Godlin Lake on the first of July they were in for a devil of a surprise. After being alone for 11 months, Ginger went plain wild when she spotted her old friends. She began whinnying, making screeching noises and jumping up in the air. She put on a memorable show for her old friends and they responded in kind.

Stan states that because there had been little snowfall, Ginger had been able to eat the abundant grass along the airstrip. She was in exceptionally good shape except for some sores she had incurred from fighting to get rid of the saddle. It must have been difficult to do, but somehow she had fought her way out of the saddle, which had turned upside down on her body and caused the sores. The saddle, which had contained the guide's rifle, was never recovered. As for Ginger, she made a habit of staying close to the pack train after having spent eleven months alone in the wilderness.

I questioned Stan at length about his experiences with swimming horses across rivers and his views seem to echo Frank Cooke's views verbatim: he mentioned that the cinch must be loosened somewhat before you force a horse to swim. Failure to do so can result in the horse being unable to get deep breaths, which can result in drowning. One example of the problems that can arise while swimming horses is well explained in his next story.

"Back in the early 70s, one of my dad's horses was sent into the water with a foamy in its pack. In a short period of time the foamy became saturated with water and became so unbearably heavy that it drowned the horse. When the drowned horse hung up on a bar, it took two men to carry the waterlogged foamy to shore. This gives some idea of the weight that the horse was suddenly subjected to when the foamy became waterlogged. This was a tragedy that could have been prevented by placing the foamy in a plastic bag where it would have acted as floatation rather than dead weight."

Since Stan has been involved in guiding since his childhood, I quizzed him at length about his experiences. He had another story of a freak accident that ended surprisingly well. His pack train was moving along a narrow passage on a steep mountainside in dense fog when one of the pack animals decided to pass another horse. Just as it was passing, the trail narrowed and the horse was forced over the edge where it dropped to what appeared to be certain death. But luck was with the horse that day because it was carrying a pack of 12 small down-filled sleeping bags, which of necessity had been piled high on its back. By some miracle the horse landed upside down and the sleeping bags all burst open and absorbed most of the shock. The horse survived and they were able to lead it off the mountain. Better yet, they even managed to collect insurance for the ruined sleeping bags. Oh for the exciting lives of big game guides and outfitters.

Make no mistake about it—the excitement and adventure is what draws so many people to the wilderness, and the same rule applied to guide and outfitter Frank Cooke and his family.

In order to give the reader a better understanding of this excitement I want to present a couple of the many letters Frank received from satisfied clients. However, I must point out that these commendations are just a few of countless that could be carried here, and they seem to compliment the many awards Frank won for getting his clients their allotment of game. Frank's most ardent supporter may well have been Warren Page, former editor of *Field & Stream*, a magazine I subscribed to and enjoyed for many years. In its July 1966 edition, Warren Page wrote an account of a sheep hunt he had with a friend named Russ Cutter. Their memorable hunt took place in Frank's guiding area in the Kechika Mountains. A portion of their successful hunt follows:

Two For The Book.

"Editor and his buddy found it easy in what may be the best Stone sheep area on the continent."

" . . . The rams—there were four of them—must already have seen the horses, since we were on the skyline as well as they, though on the opposite shoulder of a broad cup in the mountain. They may also have watched as we set up the spotting scope and argued the quality of their horns. But the sheep seemed unconcerned while Cutter took the time to decide that the lead ram, surely over 40 inches, was for him, even though this was the first day of hunting. The rams paid no attention when he and John [Tibbetts] eased over the lip and onto tumbled rocks, gave no heed when the hunters disappeared from their sight down into the bowl of the basin, and continued to rest in easy disdain on their grassy shelf as my own Indian [guide], Perry and I settled back to watch the stalk.

"That pile of boulders like a castle just below them," Russ and I had agreed. "That's the spot. If a man could crawl up that gully into that, without their spotting him, he'd have the shot made. About 250 yards, what?"

Russ Cutter and guide John Tibbets plan their attack, Colt Lake, 1965.

"The stalk into range wasn't quite that simple. For Russ and John to climb down, cross the moraine a long-dead glacier had left in the basin, and start up again took nearly an hour. Then their chosen gully turned out to be full of loose and noisy shale. Part way up they discovered that all the rams except one were obscured by their own ledge, and that one, the trophy, was lying in a position from which one jump would take him behind solid rock. And before the hunters could belly into hiding behind the castle-like promontory, the wind began whisking over them straight toward the dozing sheep. The ram got up, nervous.

"But with his 6.5 wildcat slung tight over a handy boulder Russ made the shot. He had only the one chance, but as Perry and I held our glasses on the ram it was clear that the sheep had fallen, not jumped, behind the arresting ledge . . . Our field measurements gave the splendidly wide ram a score of more than 173, easily into the Boone and Crockett record list, beyond 42 inches around the curl and a trophy for anybody's wall."

After the sheep and a caribou were taken, Warren got a fine mountain goat, then the group moved a six-hour ride by horseback from Colt Lake where they set up a spike camp. The first day out, Warren and his guide, John Tibbetts, spotted 18 rams, but the sun's glare made it impossible to ascertain their size. That evening when they returned to camp they learned that Frank and Russ had stumbled into a fine bunch of five rams on a distant mountain, and all of them at least 40 inches. The next day Warren and Frank went to the area and Warren wrote:

"My heart pounded a bit as my binoculars centred on a little group of dark-bodied sheep. Three were lying motionless; two picked about restlessly. They were down almost to the floor of the valley, perhaps 500 feet below our level and a half-mile away. Even with our 7X, the glasses showed their horns, all of them, to be majestic in weight and sweep. And when Frank got the Bushnell spotter screwed onto its tripod and motioned me over for a look, the view through 20X spurted another shot of adrenalin through my veins. Every one of those rams was a full curl; every one was in or above the 40-inch class."

Warren and Frank were stuck at that point, because the sheep were in an open area that prevented the hunters from getting within 500 yards. Their choice was simple, they had to wait until the animals moved. Warren continued:

"The waiting was interminable. The rams shifted around, alternately fed and rested, occasionally stretching their heads along the ground, as if to ease the horn weight. A small band of ewes—probably old, dry ewes long past bearing, since seldom do the sexes mix this early in the season—wandered down to join the party. They could be a complicating factor. Then the whole bunch moved down into the scrubby willow growth in the dry creek bottom to fiddle around there for an endless half hour.

"'Ah, now they're moving. The big ram just crossed the creek but the ewes are staying on this side.' grunted Frank from behind the spotter.

"The next fifteen minutes would tell the story. There were four likely bedding areas on the steep slope opposite us, little grassy flats in the shale. Two would be impossible to stalk, atop hard-rock promontories that broke the slides, but two other lying-up spots showed under those bluffs. These lower ones would be in shade the rest of the day, and we could work in over them without being seen. At least, I was keeping my fingers crossed."

"'Okay,' Frank said finally. 'They're not going to climb high. Let's back out of here while we can.' Carefully low, we scurried back toward the horses. We hadn't spotted Russ's goat, we told him, but the billy might be farther down the valley, toward the lake, and hidden in a cave or behind some rock ledge. 'Forget the goat,' he said. 'Go get the ram.'

"On the way across the valley head, a wolverine humped along within 50 yards of us. I had long wanted one of the big weasels, but not today, not with that big ram a possibility. Best Stone ram I ever seen, for sure. That realization kept me light-footed as we finger-and-toed around a dangerous cornice, scrambled down a noisy slide of small rock and sweated a quarter-mile up the other side. Slowly we traversed the first grassy bluff. The rams hadn't bedded down under that one. Must be under the next. Had to be quiet.

"The steep slope between was nasty. A different sort of clay-like rock, it was sun-hardened to the consistency of concrete, with a top layer of scattered pebbles that rolled underfoot like marbles. A fall would be easy, and disastrously noisy, but the edges of my Vibram-soled climbing boots bit and held, and finally we were peering over the edge of the bluff. Too much overhang. If the rams were below, they were in out of sight. Carefully, we edged down a series of grassy steps to a second level. There they were.

"Four of the five rams dozed in clear sight almost directly below, placidly ignorant that we were looking nearly straight down on them from perhaps 225 yards. Which was which? With the rifle still

Jack Segal of Houston, Texas with guide Herb Fellers and 42" stone ram taken out of Colt Lake.

unloaded, I edged my binoculars over the bluff. The three closest all looked good. One was light-bodied, therefore the other light ram, apparently the broomed one, was out of sight. One of the three dark rams must be our quarry. Not enough flare on that left-hand one, so the choice lay between two. One grey ram had picked the prime resting spot, farthest from the cliff on a flat shelf. Surely he must be the boss ram. If they'd only shift a bit, give us a view other than straight down.

"I was considering rolling a pebble or making some natural non-human noise when the problem was solved for us. The outside ram stood up, turned around. Then he looked straight up at us. No doubt about that flare. That one. The rifle was already loaded and lined on him when I realized the problems in the shot. At some 200 yards of range on the flat my bullet path should still be about three inches above point of aim. But shooting downhill at easily 60 degrees it would hit even higher. How much higher? If I held too low, any slight miscalculation could mean hitting, perhaps smashing, one of those magnificent horns. Better figure six inches, at a guess. A backbone hit would be fine anyway.

"With the blast of the 7 mm. Remington magnum the big ram dropped. The others started to their feet in confusion, and the other light-bodied ram appeared from under the cliff. Good. But then my ram started to his feet, moving in toward the overhang. I had missed the backbone and had to fire again. After we had worked our way cir-cuitously down, the tape showed 43.189 inches around the longer curl, with 14.190 -inch bases, and the symmetry was close enough so that when we had completed the field scoring it tallied over 175 Boone and Crockett points, up in the top quarter. I knew it might lose some in drying, but that in no sense lessened the wave of satisfaction that swept over me. Frank was pleased, too. He'd done his job, and done it properly. We had the best ram, but there were four more mov-ing off across the valley, every one of which will be as good or better with another year's growth, come the fall of '66."

This story illustrates as much as is possible the patience required to be a successful sheep hunter. Since these animals possess such astounding eyesight, any foolish move can result in a failed hunt where the animal may not be sighted again. Often several days are spent in the pursuit of the target animal and even then there is no guarantee of success.

Many people who have traveled the North use superlatives to describe Frank Cooke and Sons guiding operations. One such person is Beaver pilot Steve Buba of Prince George. Steve flew the Red Beaver, described so well in the book of the same name by Larry Whitesitt. Steve used to fly into Scoop Lake and states flat-out that Frank Cooke's camps were the best he seen anywhere in the North.

I have picked one more letter-of-thanks from the many in Frank's possession. It was from Leland Speakes, a real estate appraiser and counsellor residing in Cleveland, Mississippi:

"Few people know what it means to become a sheep hunter. There is no way for a man planning his first sheep hunt to know what his reaction will be when he looks at his first ram. It may be, 'this is too tough for me' or it may be that he is falling under the spell of the high country and is on his way to becoming a sheep hunter.

"During the 1960s, I saw Gordon Eastman's movie *High, Wild and Free*. Instantly I was hooked. It had been filmed in Frank Cooke's area of the Kechika Mountains and was a masterpiece of wilderness photography. I talked to Gordon and he informed me that Frank Cooke was the best guide and had the best Stone sheep guiding area in the entire North. He further made it plain that if I was after a good sheep hunt, then that was the place I should go.

"The fact that this was my first guided hunt may have played a part in it also being my most memorable hunt, which it turned out to be. The price was $2100 for a two-week hunt in some of the most beautiful mountains imaginable. I flew to Watson Lake, Yukon, in a commercial aircraft and from there I was flown over 100 miles south by charter plane to Moodie Lake in the Kechika Mountains. My hunt started September 15, 1970.

"I only spent one night at Moodie Lake, though, because the next morning a float plane came in and took me to Colt Lake where I met my guide, Wilmur Reed. The first day out of camp I saw more sheep than I ever imagined possible. Almost every day we spotted moose and caribou, but no shots were taken because we did not want to scare the sheep, which was our main consideration. It didn't take me very long to realize that Wilmur had a great hunting area. It was called Wilmur's Ridge for good reason—he wouldn't allow the other guides to hunt the area."

"Finally, on the fifth day, we spotted some ram tracks crossing through a high saddle and followed them. An hour or so later we topped a ridge and there within 75 yards of us were seven rams. Six

Leland Speakes and guide Wilmur Reed with fine ram.

were lying down and the other one was upright standing guard. We quietly backed off and climbed the mountain so we could get a good look at all of them. The wind was blowing so hard that it was difficult to keep our hats on, much less get a steady view through the spotting scope, but this is a normal occurrence among the peaks.

"So we studied the rams for a time and decided that one of them was decidedly bigger than the others. We marked his position among the group and snuck back down the mountain to the point where we had first seen them. As I raised my head above the ridge, I found I was looking eyeball to eyeball with the ram we had chosen. I threw my 7 mm Remington rifle to my shoulder and fired, then watched my ram rise to his feet. I fired again and hit him just behind the shoulder, then watched as the ram fell and started tumbling down the mountain. I had visions of my beautiful trophy being smashed to bits among the rocks, so I threw caution to the wind and charged downhill as fast as my legs allowed. With a bit of luck I managed to catch up to it just before it slid over a steep cliff.

"On the last day of our hunt, I managed to bag a huge goat. As well, we had a grizzly bear that hung around camp during the hours of darkness. I didn't bag him, but he sure added a touch of excitement to an already fantastic hunt.

"By the time my first hunt was over, I realized that I had contracted the serious disease 'Ovis pyrexia' or sheep fever as it is known among the mountain men. I knew that I would return and I did. Aside from that hunt, I also hunted Frank's area for Stone sheep five other times between 1970 and 1980. The guide who made these trips so memorable was Frank's son Mac, who had the eyes of an eagle, the strength of a bull, and could climb mountains like a billy goat. He knew the habits of sheep and could judge their horn size with the best of them. We spent many hours around campfires telling stories, some of which were true, and we lived the good life out there in the wilds.

"Finally, I simply can't say enough about Frank Cooke's guiding area. It has everything a hunter could dream of, such as grizzlies, caribou, mountain goats, giant moose and even wolves, which I managed to bag three of. Just to go into that country, so wild and remote—to see the guides and outfitters 100 miles from the nearest road—is a memorable experience. Tents and horses are their stock in trade and they would be in a sorry state without them. You can be assured that I will keep the memories of those trips alive forever."

The foregoing letters are just a sample of the many letters from satisfied clients that Frank has in his possession. They are proof positive that he sent many satisfied hunters homeward bound.

One day I was busy at my desk when I received a visitor. It was Frank Cooke's son, Mac. We got right down to business discussing his years of guiding, and during our conversation, I managed to get another view of the gallant old woodsman, Skook Davidson.

"The first time I went to visit Skook," Mac stated, "there was a gate I had to go through. It was on a spring, so when I let it go, it slammed shut. Skook was sitting outside watching me and he hollered, 'Get back and close that gate properly.' I didn't hear him very well so he shouted it again. I heard him plainly the second time so I went back and opened the gate, then I closed it slowly. When I got close to him, Skook shouted, 'Who the hell are you?'"

"I'm Mac Cooke."

"Are you Frank Cooke's son?"

"Yes, I am."

"Right away he shouted, 'Well it may be all right to slam gates at Frank Cooke's place but don't try it around here.'

"That was Skook, but you know he turned right around and asked me in for tea and was friendly as could be."

"Maybe he just wanted to let you know who was in charge around there, Mac, but tell me, was he as much a partier as legend would have us believe?"

"He separated his partying from his work, you know, but it didn't take long for people to find out when he arrived in town. He would

go into the bar and pin a $100 bill to the wall with thumbtacks, then he would shout to the waiters, 'There she is, boys, just give me a shout when it runs out.'

"Dad told me a story about Skook and the cheque, Jack, did he tell you that one?"

"No!"

"Well, this guy wandered in to Skook's ranch, and he didn't ask for a job or anything, he

Skook in Watson Lake bar.

just hung around and helped out a bit for the summer. When the season was over, Skook paid his help and this guy stood there waiting to get paid. Skook walked over to him and said, 'I never hired you, you came on your own but you did a fairly good job so here's a cheque for you.'

"The guy looked at the cheque and said, 'You know, Skook, if that's all your going to give me maybe you should stick it up your ass.'

"Skook grabbed the cheque back and answered, 'Well, better in my ass pocket than in yours.'

"With that, Skook stuck the cheque in his back pocket and walked off."

"Do you mean he didn't pay anything?" I asked.

"Not a cent. So the guy turned to dad and asked, 'Isn't he going to pay me?'

"Dad told him, 'No! He offered to pay you the same as the others and got an insult in return so he kept the money.'

"Anyway, the guy went back to Skook and asked for his cheque, but Skook told him, 'You're too late; you told me to stick it up my ass and that's exactly what I did and that's where it's going to stay.'

"I'm telling you that Skook was sure some kind of a guy. Rawhide told me a good story about him; my dad was there with him when it happened. They were following along the Kechika River and they were right out of grub when they found a pail hanging in a tree upside down. They checked and found a piece of plastic with some tea inside of it, so they rushed back to camp and showed it to Skook. He looked at it and said, 'There's not enough for everybody.' So he threw it out in the river.

"Dad and Rawhide were pissed off at him for that, but the next day Skook was moving horses across the river and by the time he got finished, his horse was half played out from chasing horses and running around. When he went to cross the river himself, he got almost to the shore when his horse went under. Skook had heavy clothes and his chaps were on, so he was in trouble. Dad and Rawhide watched with a long pole in their hands and waited for Skook to ask for help.

He wouldn't do it though. He kept fighting to make it to shore and went under twice before Dad and Rawhide hooked onto him and pulled him out. Once he got on the bank, Skook started bad-mouthing them until dad said, 'Goddamn you, Skook, we should have let you drown.'

"Right away Skook shouted, 'Did I ask either one of you bastards for help?' That was Skook, he sure could be a stubborn old bugger when he decided to be."

"What happened to the horse; did it survive?"

"The horse got to shore all right, but it was never the same after that; somehow it ruined him."

"Skook was quite a man, wasn't he, Mac?"

"My dad admired him so much. He treated my dad tough, but he also treated him fair. He used to call my dad, 'You long-eared maverick.' My dad thought the world of him. But the best story I ever heard about Skook came from my dad. He was flying into the Kechika years ago and there was a woman on the plane. Dad talked to her and found out that she was going to visit with Skook to get his life story. Dad told her that Skook hadn't been around women for years and that he used terribly abusive language. The woman assured dad that she could handle it and when they landed at Skook's ranch, dad helped her out of the plane and over to Skook's wagon. Dad introduced them and Skook said, 'Get up here.'

"Dad helped her up on the wagon and Skook shouted at the horses to get moving. One of them started to go but the other horse balked. Skook had a long stick in his hand so he gently tapped the horse on the rump and said, 'Get moving Doll or I'll ram this stick right up your c——.'

"Dad said the woman's face dropped, she stiffened up and looked to the side, and all dad could say was, 'I warned you, ma'am.' She hung in there, though, and went to the ranch and got her interview."

"You spent many years guiding for your father, Mac, how about recalling some other memories?"

"I have a ton of them, including some funny ones. We had an

Indian guide called Scrawny Johnny who was wanted by the police, but we did our best to hide him because we needed him for guiding. After we finished a session of guiding, we took some days off and got partying in Watson Lake and of course it didn't take very long for the police to find out we were in town. When they came to check us, Johnny seen them coming, so he ran and hid in one of the cabins. One of the policemen asked me if that was Johnny, but I told him I hadn't seen Johnny in a long time. I guess the policemen didn't believe me, though, so they ran over to the cabin and one of them shouted, 'I know you're in there, Johnny, open the door.'

"The policeman shouted like that several times but Johnny wouldn't answer. Finally the policeman shouted, 'Open the door, Johnny, or I'll kick it in.'

"That time Johnny answered by shouting, 'Not by the hair on your chinny, chin, chin.'

"There was the policemen trying to be serious and make an arrest, while at the same time they were busting a gut laughing. Finally they got organized, kicked the door in, and made the arrest. Later that day we radioed dad back in the mountains and told him that Johnny was in jail, so he told us to go and borrow the money from Hal Comish and bail him out. We did that and then went to the police station and paid $250 to get him out. Well you wouldn't believe how happy he was; he slapped us on the back and told us we were the nicest guys he had ever met. But not for long, though, in fact, only until we ran

Herb Fellers, Colin, Frankie Cooke, Scrawny Johnny and Florie Browne, 1968.

out of booze money. We considered our options and could only think of one, so we told Johnny he had to burn one for the boys. We dragged him back to the police station where we tried to trade him in so we could get our bail money back. Johnny was pleading with the police not to deal with us, while we were promising to get money the next day to bail him out again. The policeman looked at us as if he thought we were all crazy and shouted, 'What the hell do you think this is—a pawn shop?'

"Finally the police told us to get the hell out of there or they would put all of us in jail and throw away the key. All that time Johnny was saying, 'Thank you sir; thank you sir'."

"You fellows certainly played jokes on each other, didn't you?"

"We were always playing jokes on each other."

"According to Larry Whitesitt's book, you frequently spotted UFO's in the night sky. Care to comment on that, Mac?"

"Colt Lake got to the point where it was noted for UFO's. There were a lot of sightings. We would see a light up there and in seconds it would be over on the other side of the sky, and there were so many people who witnessed them with us. I was camped one time out at Denetiah Lake when my hunter got up to take a leak. He shouted at me to get up, so I jumped out of bed and there was a blue light—a monstrous blue light that lit up the whole valley. It was right above the mountain. So I hollered at the other guys and they all got up and watched it. All of a sudden it came down and passed right above us, and I mean it was travelling at a tremendous speed and in a few seconds it had crossed the sky and was gone. So many hunters watched these things that it got to the point where word got around and new hunters would mention that they sure wanted to see the UFO's."

"According to Larry Whitesitt's book, you fellows certainly got into enough fights."

"You bet! That was a good part of our entertainment. Between that and riding wild broncos and horses, it's a miracle any of us survived. But I just thought of a funny thing that happened when old Mel Hartman had a bunch of dogs at Lower Post. My dad was there at the time, and they were all sitting around having a few beers. It was just getting dark when a policeman came along and one of the dogs was really acting up. The policeman told Mel that the dog was in heat but old Mel didn't understand what he meant, so he said, 'No, she's in the shade.'

"Then the policeman replied, 'No! I mean she wants to get bred.'

"Old Mel looked at him in a strange way and said, "Go ahead, Sonny, I've always wanted a police dog'."

"Got any more humorous stories?" I asked.

"My brother Frankie and I were coming down the highway one fall—every time we came out of the bush in the fall, Frankie was always the last guy to get home. Anyway, Frankie's wife phoned me and asked if I was on my way home and I told her I was. So she asked me to pick Frankie up at Fort Nelson because he was on a big drunk there. I picked him up and along the road Frankie told me to stop at Lum and Abners, because he had to use the bathroom. We pulled in and Frankie no sooner got in the bathroom, then he came out and called me. I went over to him and he told me that someone had rubbed excrement all over the men's bathroom. Then he went into the women's bathroom to do his business. I went back to the counter and ordered two cups of coffee and then I said to the waitress, 'Did you see that big guy that came in with me?' She admitted she had, so I said, "That guy is going to rub excrement all over the bathroom."

"She gave me a funny look and replied, 'Why would he do that?'

"So I told her that he had done that every place we stopped. I don't think she believed me until Frankie came out of the bathroom and said to her. 'You better clean up the bathroom because it's a hell of a mess.' As we headed out the door, the waitress ran to the bathroom, and just as we were getting into our truck she opened the door and shouted, 'You goddamned filthy pig.'

"Frankie shouted that he hadn't done it but she called him a liar as well as several other things. Well, that was sure funny, the waitress was mad and Frankie was mad because he was accused of something

A successful hunter from Reno, Nevada, 1986.

he didn't do. I waited a long time before I admitted that I had set him up."

"You guys were a bunch of buggers, Mac!"

"You don't know the half of it. An even better one happened when we were partying at the Watson Lake Hotel and one of our guys took a gal outside to our travel-all for obvious reasons. After a while brother Terry asked me where he was but I didn't know. Terry went searching for him and found both of them passed out in our vehicle, stark naked. So he opened the back doors and backed the vehicle right up to the window of the café, which was full of people, and parked it there. We watched and pretty soon old Danny kind of sat up, gave his woman a rub, and then noticed that everyone in the café was watching them. He dove over the seat and started getting dressed, and believe me it was a long time until he lived that down."

"I have to say, Mac, that I wouldn't have wanted to be friends with you guys, it was much too hazardous."

Mac laughed as another memory came back and then began, "Another time, Rawhide, Frankie, Bill Eckert and I got left at Scoop Lake when dad decided to fly out for the day. Before he left, dad told us to take care of the place but under no circumstances were we to touch his two rifles. I think we had about 15 rifles on the wall at the time, so there was no need to use his guns, which were hand-made by a famous gunsmith named Paul Bison. Paul gave them to dad and they were worth thousands of dollars each, so you know why dad didn't want us to touch them. But as it turned out, dad wasn't gone two hours when I decided to walk up to the cabin. It was winter when this happened, and I just got out the door and there was Billy [Eckert] with one of dad's guns and it was in two pieces. I asked what happened and he told me that he had seen a wolf out on the lake so he grabbed dad's gun and went running out the door only to have his feet slip out from under him and down he came, right on the gun. Bill spent about a month trying to fix the gun—he used glue and tried everything but nothing worked. Finally he said, 'I'm going to have to tell him. He's going to kill me, but I've got to tell him.'

"Well, I can't remember all that happened, but dad was sure steamed, one day he told Bill, 'We could give you a solid steel axe, you son of a bitch and you would still break it. You break everything you touch and you touch everything.' Dad was not happy about that."

"Your dad must have had a time with all you guys the way you acted up, Mac."

"We just about drove him nuts. One time we flew back in for the last hunt of the year and dad was on the shore waiting for us with five American hunters. When the plane door opened, dad and the hunters were in for a shock. We went to get out of the plane and the first guide fell out, hit the float and then fell in the water, drunk right out of his mind. When I got out, I had two big black eyes that were swollen shut from fighting the night before. Then two other guides got out and they couldn't walk, they were so drunk. Then the last guide got out of the plane and he was all bloody with half of his ear torn off, so you can imagine what we looked like. Dad looked at us and said, 'You're fired; the whole goddamn works of you are fired!'

"So we gathered up our stuff and prepared to go out with the plane but dad was stuck; he didn't have any guides for his hunters. Finally he came into the bunkhouse and said, 'If you guys go to bed right now and sober up, I'll keep you on; I mean get your ass to bed and don't say a word or even move, and be up at five in the morning ready to go.'

"One of the guides started to say something and dad shouted, 'You're fired.' He meant it too, the guy was fired."

"I notice from your pictures that you certainly took some monster moose out of the Kechika Mountains."

"Some of the antler spreads on those moose are unbelievable. And just as unbelievable is their ability to travel through the woods with those enormous racks. But they manage somehow."

"You mentioned a story about Dall Lake, Mac, will you repeat that story?"

"Actually, I was camped at Dall Lake one time and I know that one

Mac Cooke with 63″ moose.

of the Georges was there, along with Jimmy Porter and some of his friends. I started talking with them and they told me a story that many years earlier there had been an Indian camp there—in fact, some of the log dog houses were still there—well, they told me that they were all at that lake one time when they saw 50 rams come down off the mountain and start swimming the lake. Suddenly the water started churning and all the rams went down. They saw me swimming in the lake so they told me to get out of the water because a serpent lived in the lake. When I questioned them further, they told me the story of the rams. Not once in all the intervening years had they ever entered the lake again. Just what happened to the rams is unknown; perhaps there was a minor earthquake or something of that nature. As to why they named it Dall Lake, they [the Natives] didn't know the difference between Dall and Stone sheep at that time; therefore they believed the rams were Dall sheep."

I thoroughly enjoyed my time spent with Mac Cooke, and after he left, I went back to questioning his father. I mentioned the conversation with Mac concerning how Dall Lake got its name, whereupon Frank suggested another possibility. He believed that it was named by Inspector J. D. Moodie of the North West Mounted Police who passed through the area in 1897 while engaged in a futile attempt to build a trail to the Klondike gold rush. Frank stated, "Dall Lake is not the best place for sheep. The west side of the lake is all big bluffs where mountain goats like to hang out. In the 60 years I spent in that area I never seen many sheep along the whole length of the ridge, which today is known as the Sharktooth Range. Instead, that area is locally called the mountain goat farm of the Kechika. I also think that these early–day wanderers didn't know the difference between mountain goats and sheep and therefore mistook the goats for white sheep which they probably viewed from a distance."

"Your son, Mac, told me a few stories about Scrawny Johnny. Frank, do you have anything to add? He strikes me as being a most interesting fellow."

"I remember the time I went to the police station to bail Scrawny out of jail. The policeman took me downstairs to where the cells were and Johnny was sitting there in silence. I told him to get ready to leave because I had bailed him out. I couldn't believe it when he refused and said 'I want a lawyer and I'm not going to talk to anyone but Perry Mason.'

"The policeman got tired of that nonsense and told him he had better go with me, so he did."

"I get the feeling that this Scrawny Johnny was quite a character, Frank."

"He certainly was, and I've got another story about him that just adds to the stories of tragedies in the North. I had some business at Kinaskan Lake along the Stewart-Cassiar Highway and I was surprised to find Scrawny Johnny working there. I tried to talk to him but he didn't know me, so I asked around and found out that someone had hit him on the head with a rock. I got him to my vehicle and drove all night to get him to the hospital in Watson Lake. Whenever I tried to talk to him all he would say was, 'I have to be ready at eight o'clock because I'm going to work for Frank Cooke.'

"He didn't even know me, that's the condition he was in. He never recovered from that injury."

Chapter 11

I LISTENED TO THE MANY STORIES FRANK TOLD ME, BUT it seemed there were always more questions I wanted to ask. Such as, "Did Skook ever have any women around the ranch?"

"Not in a romantic way. He did have a Native woman cook for his trail hunts. She was a first class cook who could make bread or anything on the trail. She cooked for his hunters for quite a few years. Her name was Mabel Frank and she was a sister to Rawhide, who for my money was one of the best guides ever produced in the North."

"From all I've heard and read about Skook, it seems that he was certainly well respected, is that your view, Frank?"

"Skook had built up a great reputation in the North; it was almost impossible to hear anyone say a bad word about him. He was an outstanding individual that's for sure . . . I was just reminded of an individual that Skook and I met on the trail. His name was Tom Harvey, and he was a tough old Englishman who could travel through the bush with little grub. Skook and I were travelling with his horses when we met Tom at 48-Mile Meadow. It was the first time I had met Tom and I was an impressionable youngster at the time. He and Skook talked most of the night about their experiences during the war and I got quite a good impression of this man. Tom used to have a dozen horses and he came into that country from Jasper, through Dawson Creek, Finlay Forks and right up into the Dease Lake country all by himself. I remember him telling Skook a story about how he kept people from raiding his cabin. When Tom had visitors he would make it a point to have something to eat and while doing so, he would grab the salt or pepper shaker and just be ready to use it when he would exclaim, 'Oh, my God, that's the one with the strychnine in it; I had better be careful or I'll poison myself one of these days.' Tom was always playing tricks like that on people and they didn't take any chances around his cabin unless he was there.

"Another thing, Tom had a war wound on his leg that wouldn't heal. It bothered him a lot and he suggested to Skook that some day when it got too bad that he would take some strychnine and solve the problem. When Tom died near Lower Post, there was a young Indian lad with him who claimed that Tom sat down on a log, took a few sips of tea, and then tumbled backwards off the log. As far as I know it was never proven whether he used the poison or just had a heart attack. I was at his funeral when the priest, Donald Miller, and I, took his body across the river in a boat and buried him there."

"Did Skook have a good sense of humour?" I asked.

"Skook had a great sense of humour. Sometimes he would lay a tall tale on a youngster just for a little enjoyment. The first time my son Terry flew into his cabin with me, Skook tried to hang one on Terry. He told him, 'When we were building the Grand Trunk Railway through the Hazelton area, we got involved with some other guys and picked up a whore and partied all night.

Skook's trail cook Mabel Frank at Brokenbit camp.

Pilot Terry Cooke (in white shirt) and hunters.

When morning came we found out that we had screwed her right to death.' Skook watched Terry to see how he was taking it and then added, 'We did the right thing, though, and gave her a military funeral with a ten-gun salute over her grave.' That was Skook; I guess he had lots of time in the evenings to think up these stories.

"After we left Skook's ranch and were on our way home, Terry offered his opinion of the story by saying, 'I wonder if he expected me to believe him; I think he just made that up.' Knowing Skook, I figured the last guess was the closest."

"What was the story he told those surveyors? I thought that was a con job."

"Apparently he told them that during the war he was on patrol at night for a British unit when he killed a German with his knife. He told them that he brought the head back and gave it to the officer in charge, who promptly fainted."

"Did he ever tell you that story, Frank?" I asked.

"No! I agree that he was just pulling their legs a little bit."

"Did you ever see Skook get out of hand because of excess booze?" I questioned.

"Yes! It was well known that he drank too much sometimes. He got into a terrible fight with Angus McDonald one time. We had just arrived in Lower Post—I think it was 1945— when Skook started drinking with Angus. This happened in a cabin Angus was staying in that was used by the police years earlier. The cabin was about one mile downstream from Lower Post and it was called McNab Point. Well, at first they talked and had a good time, but they ran out of booze, so they got a taxi to take them to Watson Lake where they bought some cheap booze from a bootlegger there. When they got back to the cabin, they kept drinking and finally started fighting. I knew things were getting out of hand, so when I got the chance, I emptied the cartridges out of their guns. It must have been about the fourth day, I guess, and I had just returned from checking the horses when I heard Skook holler, 'I'll blow your goddamned head off!' I ran into the cabin and Skook had Angus down on the floor. He was choking Angus with one hand and with his other hand he took his pistol and held it right against his head. I jumped and grabbed the pistol out of his hand and threw it out the door and it sailed right into the river. At the same time Skook hollered at me, 'Get out of the way; I'm going to kill this son of a bitch.' They were really going at it, and there was blood all over the floor. Angus was trying to reach his gun, but I told him it was empty. Then Angus went absolutely crazy. He attacked me and I threw a can of tomatoes at him. The first can missed him and left a mark in the wall of the cabin, but the second can hit him on the head and he dropped in his tracks. Old Phil Hankin from Telegraph Creek was there when it started, but he took off over the hill on the run.

"The next day Skook and Angus started arguing again and it got to the point where they discussed shooting it out down by the river. Maybe Phil had told the police because Johnny Betts [the policeman] came to the cabin and wanted to know what was going on. They wouldn't talk to him, though, so he finally gave up and left. I did my best to cool things around there until the next morning when Skook and I left with the horses. That was a bad scene that could have ended in death, just as so many other fights did end in death. Another thing about that gun, when we came back through there that fall we found out that Hardrock McDonald had found it when the river dropped. He turned it over to the Hudson's Bay man who gave it back to me. I took it back to the Kechika and cleaned it up and it hung on the wall there at the ranch for several years that I know of. But I'm telling you that most of the serious troubles I witnessed in the North were caused by booze.

"Something else I should mention is that Angus used to sing a song he wrote that was quite good:

My name is Black Angus and I came from the glen,
I've been roaming the wildwoods since 19 and 10.
I'm fond of fair women, good whiskey and song,
I've always been willing to help a poor man along.
When the depression came on I went to the wilds,
I rafted and walked over 300 miles.
Without any outfit which made it quite hard,
I've built many campfires on the banks of Liard.
I've fought frost and mosquitoes and slept 'neath the stars,
I've mined and prospected and lived on the barge.
Thank God I'm healthy, though I often feel dry,
If whisky doesn't kill me I'll live till I die.

"Did Skook and Angus hold a grudge over their fights?" I questioned.

"No! But there's something else I have to say about Angus: he had some big malamutes that were so strong that he used them to pull in the logs for his cabin. Those dogs would crouch down low and pull more than anyone could believe possible.

"Another thing about dogs—the Tahltan Indians from Telegraph Creek used to have little black and white dogs that would drive grizzly bears crazy. They were about the size of terriers and were kind of a breed of their own as far as I know, because I haven't seen any of them for many years. Those dogs would drive sheep right up onto the highest pinnacles where they would ignore the hunters and just watch the dogs, then the hunter could take his choice."

"I notice from the pictures that Skook had dogs around. Was that always the case?"

"Skook liked his dogs and his horses and the dogs helped keep the wolves away from his horses. Something that few people knew about Skook was that he had a hot temper. Boy, if someone mistreated his horses he just went wild. I knew one fellow that hurt his arm and because of it he left the horses tied up so they couldn't feed. Man, when Skook found out he dropped that guy with one punch and then fired him. When it came to horses, he was the smartest man I've ever known. Even when he was old, he would take his wagon down to the meadow and his voice would roar like thunder when he called them. Then they would gather around the wagon and he would feed them sugar or oats. There were some pretty wild horses that had never been ridden or carried packs, yet they would come on the run. When we were moving the horses and camping, Skook would not allow anyone to slap his horses to get them out of camp, and he would bawl you out if you ever tried. He claimed that any abuse made the horses harder to catch and of course he was right. His way of treating horses was proven right because he never had any trouble catching them and that speaks for itself. He would not work them more that six hours if they were loaded heavy. He would always give them lots of time to feed and you never saw any of Skook's horses in poor condition, even in the spring of the year. His horses were kept better than any other horses in the North, case closed."

"I think you told me that Skook had a boat for a while. Was he into machinery at all?"

"Skook and machinery didn't get along all that well. He had the mower and a boat for a while but I remember when Pat Garbett and I built that new cabin for him. He decided it would be nice to have a washing machine to do all the clothes so he bought one. One day

Skook decided he was going to wash clothes so he got Rawhide to fire up the machine for him. Well, he put the water in it and then poured most of a box of Oxydol in with it. We were working shoeing horses at the time and when Skook went back into the cabin he didn't stay there very long. He came running out the door hollering, 'She's going to blow; she's going to blow.' Rawhide ran in and shut the machine off and it took us quite a while to clean the cabin because there were suds everywhere.

"I think it was the next year that Skook got a snowmobile because he thought it would be nice to feed and check the horses without having to walk or take the dogs. He got a double-track Skidoo and when they got it ready to go, he jumped on behind Rawhide and away they went. They didn't get very far, though, because when Rawhide gave it the power Skook tipped over and landed on his back out in the field. He didn't have too much use for it after that and Rawhide was the

Rawhide, a topnotch woodsman and guide.

only person that used it when there was snow on the ground. Maybe Skook was right to stay away from machinery back in the mountains, because if you have people that don't understand how to use and care for things, then you have serious problems.

"Something that people don't know is that some of the record sheep that were supposedly shot in other areas of the North were actually poached off Skook's area. We knew who it was because he had the opportunity to hit the remote areas. But he made a mistake, though, when he started poaching on my area and I found out about it. One day my son Terry and I were flying in my Cessna 185 when we saw a plane down on one of the lakes in my area. We flew over to the spot and we recognized it was his airplane. We landed and walked over to where he and another man were standing and I challenged him about poaching in my area. He denied it, but we found their camping gear in the woods nearby. He attempted to deny it was his gear but that didn't fly because his name was on it. We had words, and then I slapped his face and told him to load his gear and get out. I can be hot-tempered when I get upset, and believe me I tore a strip off that fellow. When they took off in their airplane, we had a faster plane so we buzzed and circled them until they were completely out of the area. I had reported this fellow several times to different authorities but he had pull and so no action was ever taken. But the action I took produced results, because I never saw that fellow around my territory after that."

"Give me some names of your hunters, Frank, just for the record."

"I could go on for hours naming hunters, Glen Naperisky from California just came to mind. But there were so many. We also had Jack Leeds and his family several times. They distributed wholesale jewellery to a great number of stores and of course they were world famous."

"You mentioned guides poaching on Skook's area, do you think Skook realized just how much poaching was going on in his territory?" I asked.

"No, and I didn't tell him because he was getting old and it would have upset him. I know this, though, if Skook had have been 30 years younger that fellow wouldn't have pulled anything like that on him."

"Do you have any more stories about Skook?" I asked.

"Lots. One time before I got married, Craig Forfar and I got into the booze and started raising hell at Lower Post. We got fighting in the Hudson's Bay bunkhouse and somehow windows got broken and things like that. Len Ferrian was the policeman there at the time but he was absent that night. Well word must have got around because a couple days later Skook arrived in town. As soon as I spotted him I knew we were in trouble. He came over to us and said, 'Come on over to the police station.'

"We followed Skook to the station, and by that time Len had returned. He looked me straight in the eyes and said, 'I think you guys are getting too wild around here. If you don't slow down I'm going to take you to Fort Nelson and put you in jail.' Then he singled me out and said, 'I'll tell you something else, Frank, if it wasn't for Skook here and the fact that your dad had such a good reputation on the police force, I'd take and throw you in jail right now.' Boy, that smartened me up. I shook hands with him and assured him that it would not happen again. After that mess, Skook sent us back to the bush for a while.

"I remember another time when we tested Skook's sense of humour. We were camped about halfway between the ranch and Gataga Forks, right up at timberline. The hunt was over and we were going to return home the next morning. Well, it snowed about ten inches that night and the next morning we got up and while we were eating breakfast I knew something was going on because Rawhide, Skook's guide, winked at me. Suddenly Rawhide grabbed a tree branch that was loaded with snow and gave it a good shake, and all the snow came down right on top of Skook's bald-head. Man, you should have heard him roar; just like a grizzly bear. Rawhide and I went behind the tent and laughed for a long time. After everything quieted down and we were getting ready to leave with the horses,

Skook got a switch and gave Rawhide a couple shots with it. Then he scolded him by shouting, 'I'll bet you thought I forgot about it, didn't you? Well I didn't'."

"You young fellows must have been real hellions by the sounds of it." I commented.

"We were always up to something; I don't know why Skook put up with us. Another time Craig and I picked up some grub, and then got a ride across the river and hit it back into the Kechika. When we got in there, Skook was away on a job. He had told us to make hay, so we decided to hitch up a pinto stud and a mare he called Cannonball. Most of the horses had never seen a harness before but we figured they had to start sometime. Cannonball was a deadheaded horse, but I woke her up and found just how deadheaded she really was. When we got them hooked up, the stud wouldn't move, so I suggested Craig go up to the cabin to get Skook's bullwhip. He didn't want to go, though, because the old man had told us not to touch it. At the same time we knew that if we didn't get some hay put up that we would be in grief, too. So Craig got the whip, and we had the horses hooked up to the mower, which was in gear. I took the bullwhip and made a couple swings with it and on the second swing it wrapped around my neck and slapped me a hell of a wallop on the cheek. Man, did it ever hurt. After I got it unwrapped, I gave the horses a few shots and all of a sudden they started across the old meadow. We had cleared the meadow but there was an abundance of willows and anthills all over it. The old mower bounced over the anthills going flat out and I lost the whip. Well, we carried on like that until we reached the end of the meadow where we ended up in a pile. The horses parted company and took off through the bush and smashed the harness all to hell. The mowing machine survived but it was piled up in the ditch. After a bit of time we got the horses back, repaired the harness, and got everything organized again. But then we noticed that the whip was missing. We made our way back along the meadow and finally found the whip. It had dropped through the cycle bar and had been chopped all to pieces. We knew what we were in for if Skook found any pieces of the whip, so we gathered up all the pieces and hid them where he would never find them.

"To make matters even worse, an American came in to visit and he had an 18–year-old girl with him. Craig and I were supposed to be putting up hay, but instead we spent most of our time chasing the girl or watching each other to make sure the other guy didn't have any luck.

"When Skook got back to the ranch, the first thing he said was, 'Let's go down and see how much hay you got up.' When we arrived at the piles, he exploded, 'God damn it, is that all the hay you got up?' I just hung my head, I didn't know what else to do. As we were walking back, Skook asked, 'What's that?' I looked down and damned if it wasn't a piece of the whip that we had missed. He picked it up and said, 'That's my whip; I told you not to use my whip.' I had to confide the entire story to him and I guess he must have been young once because much to my relief he just shook his head and seemed to understand."

"When we talked on the phone you told me a story about Skook and a ladder; care to repeat it?"

"That happened when Skook worked on a ranch down in the Cariboo many years ago. The way he told it, he had a crush on a girl there and one night when he was feeling particularly horny he decided to visit her in an upstairs bedroom without her permission. But he had a problem, because each one of the steps in the stairway squeaked when you stepped on it; in fact, each step had its own sound so everyone in the house knew what step you were on. Skook considered his chances and then gave up on that idea and tried something different. He waited until everyone was asleep and then snuck out the door as quietly as possible. He got a ladder, placed it against the wall right by the young lady's window and began climbing. But he only got up a couple rungs when a voice whispered, 'Where are we going?'

"It was the girl's father who had followed Skook out the door and knew damned well what he was after. Skook was caught by surprise and must have been at a loss for words because he whispered, 'I just came down for a leak.'

"The old man wasn't fooled for a second so he whispered back, 'I know damned well what you came for but you're not going to get any, so let's go back to bed'."

"I imagine that her mom and dad took turns staying awake after that episode, Frank, but I guess that was the real Skook Davidson; he was always up to some kind of devilry in his younger days."

"That brings another story to mind about something that happened back in the Kechika during a cold spell in January. I think it was in 1945. We were staying close to the cabin and I guess we got bored because one evening Craig and I started arguing. At the same time Skook was reading an old *Reader's Digest* that was about 20 years old and one he had probably read many times before. I was trying to convince Craig that I could ride Skook's mare, Spitfire. Craig would-

n't have it, though, so we were arguing hot and heavy. Suddenly Skook let out a bellow that there would be no arguing in the cabin. Well, we waited for a while and then went at it again. That did it, Skook got off his bunk and shouted at us, 'If you're so rambunctious get outside and cut some firewood.'

"Well we went, but we didn't enjoy it because it was about 40° below zero. But we did what we were told and got the crosscut saw just

Mac's hunter and ram.

a smoking because we were trying to keep warm. Suddenly Craig said, 'Lets smoke the old bugger out of the cabin.'

"I asked what he meant and he added, 'Let's go and get some gunny sacks out of the shed and ram them down the stovepipe and smoke the old bugger right out of the cabin.' I thought that was a hell of an idea so we had a debate about who was going to do the dirty task. We finally agreed that I would, so he boosted me up to where a box was attached to the wall. I got on top of it and was just going to ram the sacks down the pipe when the box broke loose and down we came, making a hell of a racket. As soon as we hit the snow, we heard the door open so we both made a run for it. Craig jumped over the bank of Medula Creek and I bolted into the outhouse and then there was a hell of a boom as Skook cut loose with his shotgun. I heard some of the pellets hitting things around there, and believe me I made myself as low as I could on the outhouse floor. Finally Craig and I got back together and went back to the woodcutting, and we stayed at it for another couple hours until Skook came out and told us to come back in. Then he told us not to argue anymore and that's the way it was. He was quite a guy, I can tell you that. I seen him do so many things, and he would never ask anyone to do anything he wouldn't do himself.

"Something I learned about Skook occurred when I went to visit my parents and dad showed me a letter he had received about 10 years earlier. In it Skook wrote that I would either become a damned good man or else a damned bad man. He also suggested that he should keep me around for another three or four years because he could handle me. I don't deny that he was good for me because I sure was in good shape during that time. I'd snowshoe all winter and run all over the place. I was always cutting wood, building fence or look-ing after the horses. I remember the time I climbed Terminus Mountain in 55 minutes right from Skook's cabin. Kechika means windy valley in the Indian language and it was well named, because it sure can be windy. The wind howls through from the southwest and blows the snow into large drifts. That's why it's such good horse country. But the drifts can present problems for the horses because they will climb up on them and if they are icy the horses can slide down and get trapped in them and if you don't check them constantly, you will find them dead right there. At times they are afraid to come down off the drifts so they freeze to death on them. When I used to travel with my dogs I would dig out a big spot for myself and the dogs in one of these drifts, and then make a fire in there and be comfortable no matter how cold it got."

"I've heard that Skook used to keep a diary; is that true?" I asked.

"He kept a diary every day and it was all lost in the fire at the ranch in 1972. That was a terrible loss, because he had so many interesting experiences and traveled so extensively. In a sense that loss was partly my fault because he told me several times to take his diaries. Lord knows I wish I had taken them now. He led such an interesting life and got to know many famous people. One of the hunters he took out was Prince Abdarreza, brother to the Shah of Iran. Skook was never impressed by wealth, so he hollered at the Prince just the same as any other person. After the hunt was over, the Prince gave Skook a silver bowl and told him that he was the first person that treated him like a fellow man.

"Herb Kline was another person Skook used to guide. He was an oilman from Texas; he owned Trinity Oil among other things. I used to get such a kick out of him. If the weather was not suitable for hunting, he would sit and play cribbage with Skook all day long. What struck me funny was that here was this multi-millionaire playing cribbage for 1¢ a hole. One day up on a mountain I ask Herb how he made his money and he told me that when other young men were out partying and spending money that he and a friend were saving their money to drill for oil. When they hit oil he ended up with more money than he knew what to do with. I also asked him how much money he had and he replied, 'I'm not sure; I think the last time I checked it was about $180 million.' They sure were a pair, him and Skook, they got along great together and Herb was a repeat hunter.

"Skook would allow for a moose to be taken once in a while if we were short of meat, and that almost got him in trouble once. A game warden we called Shaky Don came in to the ranch and noticed some moose meat hanging in the screened-in cooler. As this was prior to the moose season, he asked where it came from and of course I said I didn't know, but thought that perhaps an Indian shot it. Don thought about it for a while and the suggested that he was going to go into the cabin and lay a charge against Skook. I stopped him in his tracks by saying, 'If you lay a charge against that old man you're going to get into a lot of grief.'

"Just then Skook walked out the door and we began admiring some big rams just above the cabin. After a moment Don said, 'I think I'll go over and drop one of those big rams.'"

"Instantly Skook replied, 'If you do then I'll drop you and take my chances with a judge and jury.'

"After Skook went back in the cabin the game warden said, 'I wonder if the old man means that.' I assured him that he meant every word and I guess the warden didn't want to push it because he left empty handed.

"Something many people are not aware of is that Skook was part of the reason for the upsurge in moose populations in the Kechika. He poisoned the wolves off and gave the moose a fighting chance. About eight or ten years later there was an abundance of moose in the area. It wasn't a big deal then, and the Game Department readily supplied Skook with the poison. Skook knew how to use it the proper way. He would freeze a beaver carcass into the ground so the wolves couldn't pack it away. That way they stayed and dug up what they could and died right there rather than in the woods somewhere. When he set the poison, he got 16 wolves in one night. But we did even better than that, because Terry and Rawhide got 54 wolves in 30 days around Scoop Lake. That gives you some idea what we had to contend with."

That brought back a memory from pilot Larry Whitesitt's book where he stated, "One afternoon when I was at Scoop Lake on a charter for Frank, I took a short flight just south of the lake and counted about 300 moose. It was like a large cattle ranch . . ."

I thought about the significance of Larry's words and then said, "Well Frank, I guess the fires and the action against the wolves must have paid off. But I want to talk about fishing, Frank; because I've heard you speak about the fishing in your area. Going by some of the pictures it must have been fantastic."

'We had secret lakes all over those mountains and I'm telling you that some of them averaged five-pound rainbows. Believe me, that sure held a hunter's interest."

Remembering a story I had read many years earlier, I asked Frank, "Is it true that Skook had up to 200 head of horses on his ranch at one time?"

"It sure is. In fact, when I was guiding at Scoop Lake I flew over to Skook's ranch and while we were shooting the breeze, 12 of his buckskin horses came in for a feed of oats. They were all the same colour, beautiful animals that had originated at Jim Beattie's ranch on the Halfway River. I knew that we would be making movies on my guideline and it occurred to me that they would look nice in the movies, so I asked Skook, 'How much for those broncos?'

"He gave me a strange look and replied, 'I thought I taught you, Kid, you don't buy horses in the fall; you buy horses in the spring.'

"I knew Skook well enough to know that you didn't wait to deal with him; if you had a chance for a deal you took it before he changed his mind. I reached into my pocket to get some money, but he stopped me by saying, 'Your money is no good around here, Kid, come back in the spring and if they are still here you can have them.'

"Well, I never did get those horses; that's just the way it was with Skook."

"He really loved his horses, didn't he?"

"His horses were his children and he showed it in every way possible. You wouldn't believe how much money he spent on them. He always had airplanes coming in with loads of oats for them and they responded to him because he could walk up and pet any of them. They knew they could trust him."

"What were some of the main things you learned while traveling with Skook?"

"On the trail, I guess most of the things I learned from him. For instance, when we were traveling through the muskegs further north we had our problems. We would take one horse across to search out a way and if that horse got bogged down then you had to get the pack off in a hurry. We always had a tucker string on our diamond hitch so that we only had to cut the tucker string to release the pack. Some horses get very good at pussy footing their way around swamps, but others get panicky and start to run and sure enough, down they go. We had a mare we called Little Lady that was about 15 years old. She would go to pieces around a muskeg and start running; next thing we knew, she was down."

"It seems to me that without the service of aircraft, you would have had a lot tougher time on those wilderness journeys."

"They were our lifeline all right, and it was nice to know that they were available if someone got seriously injured."

"I want to get back to horses swimming. Did some of them refuse to go into the water?"

"They usually have a leader, and when that horse goes into the water the others seem to follow. Some of our horses got to where a river didn't mean a thing to them. We had a horse called Bessie that would always lead the way across. We would lead her to the river edge, pull her halter off, and away she'd go. Once a horse hits swimming water you should not holler at it anymore. If you do, nine times out of ten it will turn around and swim back to you. Once it throws its ears up and hits swimming water, it will look at something on the other side and if you keep quiet, it will swim across.

"Once they come out on the other side, they like to roll. If there is a sandbar around, they will roll so you have time to catch them. If it's quite cold the horses will roll and then get up and run, so they can get warmed up. One of the things that annoyed me the most was when we got things wet. If it froze during the night we had to make sure that we dried out the ropes and everything because they would freeze and we couldn't use them. Even drying them out was a tricky business, because if you put them too close to the fire they would burn, and if you put them too far away they wouldn't dry.

"Skook also taught me a lesson that many people learned the hard way: when camping near an Indian camp in the winter, if you forgot to put your snowshoes up in a tree, then when you got up in the morning you would find that their dogs had chewed the babiche right out of them and then you were buggered as far as traveling was concerned.

"When traveling with dog teams he taught me to avoid overflow spots, where the water comes over the ice. A good lead dog will usually avoid these spots but if you get into them the sled loads up and the dogs can't pull it. Then you have a cleaning job on your hands."

"I've noticed the many awards you won for trophies, such as bears, Stone sheep and mountain goats. Surely you must look back at it all with a measure of pride, don't you, Frank?"

"Of course I do, but it was not that difficult to do when you consider the area I got from Skook. Most of it had never been hunted when I got it."

"I asked you this question before but you didn't answer it so I'll try again—in your opinion, where was the most beautiful spot in that entire country?"

"That's a tough one. I guess I have to say it's a toss-up between Skook's place and Moodie Lake."

"When you look back on your life, Frank, and the many years you spent in the wilderness of BC, how do you sum it up?"

"I guess I would sum it all up by saying that I tried; I really tried. But I guess things started to get out of hand when I forgot that I just wanted a small operation for the family. We also had a dream that we could spread out into other enterprises besides hunting, but somehow things got out of control. I sold half-interest to Bobbie Keen, a businessman from Fort Nelson, for $150,000 worth of cat work and help in other expenses. To start with, we leased 6,000 acres of land and cleared about 800 acres for horse pasture. Then we started putting up

Jewellery magnates Barbara and Jack Leeds.

buildings and cabins. One thing led to another—there was a Beaver, a Cessna 185 and a Super Cub airplane. Next came electricity, hot water and flush toilets, carpets and boats. Just the money spent on fuel, such as diesel, propane and gas was surprising."

"You must have had a good revenue to draw from, didn't you?" I asked.

"At our peak we had between 40 and 50 sheep hunters as well as hunters for other types of game, but there never seemed to be enough money to cover the expenses. Just the money paid to all the guides ran up a considerable bill. But above all else, it was the endless bureaucracy that pissed me off. I tried to work with the Game Department but that didn't happen. They went out of their way to get me, and let's face it—they can get anyone if that is their intent because they have our money to play with.

"Well, we built the ranch up to over 200 head of horses at one point. The wolves sure played hell with the colts, though. We got strychnine and used it for 11 days at one time. We got 56 wolves that we knew of, but they just kept coming in from other areas. What did they expect us to do? Were we just supposed to watch our investment being turned into wolf shit? When the Game Department pulled my licence I got fed up with the whole thing and sold out to my partner for $260,000. Bobbie kept it for about four more years and sold out to Hans Hansen and he has pumped another quarter-million dollars into the place."

"What were the main factors working against you?" I questioned.

"When word got out about the big sheep coming out of our guiding area, the resident hunters started coming into the area in droves. They came in jet boats and floatplanes and we got fed up with it all. Imagine how a hunter feels when he has paid thousands of dollars for a hunt and then climbs a mountain only to find a resident hunter packing out a sheep. The two don't mix. I suggested to the Game Department that the area be put aside for only the largest trophy sheep but they told me that if I didn't hunt them, someone else would."

"When you look back over it all, would you change it if you could?"

"No! I've had so many adventures and met so many great people. Some of the guides I hired were among the best in the business, and the hunters, some of the greatest people one could ever hope to meet. Skook Davidson was sure one of a kind. Without doubt he was the best horse packer and woodsman I ever met in my life, bar none. I used to joke about Skook's guiding crew; in fact, I wrote a little ditty about them years ago and it goes something like this:

I dreamt that I died and to heaven did go.

'Where did you come from?' They wanted to know.

When I said 'Old Skook's place' it sure made them stare.

Then they shouted, 'Come in, sir, you're the first one from there'."

"This was just written in fun because many of the people I knew around Skook's place were as fine as any and better than most."

"You mentioned his girlfriend Lil Crosina, do you know what became of that?" I wanted to know.

"Nothing; in fact she never married either. According to what he told me, Skook went to see her a couple times. Once he left with $25,000 and only got as far as Fort St. James where he ended up on a big party and blew the money. Another time he bought a Model T Ford and headed out to see her but that went haywire when he drove the car into the river near Quesnel.

"There was a story in a book about Skook flying down to visit Lil, but the story appears to be full of errors. First off, they called her Lilly when she was known as Lil. After Lil and Skook supposedly argued, the writer stated that he had to stop Skook from jumping out of the airplane. All I've got to say about that it he must have been a powerful man to stop Skook. Besides, I knew that Skook suffered unbearably from arthritis, yet suicide was never an option. He [the writer] didn't know Lil's family name, either, so I think it's a fabricated story. Besides, during all the time I spent with Skook I'm sure he would have told me about it if it were true."

"I agree, Frank, but there is one statement in that book that was worth repeating: it was to the effect that when Cataline was born they didn't throw away the mould; but when Skook was born, they certainly did. Something else that should interest you is that I have been in contact with Olive (Lock) MacKenzie of Miocene, BC. She knew Lil very well and she states that Lil took over the 153-Mile ranch after her parents' deaths. As well, I've been in contact with Lil's nephew, Willie Crosina, who forwarded a few pictures of her. He confirmed your statement that Lil never married. According to the internet, Lillian Alice Crosina passed away at 153 Mile House on August 8, 1963 at the age of 62."

"Yes, that sounds about right. As a matter of fact I recall when Skook found out that she had passed away. He never said a word; he just went for a walk, and as far as I know, that's the only time anyone ever noticed tears in his eyes."

"I wonder why Skook never sold out after his health gave out; surely he could have used the money." I suggested.

"The money didn't matter to Skook. That was his home and it was where he wanted to die. Several different people approached him about buying his line, but he wasn't interested. One summer Ted Williams and another man from Prince George flew in and offered him $100,000 for it, but it was no deal. After his death a fellow named Gary Moore bought the line for $175,000. About three years ago a man named Randy Gee purchased it for $1.3 million."

"One thing that I'm happy about, Frank, is that the mountain across the Kechika Valley from Terminus Mountain has been named Davidson Mountain by the BC Government. It sits next to and just north of Mt. Winston that was named after Churchill. Somehow it seems fitting that the two should be near each other, because they were both such courageous and freedom-loving people. But when illness forced Skook to leave, it must have broke his heart to leave the ranch."

"It sure did. I'll never forget the day Skook and I went for a walk because he was having a terrible time walking with his canes. At one point he said to me, 'Kid, this is where I want to be buried.' But it didn't work out that way because he was cremated.

"There is another story I want to tell you. When Skook was in that nursing home in North Vancouver I went to visit him with my dad, who had been visiting him almost every day. When I first went into his room I thought I noticed a spark of recognition in his eyes, but in an instant it was gone. We talked for a few minutes and then I said, 'I saw an old friend of yours the other day; you remember Frank Cooke.'

"His eyes lit up and he answered, 'Sure! How the hell is he?' He had been talking to me and didn't have any idea who I was. He died just a short time later."

"Did Skook survive off the money from the sale of his place?" I questioned.

"Yes, the $175,000 was set up in a trust fund and $1200/month was set aside to see that he got the best of care. After Skook's death the estate went to his nephew, a bank manager named Gordon Yule."

"I have read quite a lot about Skook and I wish that I would have had the pleasure of meeting the man. What was it like after he was gone, Frank?"

"It was never the same again, because we all knew that a proud old man who really cared for the wildlife was gone forever."

"What became of the people Skook trained; the ones that worked for him?" I queried.

"Several of them worked for me for many years and they were great guides. But the two that were closest to him were Rawhide [Ernest Frank] and his sister Mabel. They both died tragic deaths at a young age. Poor Rawhide, he got killed on Steamboat Mountain and it was booze that was responsible for that, too. He was on a trip from Lower Post to Fort St. John when the pickup he was riding in flipped over and he suffered a broken neck. They will have to go a long way to replace him. Without question he was one of the best woodsmen ever. But I must say something more about those Indian guides: there were three of them that kind of worked together—Rawhide, John Tibbetts and Jack George or Eagle Eye as we called him, because he could see animals that the rest of us needed spotting scopes to see— those three guys complemented each other, because what one didn't know, the others did. They could shoe horses or fix saddles or repair anything for the pack train. I'm telling you that Skook trained them well."

'Any last memories of people you guided?"

"One that comes to mind is a great gentleman I guided named Ray Spear of Spear Bullets. Now there was an interesting and knowledge-able person. He knew more about guns, ammunition and ballistics than most countries do. No! When I look back I know that I would-n't change it for the world. It was so interesting that I would do it all over again without a second's hesitation'."

"I want to get back to your family, Frank, when did your father— the renowned Const. Frank Cooke—pass away?"

"Dad died in 1988 and according to his wishes we spread half of his ashes in Stuart Lake and the other half into the Strait of Georgia. I should also mention that the famous bush pilot, Sheldon Luck, did the eulogy for my dad. They did a lot of flying together when my dad was with the police. Sheldon was one of the most famous bush pilots and he retired with over 26,000 hours."

"Your father certainly made a success of his life, didn't he?"

"He was very successful; he made a fortune in mining. It was truly his love and he pursued it as long as his health allowed."

"Several of the elderly people that I interviewed for this book offered the opinion that your father was truly one of a kind. Their admiration and abundant respect comes through loud and clear."

"Yes. Dad not only earned people's respect, but he also held it, because he treated everyone fairly and that goes a long way in this world."

"I understand that you still take people up the Kechika and Turnagain Rivers in your jet boat. Is this because you can't get the wilderness out of your life?"

Outfitter Frank Cooke stands behind Alfred Brown Jr. and Frank "Pancho" Mathew after a very successful hunt.

"I'll never get that country out of my life because it has been my life. I have so many wonderful memories of the entire area. I remember the time I guided Alfred Brown and Frank Matthews. They both got nice Stone sheep and it was nice to talk with them because they were heirs to the Tabasco Sauce Empire, so you know they were influential people."

Since my interviews with Frank I have read and reread the material I got from him. I believe that he was right in his assessment that the North has never produced Skook's equal. Another note of interest is that several years before his death, Skook asked that his poem be placed in his orbituary. When someone corrected him that it was obituary, he responded with, "No! When I die I'm not going to leave the Kechika; I'm going to hang around and around and around."

I believe that Skook's spirit will always hang around the Kechika Valley. It will be in every bird and every animal that loves to be wild and free—just as wild and free as Skook's restless spirit forced him to be. Shortly after his death a small memorial was placed at his beloved Diamond J Ranch.

Just this past summer a group got together and had a beautiful bronze plaque made to honour the memory of this outstanding individual. It is to be placed at Skook's original ranch site in the protective shadow of Terminus Mountain. Randy Gee, present day owner of the ranch has graciously offered his co-operation in the care of this memorial. On it is inscribed a brief history of Skook's life, as well as the poem he wrote from his heart during

Skook 1965.

the winter of 1949. The plaque is decorated with a horse—which exemplifies Skook's eternal love of horses—and it also contains the following:

Pioneer packer John Ogilvie Davidson was born in Scotland in 1891, and came to Canada at the age of 13. For several years he worked as a bellboy for famed packer Cataline, and in time became a frontiersman, woodsman and incomparable horse packer. At a young age he earned the title of Skookum—taken from the Chinook language—because of his renowned physical strength.

During the summer of 1939, Skook, as he became known, visited the Kechika Valley and it was love at first sight. Over the next few years he started the famed Diamond J Ranch at Terminus Mountain where he raised and maintained a herd of 200 horses. After 35 years in Kechika Valley Skook's health gave out and he spent the last few years of his life in a rest home in North Vancouver where he passed away on August 29, 1977.

During the winter of 1949 Skook wrote the following poem, which was appropriately titled:

An Ode To The North

'Tis time to live when all the North without a fence or fuss,
Belongs in partnership with God, the government and us.
When our souls sing peace and rest, beyond the great divide,
Just put us on some stretch of North that is sunny, lone and wild.

A skyline fence from east to west with room to go and come;
We liked our fellow man the best when they were scattered some.
The wolves may rob our headstones now and coyotes wail their kin,
While horses come and paw the mounds, but don't you fence us in.
Rest in peace, Skook!

Author Jack Boudreau with Skook Davidson's memorial plaque.

Index